D0745923

FROM IMAGES TO SURFACES

FROM IMAGES TO SURFACES

A Computational Study of the Human Early Visual System

William Eric Leifur Grimson

The MIT Press
Cambridge, Massachusetts and London, England

PUBLISHER'S NOTE

Second printing, 1986

Printed in the United States of America by Edwards Brothers

Library of Congress Cataloging in Publication Data

Grimson, William Eric Leifur.
    From images to surfaces.

    (The MIT Press series in artificial intelligence)
    Based on the author's thesis (Ph.D.--Massachusetts
Institute of Technology)
    Bibliography: p.
    Includes index.
    1. Binocular vision--Data processing. 2. Computer
graphics. I. Title. II. Series. [DNLM: Physiology.
WW 103 G865f]
QP487.G74   152.1'4'02854   81-13751
ISBN 0-262-07083-9   AACR2

To the memory of
David C. Marr
Scholar, Scientist, Friend

CONTENTS

SERIES FOREWORD

Artificial intelligence is the study of intelligence using the ideas and methods of computation. Unfortunately, a definition of intelligence seems impossible at the moment because intelligence appears to be an amalgam of so many information-processing and information-representation abilities.

Of course psychology, philosophy, linguistics, and related disciplines offer various perspectives and methodologies for studying intelligence. For the most part, however, the theories proposed in these fields are too incomplete and too vaguely stated to be realized in computational terms. Something more is needed, even though valuable ideas, relationships, and constraints can be gleaned from traditional studies of what are, after all, impressive existence proofs that intelligence is in fact possible.

Artificial intelligence offers a new perspective and a new methodology. Its central goal is to make computers intelligent, both to make them more useful and to understand the principles that make intelligence possible. That intelligent computers will be extremely useful is obvious. The more profound point is that artificial intelligence aims to understand intelligence using the ideas and methods of computation, thus offering a radically new and different basis for theory formation. Most of the people doing artificial intelligence believe that these theories will apply to any intelligent information processor, whether biological or solid state.

There are side effects that deserve attention, too. Any program that will successfully model even a small part of intelligence will be inherently massive and complex. Consequently, artificial intelligence continually confronts the limits of computer science technology. The problems encountered have been hard enough and interesting enough to seduce artificial intelligence people into working on them with enthusiasm. It is natural, then, that there has been a steady flow of ideas from artificial intelligence to computer science, and the flow shows no sign of abating.

The purpose of this MIT Press Series in Artificial Intelligence is to provide people in many areas, both professionals and students, with timely, detailed information about what is happening on the frontiers in research centers all over the world.

Patrick Henry Winston
Mike Brady

PREFACE

"That we see the world as well as we do is something of a miracle. What seems so direct and effortless turns out, on close consideration, to involve many rapid and complex processes the details of which we are only beginning to glimpse."

Francis H.C. Crick, David C. Marr
and Tomaso Poggio, 1980

Writing a book about human vision is difficult to motivate, because the process seems so obvious and simple. After all, we simply open our eyes and see. While an understanding of the goals of the human visual pathway is straightforward, determining the specific computations is often difficult.

Part of the difficulty lies in providing an appropriate framework within which to study the visual system. Neurophysiology has served as a framework for the study of the internal components of the visual system. Similarly, psychophysics has provided the framework for the study of the external behavior of the visual system. In this book, we consider a computational framework that may provide the bridge between the data on external and internal behavior. This computational paradigm provides a framework within which research goals may be framed and studied, and critical questions concerning the structure of the computations involved can be isolated and investigated.

This book documents one such computational study of the human early visual system. It is based upon a Ph.D. thesis, which I wrote at the Artificial Intelligence Laboratory of the Massachusetts Institute of Technology under the supervision of David C. Marr, with the financial support of the Advanced Research Projects Agency of the Department of Defense and the National Science Foundation.

Throughout the development of this book, we will have two goals in mind. The first is to take one more step in an iterative and evolving process of understanding the computations of the human visual system. Although some of the details are not yet completely determined, most of the basic concepts involved in solving the computational problem of surface reconstruction are clearly stated. Our second goal is to illustrate the computational paradigm in which those basic concepts can be elucidated. We will see the importance of the paradigm in allowing us to isolate different levels of description of a computational theory, to determine appropriate questions to be addressed at each level, and to illuminate the interactions of the different levels.

Although there are still many details left to be completed, I hope that the basis for the transformation of image irradiances into descriptions of surfaces has been sufficiently well developed to allow the reader to appreciate both the computational approach to vision and the specific models for stereopsis and visual surface interpolation. For readers interested in a more detailed description of the computational approach, and a much broader discussion of the human early visual system, I highly recommend David Marr's book *VISION: A Computational Investigation into the Human Representation and Processing of Visual Information.*

Many people have contributed to this work and provided advice and encouragement to its author. I would like to express my gratitude to:

David Marr, whose constant and timely encouragement and enthusiasm and whose insightful advice were invaluable, whose high standards are a constant inspiration, and without whom, this work would never have happened;

Tomaso Poggio, who, together with David Marr, developed the stereo theory upon which much of this book relies, who is never stumped for the correct answer, and whose enthusiasm for scientific discovery is contagious;

Berthold Horn, who provided valuable criticism on many points, and who frequently enlightened me on the details of image formation; Whitman Richards, who enlightened me on many aspects of pscyhophysics, who provided valuable criticism on drafts of this book, and who provided both financial and intellectual support; and Mike Brady, who provided valuable criticism on drafts of the original thesis as well as this book;

Patrick Winston, who exhibited unending enthusiasm about this project, who provided financial support, who suggested improvements to the presentation of this book, and who carefully maintains an atmosphere within the AI Lab that is both stimulating and supportive;

Shimon Ullman, and the other "Visionaries", who provided many useful comments and criticisms, and who are excellent sounding boards for ideas, both good and bad;

Denis Hanson, who convinced me that even a prairie boy can, on occasion, succeed;

Marilyn Matz, who carefully scrutinized many drafts of this book, and who judiciously applied a blue pencil;

Tomas Lozano-Perez, Matt Mason, Chuck Rich, and many others, who help make the AI Lab an exciting place to be, with whom I've had many discussions, and without whom the time spent in completing this work would have been far less enjoyable;

Ellen Hildreth, who read (almost) more drafts of this manuscript than I did, who provided many valuable comments, and who helped me keep my sanity throughout it all;

and my parents, who taught me long ago that few things are more valuable and lasting than a thirst for knowledge.

CHAPTER 1

THEORETICAL PRELIMINARIES

Although our world has three spatial dimensions, the projection of light rays onto the retina presents our visual system with an image of the world that is inherently two-dimensional. We must use such images to physically interact with this three-dimensional world, even in situations new to us, or with objects unknown to us. That we accomplish this task easily implies that one of the functions of the human visual system is to reconstruct a three-dimensional representation of the world from its two-dimensional projection onto our eyes. The study described in this book constitutes a computational theory of this process: *creating representations of surface shape from their images.* An example of a process which the human visual system uses to construct this three-dimensional representation is stereopsis, which refers to the use of the two viewpoints, provided by the left and right eyes, to establish the depth of surfaces around us. Illustrated in Figure 1.1 is a stereogram; the top two images represent two different viewpoints of a surface. In this case, we cannot see the surface in either image alone but when presented separately to the left and right eyes, (for example, under a stereoscope), a vivid impression of surfaces lying at different depths is perceived. The bottom figure illustrates a three-dimensional reconstruction of the perceived surfaces.

The principal question to be investigated is: *how does this three-dimensional reconstruction take place?* And, in particular, *how does this three-dimensional reconstruction take place in the human visual system?* There are many levels at which we could attempt to answer this question. Traditional methods have included neurophysiological approaches, which have sought to identify the neural structures that perform the reconstruction, and psychophysical approaches, which have sought to identify the perceptual processes involved in the reconstruction. In contrast, this book presents a new approach to the question of "how the processing takes place". This approach is the *computational paradigm* of visual processing [Marr, 1976a, 1976b, 1981; Marr and Poggio, 1977a], which we will outline in greater detail in the rest of this chapter. One of its basic tenets is that the human visual system can be regarded as an *information processor*, performing computations on internal symbolic representations of visual information. As a consequence, we can distinguish between abstract computations and the meaning of the symbols embodied in those representations on the one hand, and the physical manifestation of those symbols on the other. In other words, we can make a distinction between aspects of the visual process which are specific to biological

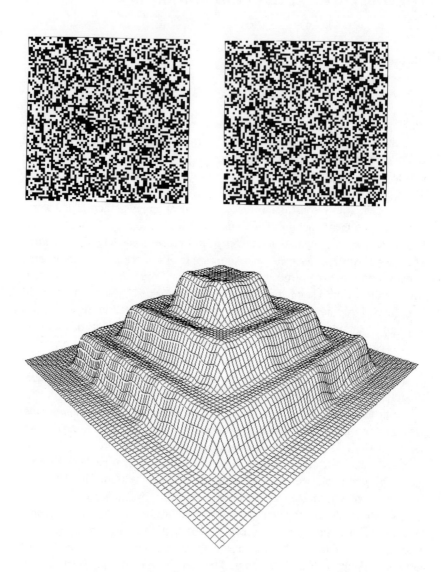

Figure 1.1
Random Dot Stereogram and Its Interpolation. Each image in the top pair is a collection
of black and white dots, constructed in such a way that they represent two viewpoints
of a set of surfaces in space. When the images are viewed stereoscopically, a series
of squares is perceived as separated in depth from the rest of the pattern, although
each monocular image contains no cue to this effect. The lower figure represents a
perspective view of the surface reconstructed by analyzing the top pair of images with
the visual processing algorithms that we will develop in this book.

hardware, and aspects of the process which are specific to the problem being solved, independent of the particular implementation of that process.

Because of this distinction, we can concentrate on the computational process that is occurring independent of the means by which that process is incorporated into the human brain. Our goal is to understand the reconstruction of three-dimensional surfaces from two-dimensional images at the level of computational theories and algorithms. While more precise definitions of computational theory and algorithm will be given in Section 1.1, we can informally consider our goal in the following manner. We begin by investigating the symbolic representations and the transformations between representations that are involved in a computational theory of the construction of surface shape. Next, we consider specific algorithms for performing these transformations, where by algorithm, we mean an ordered set of simple instructions to be performed. In general, there could be many algorithms for solving a particular computational problem. We will attempt to concentrate on the algorithm used by the human visual system. Neurophysiology and psychophysics play an important role in our investigation, by providing information about the architecture of the algorithms which are used to perform the computation, the form of the symbolic representations, and constraints on the transformations that convert one representation into another. It is my hope that computational studies such as this will help to focus research attention in the study of the human early visual system, and will provide a bridge between psychophysics, neurophysiology, mathematics and other areas that can contribute to an understanding of the visual system.

1.1 The Stages of Visual Processing

Information about the three-dimensional geometry of the visible surfaces of a scene is encoded in an image in a variety of ways. Hence, there are several sources of information in the retinal images that can be used for this three-dimensional reconstruction. One of the crucial insights of vision research is that this information can be decoded by independent processes. This will allow us to concentrate on specific modules of the visual system, such as stereopsis, without requiring an understanding of the entire system.

A schematic of the basic stages of analysis involved in early visual processing is presented in Figure 1.2. This architecture has evolved through many computational studies of vision [Marr, 1978, 1981; Marr and Poggio, 1977; Marr and Nishihara, 1978; Barrow and Tenenbaum, 1978]. It can be divided into three stages. The first stage transforms the images into a representation of the locations in an image at which there is a change in some physical property of the corresponding surface in the scene. This representation has been labelled the Primal Sketch, and constitutes the primary source of information for all later

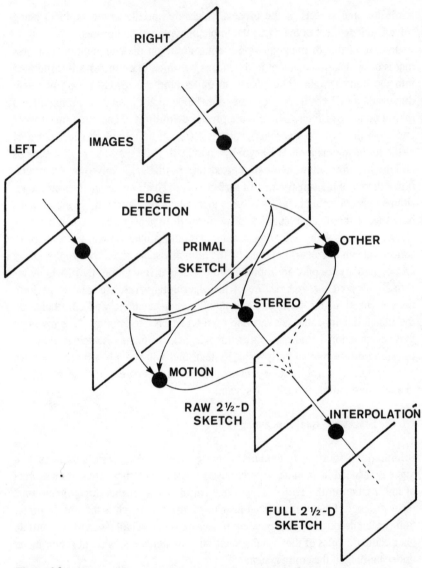

Figure 1.2
Human Early Visual Processing. This diagram schematically illustrates the different representations in the early visual system and the transformations between them. The images obtained by each eye are transformed into Primal Sketch descriptions, consisting of those image positions at which a change of intensity takes place. The Primal Sketch descriptions are then processed by stereo, motion, texture, and other modules of the system. Each computes explicit surface information at the demarked locations of the Primal Sketch. The information from these modules is combined into a single representation. This representation is interpolated, in order to compute explicit surface information at all points in the scene, yielding a representation of the shapes of the visible surfaces, called the $2\frac{1}{2}$D Sketch.

stages of processing. From the Primal Sketch, we would like to compute information about the surface shape at points in the image. A number of modules of the visual system, which to a first approximation are considered independent, perform this computation. Two of the main ones are stereo vision (using Primal Sketch descriptions from the two eyes, which are obtained at different points in space) and motion correspondence (using Primal Sketch descriptions from images which are obtained at different points in time). All of these modules feed a representation, which has been labelled the raw $2\frac{1}{2}$-D Sketch, and which consists of explicit surface information at those locations demarked in the Primal Sketch. Finally, in order to compute explicit surface information at all points in the scene, the raw $2\frac{1}{2}$-D Sketch is interpolated to yield a representation of the shapes of the visible surfaces, which has been labelled the full $2\frac{1}{2}$-D Sketch.

In this book, we will concentrate on aspects of each of the three stages: computing the basic form of the Primal Sketch [Marr and Hildreth, 1980; Hildreth, 1980]; computing surface information based on the Primal Sketches of the left and right eye, using a theory of stereo vision [Marr and Poggio, 1979; Grimson, 1980b, 1981a]; and interpolating the raw $2\frac{1}{2}$-D Sketch to obtain a complete surface description [Grimson, 1981b]. There are other sources of visual information that are important, of course. For example, one can obtain shape from *shading information* [Horn, 1970, 1975; Woodham, 1978; Ikeuchi, 1979; Silver, 1980]; *the motion of objects over time* [Miles, 1931; Johansson, 1964, 1975; Wallach and O'Connell, 1953; Wallach, 1959; Braunstein, 1976; Ullman, 1979a; Longuet-Higgins and Pradzny, 1981]; *surface contours* [Stevens, 1979; Barrow and Tenenbaum, 1981]; *texture* [Helmholtz, 1925; Gibson, 1950a, 1950b, 1966; Purdy, 1960; Bajcsy, 1972; Haber and Hershenson, 1973; Rosinski, 1974; Bajcsy and Lieberman, 1976; Stevens, 1979; Kender, 1978, 1979; Ikeuchi, 1980; Witkin, 1980]; *focusing* [Horn, 1968]; *occluding contours* [Marr, 1977]; *or stereo vision* [Kamal al-Din Abul-Hasan al-Farisi, 1433; Wheatstone, 1838, 1852; Helmholtz, 1925; Julesz, 1971; Quam, 1971; Hannah, 1974; Dev, 1975; Marr and Poggio, 1979; Binford, 1979; Barnard and Thompson, 1980; Mayhew and Frisby, 1981; Baker and Binford, 1981]. Although all of these processes transform representations of the images into representations of the surface shapes, the concentration in this book will be on stereo vision. Thus, while the method we will describe for transforming images into surfaces is not the most general possible (since it neglects sources of surface information other than stereo, for example, motion parallax, shading information, and so forth), the techniques discussed for obtaining the Primal Sketch, and the methods developed for interpolating the raw $2\frac{1}{2}$-D Sketch are generally applicable.

1.2 The Computational Approach

Although our most immediate goal is to investigate the process of creating three-dimensional representations of surface shape, we also have a more global goal of illustrating a computational approach to the study of vision. In the following section, we describe in more detail the characteristics of a computational theory of visual processing, as developed by Marr [1976a, 1976b, 1981, also Marr and Poggio, 1977a].

The motivation for this study of visual processes arose from a desire to understand and model the human visual system. As a result, the theories developed are designed to be both consistent with known evidence about that system and feasible for implementation in a biological system. Although the human system forms the basis for our study, a distinction can be made between components of the computation that are specific to the demands of implementation in a biological system and components that must be performed by any visual processor. Marr's computational approach stresses the importance of distinguishing between these two components when considering computational theories of visual processing. The human visual system can thus serve as a tool for understanding the general processing involved in computing surface descriptions, without enmiring us with details of a specific neural model for such processing in the human system. If an accurate model of the human visual system can be formed, it may also provide a method for solving the visual problem in general situations. In this book, we shall be primarily concerned with the more general questions, that is, with those elements of visual processing which apply to any visual processor.

For the computational paradigm of the visual system as an information processing system to be effective, the representations on which it performs its computations must be *useful descriptions of the visible environment.* Any information that can be obtained from the previous description of the image and that is useful for the construction of the next representation is made explicit at each stage. Thus, every proposed representation is judged by two criteria: the computability of this description, and its suitability for higher level processing (see Marr and Nishihara [1978] for a study of the application of these criteria to judging shape representations).

Marr [1978] and Marr and Nishihara [1978] argue for at least three such representations in the course of visual processing:

1.   The Primal Sketch, in which properties of the intensity changes in the image are made explicit,
2.   The $2\frac{1}{2}$-D Sketch, which describes properties of the visible surfaces for every location in the image, and
3.   The 3D Model, which makes explicit the three-dimensional shape of objects in the scene, in object-centered coordinates.

In this book, we will investigate the first two representations, formed by creating a description of image locations at which the corresponding scene location undergoes a change in a physical property, and then processing the Primal Sketch descriptions to create a description of the surface geometry.

1.2.1 Levels of Description

Critical to the computational approach is the distinction between several levels of description of a process. Since one is dealing with the manipulation of symbolic information, one can distinguish between the meaning of the symbols and the physical embodiment of those symbols. In other words, one can study the *computation* performed by the system (almost) independently of the *mechanisms* that actually perform the computation. Although a physical system, and the computation it supports, are related (by the very fact that one is computing the other), they cannot be equated. To illustrate this point, I borrow the example of an electronic calculator from Ullman [1979a, page 2]:

Some of the events in the electronic calculator have their meaning in the domain of arithmetic. Other events and components, e.g. those inside the power supply do not have such a meaning. The theory of the electronic calculator and the theory of the computation it performs are consequently distinct and non-isomorphic. But the distinction between mechanism and computation runs deeper than this non-isomorphism: the logic governing the computation is not entirely expressible in terms of the physical system. For example, the fact that a standard pocket calculator presents only the first eight digits of the square root of the number 2.0 is a property of the particular device in question. The fact that this number cannot be represented by *any* finite decimal belongs to a different realm, i.e. to the theory of arithmetic. Furthermore, the theory of the mechanism and the theory of the computation deal with different entities. The theory of the calculator deals with electronic circuits, currents, and voltages. The theory of what is being computed, on the other hand, deals with arithmetic objects.

In applying the computational approach, we will study the processing of the visual system at three different levels: the computational theory, an algorithm to solve the theory, and the underlying implementation of the computation [Marr and Poggio, 1977a].

At the level of the computational theory, we must determine the physical constraints that restrict the problem sufficiently to allow the process to do what it does. In general, the problems faced by modules of early visual processing appear to be insoluble if one attempts to solve them from the image alone. But if we can identify additional constraints on the process, imposed naturally as a consequence of the way the world is made, we can restrict the result sufficiently to allow a correct solution to be found. For example, Ullman's [1979a] *rigidity assumption* in the interpretation of three-dimensional structure from motion, Marr and Hildreth's [1980] *condition of linear variation* and *spatial coincidence assumption* in the analysis of intensity changes and Marr and Poggio's [1979] assumptions of *uniqueness* and *continuity* are instances of physical constraints that restrict the problem at hand. This enunciation of additional valid or plausible constraints is a crucial step in the formulation of the computational theory.

Once the additional information has been isolated, one can incorporate it into the design of a process. There are a number of ways in which a process may utilize a constraint. The constraint may be treated as an assumption that is taken always to be true with or without verification (optical illusions often illustrate situations where these assumptions are not valid). An example of this is the case of linear variation [Marr and Hildreth, 1980]. In contrast, some other process might explicitly "look for" the satisfaction of the constraint; if it is consistent with visual input, the constraint is assumed to be true. An example of this is the rigidity constraint [Ullman, 1979a]. Alternatively, the constraint may be explicitly embedded in the process, such as the continuity and uniqueness assumptions in stereo [Marr and Poggio, 1979].

At the level of the computational theory, we must consider representations as well as constraints. All the processes of early vision take properties of the image as their input and compute properties of surfaces, either relating to their geometry or their reflectance, as their output. In the stereo process, it is important to determine the representation of the input to the process, the means of transforming this information into a representation of surfaces, and the nature of this surface representation. Although these questions can be addressed for visual processing in general, it is desirable to have the theory be consistent with processing in the human system. Thus, psychophysical evidence concerning the nature of these representations, and the processes by which they are transformed, will be important for answering these questions.

A fundamental assumption is being made at the level of the computational theory: that the human visual system is an inherently modular system, allowing us, for example, to study the process of stereo vision in isolation. At first glance, it is not clear to what extent stereoscopic processing is independent of the monocular analysis of each image. One method for testing whether a process can be studied in isolation is to present the visual system with images in which, as far as possible, all but one type of information have been removed. The objective is to determine whether one can make use of just that one type of information. For stereo this can be demonstrated by the random-dot stereogram, invented by Julesz [1960]. Each of the images in Figure 1.1 is a collection of black and white dots, identical except that a centrally located square-shaped region is shifted horizontally in one image relative to the other. Other than this disparity, the images contain no information about visible surfaces. Yet, when the pair is viewed stereoscopically and fused (the two images are brought into correspondence), one clearly and vividly perceives a square floating in space above the plane of the background. This illustrates that disparity alone can cause the sensation of depth. The fact that neither image contains any recognizable monocular organization implies that the stereo process may be studied in relative isolation from other visual processes.

The idea that a large computation should be divided and implemented as a collection of small sub-parts that are as nearly independent of one another as the overall task allows, is what Marr [1976b, 1981] calls the *principle of modular design*. This principle forms a cornerstone to the approach. Its importance lies in its heuristic value, that is, without modularity, a small change in one place in a process could have consequences in many other places. This means that the process as a whole becomes extremely cumbersome, and difficult to debug and analyze. While the main role of the principle of modular design is to enable us to derive computational algorithms for particular visual problems, it is worth noting that many of the components of the human visual system exhibit, to a first approximation, some aspects of modularity. The example of the random dot stereogram (Figure 1.1) in stereo vision, and the two cylinders demonstration in the structure-from-motion computation [Ullman, 1979a] both serve to illustrate that the human early visual system can, as a first approximation, be considered a modular one. Of course, we do not necessarily imply that the human visual system is strictly modular, since clearly computations performed by one visual component can influence the computations performed by another. We shall use the principle of modular design as a basic guide for first creating computational algorithms that are modular, and will then consider extensions of the system to account for interaction among the modules.

Having developed a computational theory of the processing involved in a visual task, one can then turn to the design of a particular algorithm to achieve the task. We are ultimately interested in the algorithm used by the human visual system. However, a second purpose for studying an algorithm is that it serves as an excellent source of review for the computational theory. Any implementation of a theory uncovers otherwise unnoticed difficulties with the task and demonstrates the adequacy of the theory. Furthermore, any assumptions made by the theory are tested not just by having an implementation, but by running the implementation on examples. Chapter 4 of this book will detail how a particular implementation of a theory of human stereo vision helped to refine the theory, both through the act of implementation and through the use of the implementation on trial data.

Marr [1976b, 1981] outlines two other criteria that can also be used to guide the design of algorithms, and that ought to be satisfied by any serious candidate for an early process in the human visual system. The first, the *principle of graceful degradation*, says that whenever possible, degraded or impoverished data should not prevent the delivery of at least some of the answer. The second, the *principle of least commitment*, says that nothing should ever be done that may later have to be undone.

It is important to note that there may be several possible algorithms for embedding a particular computational theory. In many cases, one can distinguish between the acceptability of different algorithms. For models of the human visual system, I shall adopt a set of algorithmic criteria, outlined in Chapter 7, that support biological feasibility [Ullman, 1979b].

The third level of description is that of the implementation. We are ultimately interested in understanding the neural implementation used by the human system. It would be nice to be able to give general rules about processes at the level of the neural implementation. Unfortunately, only a few theories have been developed to the point where specific neural implementations can be proposed [for example, Marr, 1969], and none have been confirmed experimentally in every detail. Thus, it is not yet possible to formulate such rules.

Although I have outlined the three levels of description in order from computational theory through algorithm to implementation, this should not be taken as an implication that the process of solving a computational problem also follows this order. Rather, as in any scientific endeavor, the different levels interact in a wide variety of ways, each one serving to provide useful feedback for the other levels. For example, when considering algorithms for solving a particular problem, it is useful to keep in mind the types of architecture which the human system has available for implementing its algorithms. Similarly, while the computational theory is important in providing constraints on an algorithm, the development of the algorithm itself can serve to illuminate constraints on the computational theory which might otherwise have been overlooked. The importance of the levels of description is to identify which questions are particularly relevant to the different aspects of the entire computational problem.

Finally, I wish to note that for a particular computational theory, there may be many algorithms, even with the overall structure that we will derive here, and many more implementations of the algorithms. The algorithms that are developed in this book are one possible set of methods for constructing three-dimensional representations from pairs of images, and there may be many ways of modifying or improving these algorithms. The computational theory is expected to have somewhat more permanency, however. The intent of the computational theory, especially the constraints derived as a part of that theory, is to capture those aspects of the problem that are inherent to any solution of that problem. We now turn to a brief outline of the derivation of a computational theory of three-dimensional surface representations, and specific algorithms for performing the surface reconstruction.

1.3 Overview

The remainder of this book is devoted to a discussion of computational theories of the processing of the human early visual system. Figure 1.2 illustrated schematically the stages of processing used by the human system to transform retinal images into a representation of surface shape.

Initially, the images obtained by each eye are transformed into *Primal Sketch* descriptions, which make explicit those places in an image at which some physical property of the underlying surface changes in a noticeable manner [Marr, 1976b, Marr and Hildreth, 1980, Hildreth, 1980]. In Chapter 2, we examine this process within the context of stereo vision.

We first illustrate the basic problem of stereo, which is to locate points in the images of the right and left eye that correspond to the same location on a surface. We show that if such locations can be found, the difference in the positions of the two retinal locations can be used to compute the distance to the surface. We argue that to perform this correspondence computation, we need to describe image attributes that can be unambiguously identified with specific surface locations. In general, positions on a surface at which a physical property, such as surface material, surface texture, or surface shape, changes radically will satisfy our requirement and such surface locations can be identified in the image by a sudden change in image irradiance. We then derive a method for extracting a description of these image locations, specifically by isolating the *zero-crossings* of the convolution of the image irradiances with a filter whose form is a Laplacian of a Gaussian (Section 2.3). We also show that this processing is consistent with current psychophysical information about the human early visual system.

Given these basic descriptions of the images, we must address the problem of determining the correspondence between descriptors in each image. We state two simple rules, based on the physical structure of objects, to apply to the computation. These are: each descriptor from one image should match at most one descriptor from the other image, and the difference in retinal position of matching descriptors should change smoothly over the image. To apply these rules, we must face the *false targets* problem: since the basic descriptors are relatively simple, there may be several possible descriptors in one image which could correspond to a particular descriptor in the other image. The false targets problem is directly proportional to the range and resolution of depth information over which a match is sought. We show that we may solve the false targets problem without sacrificing either, by matching descriptions obtained at several levels of resolution, and using the rough depth information obtained at a coarse resolution to guide the matching at a fine resolution, by changing the orientation of the eyes. The algorithm we use, derived in Section 2.5, is that proposed by Marr and Poggio [1979]. In the remainder of Chapter 2, we show the relationship between the Marr-Poggio algorithm and currently available psychophysical and neurophysiological information about the human stereo system.

Having developed the stereo problem and an algorithm for solving it, we turn in Chapter 3 to an implementation of the algorithm, first discussed in Grimson [1981a]. Each step of the algorithm is specified in detail. In Chapter 4, we examine the performance of the Marr-Poggio stereo algorithm using the implementation described in Chapter 3. Since the algorithm was developed as a model of the human stereo system, we evaluate its performance by comparing the results of the algorithm to human perception for a wide range of random dot stereograms, (see also [Grimson, 1980a, 1980b, 1981a]). We further demonstrate the capabilities of the algorithm by considering its performance on a series of natural images. Sections 4.3 and 4.4 discuss various aspects of the algorithm and its implementation. Finally, we develop the computation of depth from disparity.

While our first few chapters focus on the process of stereo vision, there are other early visual modules, such as structure-from-motion [Ullman, 1979a], which also compute descriptions of surface shape from Primal Sketch descriptions. Both of these algorithms compute specific surface information only at certain isolated points in the images — in this case, the zero-crossings of the convolved images. (Note that the important point here is not whether zero-crossings or some other descriptor are used as the basic representation on which the computation is performed, but rather that explicit surface information is available only at such points.) In Chapter 5, we argue that such a surface description is not sufficient. We show both computationally and psychophysically that the representation of surface shape should be complete, in the sense of containing a specific depth value everywhere in the representation, rather than just at a set of scattered points. The problem we consider in Chapters 5 through 9 is how to create a complete surface representation, given the results of the stereo algorithm (or the structure-from-motion algorithm).

In principle, there are infinitely many surfaces which could fit any given set of boundary conditions, as provided by the stereo algorithm. In Sections 5.3 and 5.4 we show that most of these surfaces are not consistent with the known information. In particular, a surface whose orientation undergoes a series of radical changes should generally give rise to image irradiances which also undergo a series of radical changes. Such changes would then give rise to zero-crossings in the convolved image. If there are no corresponding zero-crossings in the Primal Sketch, such a surface is inconsistent with the information in the image. We use this argument to derive the *surface consistency constraint* [Grimson, 1981b] which states that

The absence of zero-crossings constrains the possible surface shapes.

In Section 5.5, we review the factors which combine to form the image irradiances and derive Horn's image irradiance equation [Horn, 1970, 1975, 1977]. In Section 5.6, we use this equation to make the surface consistency constraint precise, by the *surface consistency theorem* that relates the probability of a zero-crossing to the variation in surface orientation [Grimson, 1981b].

The surface consistency constraint states that to find a complete surface to fit through the known points, we should choose a surface which is most consistent with that known information. The surface consistency theorem of Section 5.6 indicates that one way of measuring surface consistency is to measure the amount of variation in surface orientation over a region of the surface. In Chapter 6, we consider the problem of measuring this variation. In general, the problem is to determine, given two possible surfaces, which one is more consistent with the zero-crossings. A traditional method for comparing two surfaces is to assign to each surface a real number. Then, in order to compare two surfaces, one need only compare the corresponding real numbers. To do this, we need to define a functional, mapping the space of possible surfaces into the space of real numbers, $\Theta: X \mapsto \mathcal{R}$. This functional should be such that the more consistent the surface, the smaller the real number assigned to it. In this case, the most consistent surface is that which is minimal under the functional. The development of Chapter 5 leads to a functional that measures variation in surface orientation.

We also require that the problem of finding a most consistent surface be well-defined, that is, that there be a unique most consistent surface. This is not just a mathematical nicety, but follows from the notion that if we create a local, parallel, iterative algorithm to compute the most consistent surface, we need to guarantee that the computation will converge to a unique answer. In Chapter 6 we derive a simple set of mathematical conditions on the functional which guarantee a unique family of solutions. We also show that there are many possible functionals which measure surface consistency and satisfy these conditions. To determine the best functional to use, we investigate the differences in the solution surfaces corresponding to each of these functionals. We also consider the conditions under which the family of solutions will consist of only a single minimal surface. Based on these facts, we argue in Section 6.5 that the best functional to use is the *quadratic variation*. We claim that the *visual surface interpolation problem* is solved by finding the unique surface which minimizes the quadratic variation, while passing through the known points provided by the stereo algorithm (or the structure-from-motion algorithm).

In Chapter 7, we consider what types of algorithms are best applied to solving the interpolation problem. Based on a series of algorithmic constraints, we suggest that the techniques of mathematical programming are appropriate to our problem. We review the *conjugate gradient method*, appropriate to the problem of approximating the surface, and the *gradient projection method*, appropriate to the problem of interpolating the surface.

In Chapter 8, we create explicit algorithms, based on both of these methods, for solving the visual surface interpolation problem. We demonstrate the suitability of the surface interpolation theory by testing the algorithms on a set of synthetic examples. Finally, we complete our original task, by processing a series of stereo images with the Marr-Poggio algorithm, and then creating a complete surface description by applying the interpolation algorithm. Thus, we complete the task of computing surfaces from images.

To complete our discussion, in Chapter 9, we analyze the performance of the algorithm and sketch additional modifications which should improve the performance of the system. We consider the possible benefits of improving the initial input to the stereo algorithm, the interactions between the stereo module and other components of the early visual system, and the problem of detecting discontinuities and their role in the interpolation process. Finally, we indicate some of the implications of this theory for neurophysiology and psychophysics.

Thus, we will develop a theory of stereo vision, which transforms the images into Primal Sketch representations and then transforms these representations into the Raw $2\frac{1}{2}$-D Sketch, and a theory of visual surface interpolation, which transforms the Raw $2\frac{1}{2}$-D Sketch into the Full $2\frac{1}{2}$-D Sketch. Throughout this study, our focus will be on the development of computational theories and algorithms.

CHAPTER 2

A COMPUTATIONAL THEORY OF STEREO VISION

In this chapter, we begin the discussion of the process of transforming a set of images into a representation of the shapes of the visible surfaces. We consider first the basic operations involved in solving the stereo problem. Much of the discussion is based on a theory of edge detection developed by Marr and Hildreth [1980; also Hildreth, 1980] and a theory of stereo vision developed by Marr and Poggio [1979] and implemented in Grimson [1980a, 1980b, 1981a].

2.1 The Correspondence Problem

If two objects are separated in depth from a viewer, then the relative positions of their images will differ in the two eyes. This is illustrated in Figure 2.1, and can be demonstrated in the following manner. Hold your thumb at arms length, and view it first with the left eye closed, then with the right eye closed. You will notice that the background shifts relative to the position of the thumb in the two images. The process of stereo vision, in essence, measures this difference in the relative positions and uses it to compute depth information for visible surfaces in the scene.

To avoid confusion, three terms relating to stereopsis are defined here. The term *disparity* refers to the angular difference in position of the image element in the two eyes (see Figure 2.1). *Distance* refers to the objective physical distance from the viewer to the object, usually measured from one of the two eyes. Finally, *depth* refers to the subjective distance to the object as perceived by the viewer, usually measured relative to the fixation point or some other three-dimensional point.

It can be seen from Figure 2.1 that disparity varies with the relative positions of objects. Suppose the eyes are fixating at a particular point, as indicated by the circle in the figure. Objects in front of the fixation point have convergent (or crossed) disparities relative to the fixation point (for example, d_3 in the figure). Objects beyond the fixation point have divergent (or uncrossed) disparities relative to the fixation point (for example, d_1 in the figure). As an object moves closer to the viewer, its disparity increases in magnitude.

This can again be demonstrated with a simple example. Hold a finger in front of you and fixate on it (that is, center your eyes on it). Now place a second

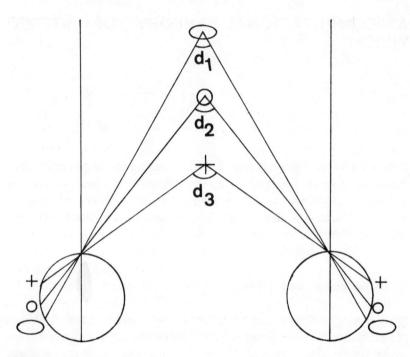

Figure 2.1
Definition of Disparity. The disparity of a point refers to the angular difference in position of the image element in the two eyes. Given a fixation point, such as the circle in the figure, disparities may be crossed (d_3), uncrossed (d_1), or zero (d_2), relative to the fixation point.

finger in front of it, aligned with the first when viewed from the right eye. If you now view the fingers from the left eye, you will note that the nearer finger appears to move to the right. Repeat the same process with the second finger behind the first, again aligned with respect to the right eye. Now the second finger appears to move to the left when viewed with the left eye. Thus, we see that, relative to the fixation point corresponding to the first finger, both the depth and the disparities associated with positions in front of and behind the fixation point are different, corresponding to shifts in the image in different directions. Fixate again on one finger, and place a second finger in front of it. In order to fixate on the second finger, you must change the alignments of the eyes. In particular, you must cross them to align the images of the second finger. As a consequence, disparities associated with such relative depth positions are referred to as *crossed*. If the second finger is placed behind the first, one must uncross the eyes to change the fixation to that finger. Disparities associated with such relative depth positions are referred to as *uncrossed*.

This relationship between distance and disparity suggests that one could determine the distance to objects in a scene by measuring their disparity. But how does one measure this disparity? Marr [1974] proposes that there are three steps involved:

1. A particular location on a surface in the scene is selected from one image;
2. The same location is found in the other image; and
3. The disparity between the two corresponding image points is measured.

Once two corresponding image points are identified, the actual computation of distance involves a simple geometric transformation, and hence does not pose any major difficulties.

The heart of the problem lies in identifying elements in each image which correspond to the same element in the scene. If a specific location could be identified beyond doubt in the two images, then steps (1) and (2) could be avoided and the whole process would be simple. For example, if we illuminate a spot in the scene with a narrowly focused beam of light, we can identify that spot unambiguously in the two images. Matching the two spots and computing their disparity is then trivial. Although this is a perfectly valid method for solving the correspondence problem, [Agin, 1972; Shirai and Suwa, 1971; Lewis and Johnston, 1977], it is clearly not applicable to the human system. We are not, unfortunately, equipped with lasers in our foreheads, and hence cannot perform depth computations based on the matching of spots of light in the images. The human system requires a more passive method for sensing the environment.

Thus, the problem of the identification of corresponding image points cannot be avoided. There are two parts to the correspondence problem: determining what elements from an image are to be matched; and given an element from one image, evaluating candidates from the other image according to some matching criteria.

To solve the correspondence problem, we must first decide on the nature of the elements to be matched in the two views. Are they intensities? objects? something else? The answer to this question will have a strong influence on the second problem of how to match these elements. In fact, there is a trade-off between the complexity of the monocular analysis used to extract the elements to be matched, and the complexity of the process which matches them.

At one end of the spectrum, we could perform object recognition before stereo matching. That is, we could first process each monocular view, identifying the various objects contained therein. Since in most scenes, the probability of having two or more "identical" objects is small, the matching problem becomes simple. To determine the disparity, a particular object, say a desk, would be located in each of the two images, and the disparity would be computed. The solution of the correspondence problem — which element in one view matches which element in the other — is greatly reduced at the expense of identifying and locating objects in a scene, which is a non-trivial task. Under such a scheme, the stereo process would be a later visual process, following earlier processes which would analyze each monocular image. Of course, we have already seen that this is not the case for the human stereo system. The example of Julesz random-dot stereograms (Figure 1.1) showed that stereopsis occurs very early in the visual process and is relatively independent of other forms of visual processing.

If the human stereo process is an early one, then much more primitive matching elements are used. In the example of the random dot stereogram, there is no monocular structure at the level of objects. The only information available from the images is at the level of irradiance values, the dots themselves, the edges of the black and white clusters of dots and so forth. If we choose to match these more primitive sorts of elements the number of potential matching elements will increase because their density is so great, and the difference between possible elements is small. For example, suppose we chose to match dots; their only distinguishing feature is being black or white. For a particular white dot in the left image, there are many white dots in the right image to which it could correspond. For any primitive descriptor of the left image there is likely to be a large number of possible matching descriptors in the right image. All but one of these will be incorrect. Thus, at the other end of the spectrum, the correspondence problem is more difficult, although the extraction of elements to be matched is simplified.

2.2 The False Targets Problem

The task of identifying corresponding locations in the two images is a difficult one because of what is called the *false targets problem*. An example of this is shown in Figure 2.2 (after Marr and Poggio, 1979). Each eye sees four dots, but which are the correct matches? Which dot viewed from the left image corresponds to a particular dot viewed from the right image? *A priori,* any of the 16 possible matches is a plausible candidate, but in fact when we observe such a stereo pair, we make the correspondence shown with the filled circles, and not any of the correspondences shown with open circles. These alternate candidates are called *false targets.*

That we always make the correspondence shown with the filled circles is somewhat surprising since there seems to be little reason to distinguish one match as more favorable than another on the basis of the elements being matched. Moreover, as Marr observes, there is another solution to this particular correspondence problem which seems just as "valid", namely the four central vertical matches in which R1 is paired with L4, R2 with L3, R3 with L2, and R4 with L1. But we never "see" this match, which would correspond physically to a set of circles in a line receding from us. Why?

To answer this question, additional information is needed to decide which matchings are correct. This information will be derived by examining the basis in

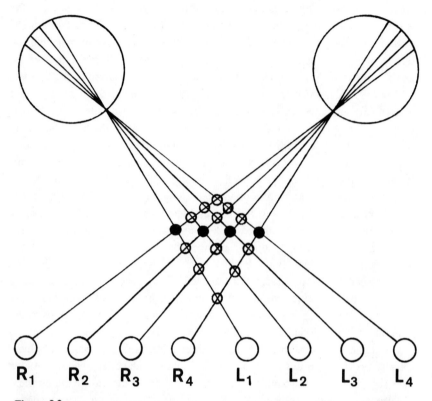

Figure 2.2
The False Targets Problem. Each of the four points in one view could match any
of the four projections in the other view. Of the 16 possible matches indicated by
the circles, only those indicated by the filled circles are actually perceived. (Redrawn
from Julesz [1971, fig. 4.5-1], and Marr and Poggio [1979, p.302]).

the physical world for making a correspondence between two images. Marr and
Poggio [1979] [also Marr, 1974] describe two physical constraints that are relevant
to the stereo process:

1. A given point on a physical surface has a unique position in space at any one
time.

2. Matter is cohesive and separated into objects. Furthermore, the surfaces of
objects are generally such that the changes in the surface are very small compared
with their distance from the viewer.

Let us briefly return to the example of Figure 2.2, to see how these constraints
can reduce the number of possible surfaces. In principle, each dot from the left
image could be associated with any dot from the right image. Since the association (or matching) need not be a one-to-one or onto mapping, this means there

are $2^4 = 16$ possible associations of dots from the right image to any dot in the left image. Each one of these could be part of a matching of the two images, so that, in principle, there are $(2^4)^4 = 65,536$ possible ways of matching the dots from the two images. (Note that in this context, the word matching does not imply a one-to-one or onto mapping, but simply any association of the two sets of dots.) These associations range from the case of none of the dots in the left image being associated with any of the dots in the right (giving rise to two disjoint images being superimposed) through to the case of all dots in the left image being associated with all dots of the right. Clearly many of these associations corresond to physically unlikely (or even impossible) situations. For example, the first constraint essentially states that in general, excluding accidental alignment of objects, there should not be more than one match along any line of sight from either eye. Even if we allow some (or all) of the dots to be unmatched, the number of possible associations is reduced to 209, corresponding to situations in which zero or one match is made along each line of sight. If we further restrict the associations to only include those which have exactly one match along each line of sight, there are 24 possible associations left. The second constraint essentially states that, barring other information, the most likely of these 24 matches is the one actually chosen in Figure 2.2. This is because this match corresponds to the "smoothest" object (relative to the other 23 matches).

The significance of Marr and Poggio's observations is that properties of physical surfaces constrain the way in which positions on the surface behave. As we have seen in the above example, such constraints can greatly reduce the problem of false targets, and in principle should be sufficient to solve the correspondence problem.

2.3 Determining What To Match

We have argued from the evidence of random dot patterns that the extraction of a matchable description of the scene must be, at least in part, an early visual process. That is, while the evidence of random dot stereograms does not imply that only primitive analysis is done, it does imply that stereo vision must be capable of operating on primitive descriptions. The creation of a description of surface locations suitable for matching between the images is somewhat difficult. As we have seen, if a surface location could be chosen in some absolute way — such as by shining a narrow beam of light onto it — the problem would be simple. However, we are not able to do this. Thus the problem of identifying surface locations from their image projections must be addressed.

We saw that Marr and Poggio's observations may be sufficient to solve the false targets problem. It is important to note, however, that these observations relate to surface locations in a scene. The stereo matching process must operate from descriptions of images. Thus, we want to match "features" of surfaces in the scene, by way of properties of the images. Can we transform Marr and Poggio's observations about physical constraints which apply to surfaces into equivalent constraints which apply to elements of the images?

To do this requires the capability of making assertions about surface locations solely on the basis of information in the image. In general this is not possible, since it is unlikely that we can unambiguously identify surface locations from the images themselves, at all points in the images. Consider, for example, a smooth featureless surface such as a matte white wall. Attempting to perform the correspondence computation in this case is virtually impossible. Suppose we extract an irradiance value from a position in one image. In the second image, we have little hope of locating the position of the corresponding point, since irradiance everywhere is nearly uniform. As a consequence of this difficulty in identifying image locations that accurately reflect specific surface locations, the physical constraints proposed by Marr and Poggio are not directly applicable.

While portions of a uniform surface such as the matte white wall cannot be distinguished, this will not be the case for scratches, texture, or other markings, or for boundaries between surfaces. Such features will give rise to sharp changes in the reflective properties of the surface, and will in general cause changes in the irradiances of the image. As a consequence, there should be a direct correspondence between the changes in irradiances and specific surface locations. If we can reliably locate such irradiance changes, then we should be able to apply the two physical constraints to them. Marr and Poggio propose [Marr, 1974; Marr and Poggio, 1979] that the computation of disparity takes place by comparing symbolic descriptions of features in an image that correspond to changes in irradiance, and hence to locations on a surface where some physical property is changing.

We now turn to the problem of detecting these changes in irradiance. Consider first the case of a one-dimensional irradiance profile. A step change in irradiance is shown in Figure 2.3(a). The first derivative of this profile is shown in Figure 2.3(b), and its second derivative in Figure 2.3(c). It can be seen that the sharp change in irradiance gives rise to an extremum in the first derivative and a zero-crossing in the second derivative. When we turn to two-dimensional arrays of irradiance, such as an image, the same observations hold true. A sharp change in the irradiances gives rise to an extremum in a first directional derivative, and a zero-crossing in a second directional derivative. Thus, we could propose that to extract the symbolic descriptions of the image necessary for stereo matching, we should isolate the locations corresponding to a zero-crossing in a second directional derivative (or equivalently, an extremum in a first directional derivative).

In order to find the zero-crossings, we need to determine which directional derivative to use, that is, in which direction should the derivative be taken? It is not sufficient to choose zero-crossings of the second derivative in any direction. To see this, consider a uniform irradiance change running down the y-axis, as

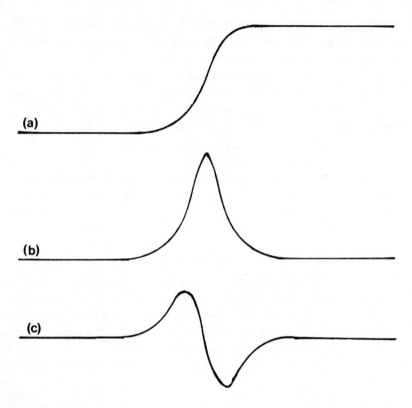

Figure 2.3
One-Dimensional Problem of Detecting Image Changes. Figure (*a*) illustrates a one dimensional step change in irradiance. The change is associated with an extremum in the first derivative (*b*) and a zero-crossing in the second derivative (*c*).

shown in Figure 2.4 (after Marr and Hildreth, 1980). At the origin the second directional derivative is zero in every direction, but it is non-zero nearby in every direction except along the *y*-axis.

The properties of the surfaces which cause the irradiance changes (such as changes in reflectance, illumination, surface orientation, or distance from the viewer) are spatially continuous and can almost everywhere be associated with a direction that projects to an orientation in the image. The orientation of the directional derivative should therefore be chosen to coincide with the orientation formed locally by its zero-crossings. (In Figure 2.4, this direction is the *y*-axis, and the appropriate directional derivative is $\partial^2 E / \partial x^2$, where E is the image irradiance function.)

It can be shown [Marr and Hildreth, 1980, Appendix A] that this direction coincides with that in which the zero-crossing has maximum slope (the rate of

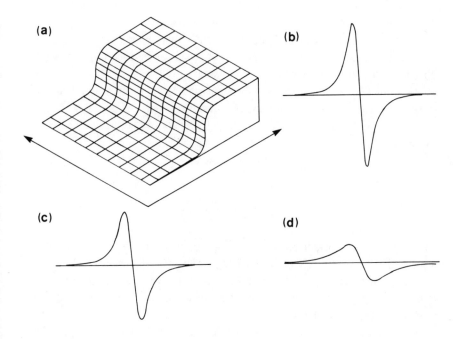

(a)

(b)

(c)

(d)

Figure 2.4
**(From Marr and Hildreth, 1980) Spatial and directional factors interact in the definition
of a zero-crossing segment.** Figure (*a*) shows an irradiance change, and (*b*), (*c*) and (*d*)
show values of the second directional derivative near the origin at various orientations
across the change. In (*b*), the derivative is taken parallel to the *x*-axis, and in (*c*)
and (*d*), at $30°$ and $60°$ to it. There is a zero-crossing at every orientation except for
$\partial^2 E / \partial y^2$, which is identically zero (here E is a function denoting the image irradiance
values obtained at any point). Since the zero-crossings line up along the *y*-axis, this
is the direction that is chosen. In this example, it is also the direction that maximizes
the slope of the second derivative.

change of the second directional derivative across the zero-crossing), provided the
condition of linear variation holds:

*The irradiance variation near and parallel to the line of zero-crossings should lo-
cally be linear.*

Although it is possible to design an algorithm for determining the appropriate
directional derivative, applying it to the image, and locating the zero-crossings,
Marr and Hildreth [1980] suggest that it may not be necessary to use such derivatives. In practice, if we are to use directional derivatives, we must consider convolving the image with a set of operators, one for each of a number of directions.

Convolutions are computationally expensive, and it would be useful if their number could be reduced, for example, by using just one non-directional operator.

The only non-directional second-order differential operator is the Laplacian, ∇^2. Marr and Hildreth [1980, Appendix A] show that under weaker conditions than the condition of linear variation, the Laplacian can be used in place of the directional derivatives to locate the zero-crossings.

We could straightforwardly apply the Laplacian to the images. For practical reasons (to reduce sensitivity to noise, quantization of irradiance and so forth), however, we will first smooth the image slightly by convolution with a Gaussian function:

$$G_\sigma(x, y) * E(x, y)$$

where the Gaussian is given by

$$G_\sigma(x, y) = \sigma^2 e^{-(x^2+y^2)/2\sigma^2}$$

and E is the image irradiance function, $E(x, y)$ denoting the irradiance value associated with location (x, y) in the image. The Gaussian is a band-limited operator, which means it will be sensitive to a particular range of frequencies. In terms of the image, this means that the Gaussian in some sense blurs the image by an amount dependent on its size.

To obtain the symbolic descriptions of the changes in the image, we apply the Laplacian

$$\nabla^2 = \frac{\partial^2}{\partial x^2} + \frac{\partial^2}{\partial y^2}$$

to the filtered images, and locate the zero-crossings of the result. Mathematically, we are proposing that the image be filtered using the following set of operations:

$$f(x, y, \sigma) = \nabla^2[G_\sigma(x, y) * E(x, y)]$$

which by the derivative rule for convolutions becomes:

$$f(x, y, \sigma) = \nabla^2 G_\sigma * E(x, y).$$

The convolution operator $\nabla^2 G_\sigma$ is given by

$$\nabla^2 G_\sigma(r, \theta) = \left(\frac{r^2 - 2\sigma^2}{\sigma^4}\right) \exp\left(\frac{-r^2}{2\sigma^2}\right)$$

where

$$r = \sqrt{x^2 + y^2}.$$

This is a rotationally symmetric function, with one free parameter σ, which determines the spatial size of the function. Its cross-section is shown in Figure 2.5.

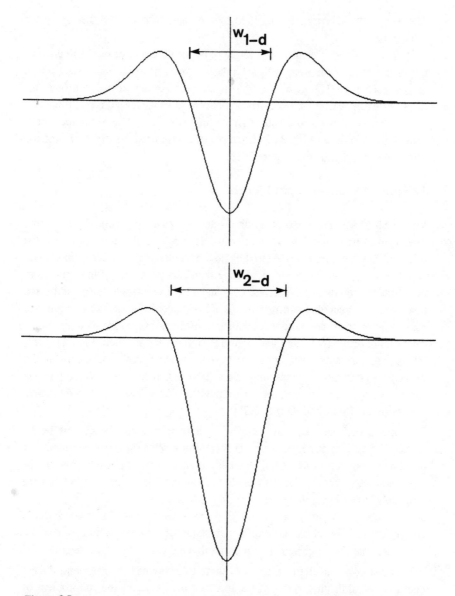

Figure 2.5
The Primal Sketch Operator. The top figure shows the one-dimensional operator. The bottom figure shows a cross-section of the equivalent, rotationally-symmetric, two-dimensional operator. The sizes of the operators are determined by the values of w_{1D} and w_{2D}.

Note that the width of its central negative region, denoted by w_{2D}, is given by:

$$w_{2D} = 2\sqrt{2}\,\sigma.$$

The size of the filter may be specified by the value of σ or equivalently by the value of w_{2D}.

Thus, we can locate changes in irradiance by locating zero-crossings in the output of the image convolved with a Laplacian operator, (that is, we seek points (x_0, y_0) such that $f(x_0, y_0, \sigma) = 0$). In the next section we will see how this description can be developed further, in order to solve the false targets problem.

An example of this processing is shown in Figure 2.6. The $\nabla^2 G$ operator is applied to the images of Figure 2.6(a), the result is shown in Figure 2.6(b) and the zero-crossings are shown in Figure 2.6(c).

2.4 Solving the Correspondence Problem

We have indicated that the basic symbolic descriptors to be matched by the stereo process must be on the level of zero-crossings of a $\nabla^2 G$ operator applied to the image. (Note that the original Marr-Poggio theory also required that *terminations*, corresponding to breaks in oriented edge segments, or points of high curvature in oriented zero-crossing segments, be matched.) The problem to be addressed now is that of matching two primitive symbolic descriptions. The two physical constraints on the correspondence problem must be translated into computational rules that govern how the left and right descriptions are matched. In making this translation, it is necessary to ensure that the items to which the rules apply in the image are in one-to-one correspondence with well-defined locations on a physical surface (such as the zero-crossings). Computational analogues of the two physical constraints are [Marr and Poggio, 1979]:

1. *Uniqueness.* Except in rare cases, each item from either image may be assigned at most one disparity value. This condition relies on the assumption that an item corresponds to something that has a unique physical position. The exceptions can occur when two features lie along the line of sight from one eye, but are separately visible in the other eye.

2. *Continuity.* Disparity varies smoothly almost everywhere. This condition, a consequence of the cohesiveness of matter, states that only a small fraction of the area of an image is composed of boundaries that are discontinuous in depth.

We must now consider how to apply these rules in practice. Marr and Poggio note that the difficulty of the correspondence problem and the subproblem of eliminating false targets is directly proportional to the range and resolution of disparities considered and to the density of matchable features in an image. In other words, the greater the range of disparity over which a match is sought, the greater the number of false targets. At the same time, the finer the resolution

Figure 2.6
Examples of $\nabla^2 G$ Convolution and Zero-Crossings, Fine Filter. Sample images are shown in (a). The convolution of the images with a fine $\nabla^2 G$ operator are shown in (b). In (c) the zero-crossings of (b) are illustrated.

at which features are detected, the greater the density of features and thus the greater the number of potential false targets.

Thus, one can avoid the false targets problem either by reducing the range of the disparities accepted or by reducing the resolution of the disparities accepted. It would, however, be preferable if the system could obtain both large range and fine resolution in its disparity processing, since the system needs both to be able to compute depth over a large range, and to obtain fine detailed depth information. One method for obtaining both range and resolution of disparity information is to use a series of symbolic descriptions. First consider a very coarse symbolic description of the irradiance changes in an image, similar to what one might see through a severely defocused camera. At this coarse resolution, the density of elements is low, so if we locate an element in the left image, we can search over a large area in the right image for a corresponding element, without encountering many false targets. For example, Figure 2.7 shows the zero-crossing descriptions obtained for the images of Figure 2.6, using a coarser filtering of the image. The drawback is that fine detail information will be lost and the disparities detected will be coarse.

To obtain the fine disparity information, we need to perform the matching on a fine resolution symbolic representation, such as in Figure 2.6. But here, the range over which a match can be sought must be greatly reduced, if we are to avoid the false targets problem. How can we give such a fine representation a large effective disparity range, while maintaining the small actual disparity range needed to avoid the false targets? If we were to solve the correspondence problem for a coarse symbolic description of the images, this would provide us with rough information about the disparities associated with different portions of the image. We could use that as a guide for matching elements at finer resolutions.

Consider a point in the left image at position (x, y) and suppose that its corresponding point in the right image is located at position $(x + d, y)$ (see Figure 2.8). Further, suppose that in order to avoid the false targets problem, a match is sought for the coarse symbolic description over a range $\pm w_c$ while a match is sought for the fine symbolic description over a range $\pm w_f$. Finally, assume that $w_f < d < w_c$. Attempting to find the disparity associated with this point using only the fine symbolic description will not succeed, since the matching point is beyond the range that we can search. The matching descriptions are within the search range of the coarse matcher, however. In this case, due to the coarseness of the filter, the disparity assigned to the point will not be exact, say $d_c \neq d$. It is the case, however, that the disparity obtained by matching the coarse symbolic descriptions will be a rough estimate of the actual disparity. If we choose the sizes of the filters appropriately, we can ensure that $|d_c - d| < w_f$. Thus, if we use the rough estimate of the disparity to align the images, the search for a match in the fine symbolic description of the right image will be centered about

Figure 2.7
Examples of $\nabla^2 G$ Convolution and Zero-Crossings, Coarse Filter. Sample images are shown in (*a*). The convolutions of the images with a coarse $\nabla^2 G$ operator are shown in (*b*). In (*c*) the zero-crossings of (*b*) are illustrated.

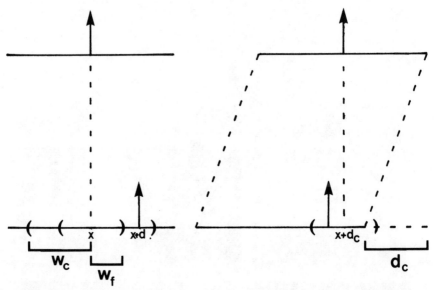

Figure 2.8
Matching of Coarse Filtered Images can Facilitate Matching of Fine Filtered Images.
The left figure shows a one-dimensional example of a matching problem. The arrows
indicate the positions of zero-crossings. The two corresponding zero-crossings are
separated by a disparity d, such that $w_f < d < w_c$ where w_c is the range over which
a match is sought in the coarse description and w_f is the range over which a match
is sought in the fine description. It can be seen that the correspondence lies beyond
the range of the fine matcher, but within the range of the coarse one. We can use
the coarse disparity estimate d_c to align the images, as in the right figure. Now, the
correspondence lies within the range of the fine matcher, and the correct disparity d
can be computed.

the point $(x + d_c, y)$ rather than the point (x, y). In this case, we can now successfully match elements in the finer description. Even though the range over
which a match will be sought is reduced in this finer representation, we are able
to find the appropriate match, since we have centered our search in roughly the
correct region of the image. Thus, by combining the processing of coarse and
fine filtered images, fine resolution disparity can be detected over a large disparity
range, while avoiding the false targets problem.

Passing information from a coarse filtering to a finer one could be accomplished in several ways. One could consider the symbolic representations
as internal data structures. To match the fine resolution descriptions, one could
simply offset the internal representations relative to one another, by an amount
specified by the disparity information from the coarse descriptions. This would

require that the mechanism that feeds information to the matcher be capable of changing the locations in the two representations from which it obtains its data. This is perhaps more complicated than is necessary.

There is a second method for controlling the interaction between coarse resolution correspondence and fine resolution correspondence. Suppose we require that the mechanism which feeds the matcher must always access the same locations in the symbolic representations. If we change the relative orientations of the two eyes, the alignment of the symbolic representations will also change. Thus, we could accomplish the interaction between coarse and fine resolution correspondence by allowing the disparity information obtained by the coarse filtering to control the vergence movements of the eye muscles, thereby aligning the two images in such a way as to facilitate the matching of the finer symbolic descriptions. The vergence movements of the eyes can be appreciated by noting what happens to your two eyes if you fixate on a finger held at arm's length and maintain fixation on the finger as you move it towards the end of your nose.

2.5 The Marr-Poggio Stereo Algorithm

Marr and Poggio [1979] have proposed an algorithm for solving the correspondence problem which basically operates in the manner described above. The algorithm consists of the following steps:

1. Irradiance changes are detected for a set of different resolutions. Matching takes place between corresponding descriptions from the two eyes. The range of disparity values over which a match is sought is of the order of the resolution of irradiance changes.

2. The matching of coarse descriptions controls eye vergence movements, thus allowing finer descriptions to be matched.

3. When a correspondence is achieved, it is held and written down in a memory somewhere.

4. The memory can control the positions of the descriptions, allowing one to fuse any piece of a surface easily once its depth map has been established in the memory.

(Since the development of the Marr-Poggio algorithm, a number of interesting modifications have been proposed by Mayhew and Frisby [1981].)

There are two tasks left to consider. The first is the form and size of the operators which perform the filtering of the image at different degrees of coarseness. The second is to specify the matching procedure used in step 1.

We have argued that in order to obtain both range and resolution of disparity information, we need to obtain a range of symbolic descriptions of the changes in the image, each description reflecting a different coarseness. Although there are many possible ways of filtering the image at different degrees of coarseness, Marr and Hildreth [1980] suggest that the Gaussian is one of the best filters to use. In particular, they propose that the image should be filtered by convolution with a series of different sized $\nabla^2 G$ operators, and the zero-crossings of each output be located.

The Gaussian is a band-limited operator; in terms of the image, this means that the Gaussian in some sense blurs the image by an amount dependent on its size. Thus, the application of a large Gaussian will tend to enhance gross features of the image, while the application of a small Gaussian will tend to enhance fine features of the image. One can obtain descriptions of the image with varying degrees of resolution by filtering the image with a series of $\nabla^2 G$ operators, each with a different size Gaussian. For reasons that will become apparent in the discussion of human psychophysics, the separation of these filters should be roughly one octave. This means that if the size of the smallest filter is given by its central diameter w, the other filters should have sizes specified by central diameters of $2w$, $4w$, and $8w$.

Having filtered the image $E(x, y)$ to obtain the convolved image $f(x, y, \sigma)$, the zero-crossings of f are located. Two features of zero-crossings can be computed and will be of use in the stereo matching problem. One is the sign, or contrast, of the zero-crossing. This is computed simply by noting whether the convolution values change from positive to negative or negative to positive while scanning from left to right across the zero-crossing. The second feature is the local orientation of a zero-crossing on the image plane. This is found by computing the gradient of the convolution values across the zero-crossing and taking the orientation of the projection of the gradient onto the image as the orientation of the zero-crossing.

Thus, the problem of what is to be matched in determining disparity in a scene has been solved. Specifically, the image will be filtered with operators whose form is a Laplacian of a Gaussian and the resulting convolution values will be searched for zero-crossings. This will give rise to a series of zero-crossing contours and it is this symbolic description of changes in an image that will be matched to obtain disparity information.

Having determined the form of the symbolic descriptions, we turn to the procedure for determining the correspondence between them. The correspondence problem is straightforward only if false targets are rare. By performing the matching for different resolutions, and using the results of the larger channels to drive the alignment of the smaller channels, fine disparity information can be achieved over a wide range of disparities while avoiding the problem of false targets. In general terms, for each pair of filters of a given size, the correlation process consists of matching symbols of the same type. We shall use two attributes to determine type, the contrast sign of the zero-crossing and the orientation of the zero-crossing in the image plane.

To evaluate their design, Marr and Poggio [1979] performed a statistical analysis of the zero-crossings to determine the probability distribution of the interval between adjacent zero-crossings of the same sign in the filtered image. Suppose that a zero-crossing L in the left image matches some zero-crossing R in the right image, and let w denote the diameter of the central region of the filter. The probability distribution derived by Marr and Poggio states that the probability of another zero-crossing of the same sign within $\frac{w}{2}$ image elements of R is less than 0.05. This means that if the disparity between the two images for this region of the image is less than $\frac{w}{2}$, a matcher that searches for possible matches in the range $\pm\frac{w}{2}$ will find only the correct match with probability 0.95, and the correct match will almost always be found. According to this analysis, if one wishes to avoid false targets altogether, the disparity range over which a match is sought must be restricted to $\pm\frac{w}{2}$.

To enlarge the range of disparity accepted, the following modification is possible. Suppose the size of the search region is expanded to $\pm w$. Then, if the disparity between the two images is less than $|w|$, Marr and Poggio show that 50% of all matches will be correct and unambiguous. The remaining matches will be ambiguous, usually with two alternatives, one convergent (in the range $(0, w)$) and one divergent (in the range $(-w, 0)$), one of which is always correct. For these ambiguous cases, the correct alternative can still be found by making use of the sign of the disparity of the neighboring unambiguous matches. (By the sign of the disparity, I mean the sign of the direction of the matching zero-crossing: crossed or convergent, uncrossed or divergent, and zero.) One may choose between the convergent and divergent alternatives by selecting the one with the same sign as the dominant sign of the neighboring unambiguous matches. Such a procedure is based upon the continuity constraint, since it expects disparity to change as little as possible.

Finally, the above discussion concerned the situation in which the disparity of the elements is less than $|w|$. If the disparity exceeds the operating range, one wants to ensure that the algorithm is capable of detecting this fact. Marr and Poggio show that given that the images are outside the acceptable disparity range $|w|$, the probability of a random match is about 0.7. Thus the probability of a zero-crossing having no candidate match is 0.3 if the images are outside the acceptable disparity range, and 0.0 if the images are within the acceptable disparity range. This situation can easily be detected (by calculating the percentage of unmatched points, see Chapter 4) and used to remove random matches. In this way one can ensure not only that correct disparities are computed where available, but also that incorrect disparities are avoided. A precise statement of the algorithm will be presented in Chapter 3.

2.6 Previous Models

Earlier work on the correspondence problem has come from two sources, image processing and psychology. The work in image processing has been generally concerned with finding a solution to the correspondence problem, irrespective of its relevance to the human system, while work in psychology has been centered around modelling the human stereo system.

Although models in image processing have concentrated on the correspondence problem without specific regard for the human system, correlates of some aspects of the human system have appeared in the image processing literature. Of particular note is the use of several scales of resolution [Moravec, 1977, 1979; Baker and Binford, 1981]. While many models have attempted to match the raw irradiance values, some have defined a set of "interesting points" (similar, in principle, to the points detected by the Marr-Hildreth theory of edge detection) in the images [Quam, 1971; Lillestrand, 1972; Levine, et al., 1973; Sutro and Lerman, 1973; Hannah, 1974; Nevatia, 1976; Burr and Chien, 1977; Moravec, 1977, 1979; Arnold, 1978; Kahl, et al., 1978; Binford, 1979; Baker, 1980; Barnard and Thompson, 1980; Baker and Binford, 1981]. Such methods usually use either a cross-correlation or a mean-square difference technique to measure the similarity between nearby regions of the "interesting" points. Other methods have segmented the monocular images before performing a correlation based on properties of the segments [Price and Reddy, 1977].

Several strategies for limiting the search in the cross-correlation techniques have been explored. Some have used a fixed camera model to constrain the search to one dimension [Levine, et al., 1973; Mori, et al., 1973; Hannah, 1974; Nevatia, 1976]. Others have used a coarse search to obtain a rough estimate of the matching points, followed by a fine search to refine the disparity estimate [Levine, et al., 1973; Gennery, 1977; Tanimoto, 1978], or have used a sequential similarity detection scheme, [Barnea and Silverman, 1972].

The image processing models listed above are not directly applicable to the human visual system, nor are they intended as models of that system. Even so, many of the aspects of these methods are of interest to the modelling of the human stereo system.

In the psychological literature, there have been many classical models of stereoscopic vision, for example, [Muller, 1826; Wheatstone, 1838, 1852; Brucke, 1841; Brewster, 1856; Panum, 1858; Helmholtz, 1925; Koffka, 1935; Ogle, 1959]. More recently, there have been models based on grey-level correlation [Sperling, 1970] and cluster seeking [Julesz, 1963a]; a spring-dipole model [Julesz, 1971, page 203ff; Julesz and Chang, 1976] and several neural models [Nelson, 1975; Dev, 1975; Hirai and Fukushima, 1976; Sugie and Suwa, 1977; Marr and Poggio, 1977b].

2.7 Psychophysical Evidence

Having proposed and outlined an algorithm for solving the stereopsis problem, we can now turn to the question of how well the algorithm fits the known evidence about the human stereo system. The evidence will be roughly broken into two groups, psychophysical data and neurophysiological data.

A large body of literature is available concerning the psychophysics of stereo vision. The interested reader is referred to Julesz [1971], Richards [1975] and Gulick and Lawson [1976] for extensive bibliographies and reviews. In this section we briefly consider the psychophysical evidence relevant to the Marr-Poggio algorithm. A more complete analysis may be found in Marr and Poggio [1979].

The theory proposed by Marr and Poggio differs in several ways from previous approaches. In examining the psychophysical evidence we will consider both evidence directly bearing on the structure of the Marr-Poggio algorithm and evidence relevant to the difference between the Marr-Poggio algorithm and several of the psychological models mentioned above.

2.7.1 The Primal Sketch Filters

The first stage of processing consists of applying a set of $\nabla^2 G$ operators to the images, and locating the zero-crossings of the resulting convolved image. What evidence is there that such filters exist in the human visual system?

The existence of separate spatial-frequency tuned channels in the human visual system has long been known [Campbell and Robson, 1968]. Recently, Wilson and Giese [1977] and Wilson and Bergen [1979] presented a careful analysis of these channels, which incorporates virtually all of the previous evidence. They have found strong evidence that at each point in the foveal region of the visual field there exists at least four and possibly five independent channels in the human early visual system (see also Richards and Polit, [1974] concerning the hypothesis of four spatial channels). The point of interest in this context is that the form of the filters, as analyzed by Wilson and collaborators, very closely fits the shape of a difference of two Gaussians. The stimuli used by Wilson and collaborators were one-dimensional gratings, which means that only the cross-section of the filter can be determined. Thus, they do not directly address the question of whether the full two-dimensional operator is rotationally symmetric (and hence orientation independent). However, it is worth noting that in two dimensions, a difference of Gaussians is a close approximation to the Laplacian of a Gaussian [Appendix B, Marr and Hildreth, 1980].

Thus, the operator for detecting features of a visual scene that was developed on basic information processing grounds is closely related to the operator that appears to be used by the human visual system. Wilson and collaborators also observe that the peak sensitivity wavelength of these channels increases linearly with retinal eccentricity from some initial value in the fovea.

Given the form of the operators, only the size of these filters is left to be determined. Wilson and Bergen's data indicated difference of Gaussian filters whose sizes — specified by the width w of the filter's central region — range from $3.1'$ to $21'$ of visual arc. The variable w is related to the constant σ of $\nabla^2 G$ by the relation:

$$\sigma = \frac{w}{2\sqrt{2}}.$$

If the visual input to the operator is a one-dimensional grating, then the response of the operator is equivalent to that obtained by applying a one-dimensional operator to the one-dimensional input. This one-dimensional operator is obtained by projecting $\nabla^2 G$ onto a line, and is given by

$$D_{xx}G = \sqrt{2\pi}\left(\frac{x^2 - \sigma^2}{\sigma^3}\right)\exp\left(\frac{-x^2}{2\sigma^2}\right).$$

This operator is illustrated in Figure 2.5 and has a central region width of

$$w_{1D} = 2\sigma.$$

Wilson and Bergen's values for w were obtained by using oriented line stimuli. To obtain the diameter of the corresponding circularly symmetric center-surround receptive field the values of w must be multiplied by $\sqrt{2}$. The resolution of the initial images should roughly represent the resolution of processing by the cones of the retina and the size of the filters should represent the size of the retinal operators. In the most densely packed region of the human fovea the center-to-center spacing of the cones is 2.0 to $2.3\mu m$, corresponding to an angular spacing of 25 to 29 arc seconds [O'Brien, 1951]. Accounting for the conversion of Wilson and Bergen's data, and using the figure of 27 arc seconds for the separation of the cones in the fovea, one arrives at values of w in the range 9 to 63 image elements, and hence, values of σ in the range 3 to 23 image elements.

Although Wilson and collaborators have found definite evidence only for four different sized channels, it has recently been proposed [Marr, Poggio and Hildreth, 1980; Crick, Marr and Poggio, 1980] that an additional smaller channel may also be present, in order to account for experiments on human acuity. This filter would have a central diameter of $w = 1.5'$, roughly corresponding to 4 picture elements. (One picture element, or *pixel*, corresponds roughly to one receptor in the human retina.)

The Wilson and Bergen studies provide evidence only for the size of the one-dimensional cross section of the filters. We have proposed, on computational grounds, that the full two-dimensional operator be orientation independent, (for example, the Laplacian ∇^2). The use of non-oriented filters was also arrived at independently on psychophysical grounds by Mayhew and Frisby [1978a].

At this point, it is worth noting several asides regarding the Primal Sketch. The first concerns the role of the development of the stereo theory in the refinement of the Primal Sketch. The framework for the Primal Sketch was first developed by Marr in 1976 [Marr, 1976]. However, many of the details of that theory were not explicitly implemented in an algorithm, and hence not carefully tested. During both the development of the stereo theory and, in particular, during the implementation of the stereo algorithm, many of the details of the Primal Sketch were tested and found to require refinement. These refinements in part led to the revamping of the Primal Sketch theory, discussed in detail in Marr and Hildreth [1980].

The importance of this point is really one of methodology. A major aspect of Marr's computational paradigm is that the creation of a specific algorithm to solve a computational theory provides a major source of feedback for that theory. The creation of an algorithm, and the testing of it via a computer implementation, allows one to discover previously overlooked problems, to illuminate errors or unwarranted assumptions in the theory, and to generally refine the theory itself. The development of the stereo algorithm is an example of this process.

An example of this refinement concerns the use of non-directional operators and the use of zero-crossings. In the original Marr-Poggio theory, it was proposed that the initial convolutions of the images use directional operators. This was based in part on the proposal that the neural units responsible for this operation were the simple cells of visual cortex, which are known to be orientation dependent [Hubel and Wiesel, 1962, 1968]. In principle, of course, there is no difference between locating the zero-crossings of a second directional derivative and the peaks of a first directional derivative. Indeed many earlier edge detection algorithms did, in fact, localize peaks of first derivatives [see reviews in Davis, 1975; Rosenfeld and Kak, 1976; Pratt, 1978]. Why do we rely on zero-crossings of second derivatives, and why do we use non-directional operators?

Any first derivative operator that could be used must be directional, that is, must have a preferred direction of sensitivity. Such operators have several practical problems associated with them (see Hildreth, [1980] for a more complete discussion of these problems). Two effects are particularly relevant to the stereo process. The first is that oriented bar-shaped filters smear or stretch zero-crossings in the direction of the orientation of the filter, relative to the actual edges in the image. For example, a vertically oriented bar filter converts a circular object in a scene into an oval zero-crossing contour. This is undesirable, since any matching performed on smeared zero-crossings will result in disparity values being assigned to locations in the image for which there is no evidence that such assignments are valid. Any matching process that assigns disparities based on such descriptors will be assigning disparity values that do not accurately reflect the structure of the underlying surface.

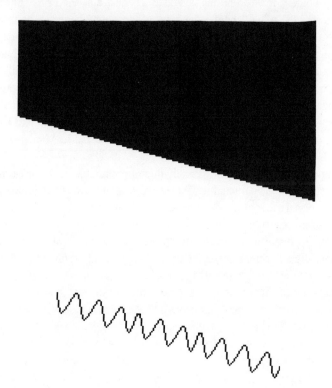

Figure 2.9
The Snake Effect. The ideal edge of the top figure was processed with an oriented filter whose orientation differed from that of the edge by 70 degrees. The zero-crossing in the bottom figure has the same overall orientation as the edge, but exhibits a wide fluctuation about this orientation.

While in principle it is possible to use several directional filters, with different orientations, and to select zero-crossings only from the filter with the maximal response, in practise, it is difficult to perfect such a scheme. The use of a non-directional filter would remove these difficulties.

As might be expected, some experiments with the aspect ratio of such bar shaped filters indicated that the lower the aspect ratio, the smaller the amount of stretching of the zero-crossing contours. (The aspect ratio refers to the ratio of the size of the oriented filter parallel to and perpendicular to its orientation.)

A second effect concerns the case of an edge with an orientation different from that of the filter, illustrated in Figure 2.9. In this case, instead of producing a straight zero-crossing contour along the orientation of the edge, the filter produced a zero-crossing contour with the same overall orientation as the edge, but which curved about the edge in a snake-like fashion. Thus, the resulting zero-crossing contour had a significant number of segments consisting of components in the direction of the filter orientation, rather than in the direction of the edge. Again, any matching process that assigns disparities based on such descriptors will be assigning disparity values that do not accurately reflect the structure of the underlying surface.

In order to avoid these types of difficulties, it is necessary to seek a non-directional operator. The operator with lowest order that satisfies this is necessarily second order, namely the Laplacian. In addition to the justifications offered by Marr and Hildreth [1980] and the psychophysical evidence of Mayhew and Frisby [1978], there are computational reasons for using non-directional operators.

A second computational reason for relying on zero-crossings concerns the use of interpolation for human hyperacuity. Hyperacuity refers to our ability to compute the position of a feature in an image to a resolution of a few seconds of arc, about $\frac{1}{5}$ the size of a foveal receptor, [Westheimer and McKee, 1975, 1976, 1977; Westheimer, 1976, 1977; Beck and Schwartz, 1978; Burr, 1979]. Marr, Poggio and Hildreth [1980] argue that in order to account for such hyperacuity, given the sampling density of the receptors and ganglion cells, one must postulate an interpolation process to isolate the zero-crossings to an accuracy finer than that of the receptor spacing. It can be shown that in the case of interpolating the zero-crossings a straightforward linear approximation between the adjacent convolution values will suffice. If we utilized peaks in the output of a first derivative operator, a non-linear interpolation would be required to account for hyperacuity, which in turn requires the values of the derivatives of the convolution values. This would, however, involve an estimation based on the discrete convolution samples and would introduce a significant error. Hence, the use of second derivative operators makes the localization of zero-crossings to fine resolutions a straightforward computation, while the use of first derivative operators makes the localization of peaks a non-trivial computation with serious error problems.

2.7.2 Eye Movements

What is the relative importance of neural fusion and eye movements? We have argued that disparity information from the coarser channels can be used to align the symbolic descriptions of the finer channels, thereby facilitating the solution of the correspondence problem for those finer channels. This alignment of the symbolic descriptions could be strictly a neural process (that is, occurring within an internal representation in the visual pathway). On the other hand, it could be accomplished by aligning the images through control of vergence movements. A vergence movement of the eyes changes the relative alignments of the two eyes by differentially moving them towards or away from the nose.

In principle, all of the previous human models [Sperling, 1970; Julesz, 1963a, 1971, page 203ff; Julesz and Chang, 1976; Nelson, 1975; Dev, 1975; Hirai and Fukushima, 1976; Sugie and Suwa, 1977; Marr and Poggio, 1977b] have the ability to interpret random dot stereograms without the use of eye-movements, while the Marr-Poggio algorithm relies on them. Thus, the question is of critical importance in determining the relevance of such models. Unfortunately, almost all studies using random-dot stereograms proceeded by viewing the pairs with free eye movements [Julesz, 1971; exceptions are Fender and Julesz, 1967; Evans and Clegg, 1967; Richards, 1977]. Two observations can be made, however. The first is that the small size of Panum's fusional area (the psychophysical estimate of the range of disparities which can be matched for a single fixation) [Fender and Julesz, 1967] suggests that eye movements may be important for performing stereo matching. The second is that although some observers can see depth in simple random-dot stereograms that are presented in a flash or under stabilized image conditions, eye movements or the associated retinal motion are essential for many observers for simple stereograms. Even then, the perceived depth may be ambiguous or inappropriate [Richards, 1977], except possibly in the disparity range 0-13 minutes [Mayhew and Frisby, 1978b]. For complex stereograms such as Julesz's spiral [1971, Figure 4.5-4], eye movements are probably essential [Frisby and Clatworthy, 1975; Saye and Frisby, 1975]. Stabilized conditions refers to situations in which the image is maintained in a fixed position on the retina, independent of any eye movements. Presenting stereograms in a flash eliminates the influence of eye movements since the visual input is removed before the system has an opportunity to perform an eye movement.

If eye movements are used by the stereo system to align the images, one would expect the system to exhibit a fine degree of control over such movements. The psychophysical evidence is consistent with this expectation: vergence movements may be controlled with an extremely high degree of precision [Riggs and Niehl, 1960; Rashbass and Westheimer, 1961].

2.7.3 Disparity Layers

Most of the previous, cooperative models of the human stereo system lead to the expectation of a series of disparity layers, each of which is finely tuned to a particular disparity. Richards [1970, 1971], however, proposes that the mechanisms underlying stereoscopic depth perception are organized into at least two pools, roughly corresponding to crossed and uncrossed disparities. (The notion of two pools roughly corresponds to having neurons that are sensitive to a wide range of disparities, either crossed or uncrossed, rather than specifically tuned to a narrow disparity range.) Richards bases this proposal on a study of "stereoanomalous" observers, who are able to process one of these kinds of disparities more strongly than the other. It is interesting to note that some confirmation of this proposal has been found in the monkey visual cortex [Poggio and Fischer, 1978].

As Marr and Poggio observe, although these data do not rule out the existence of many functional layers, they do suggest the genetic importance of the two pools idea and hint at its functional implications. We shall also see in the next section that the neurophysiological data seem to support the notion of pools rather than layers.

2.7.4 Several Channels

What is the structure of the disparity detectors? Kaufman [1964] and Julesz [1971, 3.9 and 3.10] found that one can simultaneously experience both binocular rivalry and fusion of different spectral components in a stereogram. Binocular rivalry refers to the existence of two possible depth interpretations corresponding to two different solutions to the correspondence problem. In this situation, our perception flips back and forth between the two interpretations. Julesz and Miller [1975] expanded this finding in the following manner. They selected masking noise bands, containing equally effective noise energy, such that their bands either overlapped the stereoscopic image spectrum or were two octaves distant. The first case resulted in rivalry while in the second, stereoscopic fusion (and the subsequent perception of depth) could be maintained despite the presence of strong binocular rivalry caused by the masking noise.

This finding suggests that disparity information might at some stage be conveyed by independent stereopsis channels, tuned to different spatial frequencies, and roughly one octave wide. (Such channels are probably the same as those analyzed by Campbell and Robson, [1968] and others.) The findings of Mayhew and Frisby [1976] using rivalrous texture stereograms are also consistent with the idea of independent spatial-frequency tuned stereopsis channels.

The evidence for independent channels raises the question of whether channels separated in the frequency domain are also separated in the disparity domain. In other words, are the channels further distinguished by the range of disparity values that they can convey? The Marr-Poggio algorithm critically relies on the proposal that the range of disparity detected by a channel is directly related to its frequency range. Felton, Richards and Smith [1972] reported that, over the 1 degree disparity range they examined, high spatial-frequency detectors feed small disparity mechanisms whereas low spatial-frequency detectors feed large disparity mechanisms.

Marr and Poggio also argue that indirect evidence about this point may come from the differing reports of the size of Panum's fusional area. Fender and Julesz [1967] gave a figure of 6 minutes for Panum's fusional area for random-dot stereograms with a dot size of about 2 minutes. Julesz and Chang [1976] flashed stereograms with a range of disparities, implying that those up to ±18 minutes were fused. Marr and Poggio propose that one explanation for this discrepancy is that Panum's area depends on the dot size, since Julesz and Chang's dots were 6 minutes square.

The evidence concerning the size of Panum's area is important since it bears on the question of the range of disparity which can be matched by one channel. If the correspondence process takes place over a range of disparities governed by $\pm w$, then the data of Wilson and Bergen [1979] imply an estimate of Panum's area on the order of 6 to 21 minutes, depending on which of Wilson's channels is performing the matching.

2.7.5 Hysteresis

It is also important to consider the role of hysteresis in stereopsis demonstrated by Fender and Julesz [1967]. They showed that once a binocularly stabilized random-dot stereogram had been fused in the 6 minute Panum area, the images could be pulled apart symmetrically by about 2 degrees in the horizontal direction without loss of stereopsis. Julesz and Fender, along with many later researchers, interpreted this result as indicating that binocular fusion is a cooperative process. A cooperative process is one that is characterized by a series of locally interconnected elements that performs an iterative computation of the problem at hand. In general, the value of a cell at some time t is determined by the value of the cell at time $t - 1$, as well as the values of neighboring cells at time $t - 1$. As a consequence, the system of interconnected cells tend to "cooperate" in determining their solution, since each cell's computation is affected by the current values of the neighboring cells.

Additional support for this view included:

1. disorder-order transitions and multiple stable states in stereopsis [Julesz and Chang, 1976, p.117], which are reminiscent of other cooperative processes,

2. the pulling effect with ambiguous random-dot stereograms [Julesz and Chang, 1976], (the pulling effect refers to the fact that the addition of a slight amount of noise along the border of an ambiguous area, which is biased towards one of the two possible interpretations, is sufficient to force the perception of only one of the interpretations),

3. Julesz's conclusion [1971, p. 200] that "stereopsis is a parallel process in which each depth plane is simultaneously processed."

In their original paper, Julesz and Fender concluded that the labelling of corresponding points can occur only within Panum's fusional area, but that under appropriate conditions, these correspondences could then be preserved for large retinal image shifts. Marr and Poggio [1979] argue that although the data of Julesz and Fender indicate the presence of a "simple memory process" (which they called hysteresis) there is no evidence that this hysteresis is intrinsic to the process of assigning correspondences (which would be the case if stereopsis were a cooperative process). As evidence, Marr and Poggio point out that the phenomenon of hysteresis occurs over a disparity range of 2 degrees, which is much larger than the estimates for Panum's area. Hence, they conclude that the observed hysteresis cannot be a direct consequence of the correspondence problem.

2.7.6 Matching Attributes

The final question concerns the attributes of the zero-crossings used by the matching process. The use of the sign of the zero-crossings as a matching attribute has some backing in psychophysical evidence. Julesz [1963b] demonstrated that it is extremely difficult to fuse a random dot pattern and its negative image.

2.8 Neurophysiology

In order to distinguish between the Marr-Poggio algorithm and previous algorithms based on cooperativity, we can also turn to the neurophysiology literature and ask four basic questions:

1. Are there disparity detectors?
2. If so, how finely tuned are they, and what range of disparities is covered by their peak sensitivities? For example, are there many, or are there just two or three (crossed, uncrossed, and possibly zero disparity)?
3. Are they organized into layers or columns of equal disparities?
4. Are the disparity detectors sensitive to specific spatial features?

Unfortunately, in part due to the tremendous technical difficulties involved in experiments on stereoscopic disparity, the available physiological evidence is not decisive.

Most physiologists believe that disparity detectors do exist, although there is some uncertainty about which cortical area is involved. Disparity sensitive units have been found in the visual cortex of the cat [Barlow, Blakemore and Pettigrew, 1967; Pettigrew, Nikara and Bishop, 1968; Nelson, Kato and Bishop, 1977; Hubel and Weisel, 1973], as well as areas of the visual cortex of the macaque monkey [Hubel and Weisel, 1970; Poggio and Fischer, 1978].

There are a number of different findings concerning the range and resolution of the disparity tuning of the cells. Barlow et al. [1967, Figure 3] reported disparity sensitive cells in the cat that had a range of about 6.3 degrees of arc at 5-15 degrees eccentricity (that is, the cells were found at an angular displacement of 5-15 degrees from the center of the visual field). Pettigrew et al., [1968, Figure

11] reported cells at an eccentricity of 8 degrees that were tuned to a disparity of about 3 degrees [see also Figure 9 of Nikara, Bishop and Pettigrew, 1968].

There are also several findings concerning the sharpness (or resolution) of disparity tuning. Nelson, *et al.* [1977] report a disparity-sensitive cell in the cat, tuned to an unknown disparity value, that had an accuracy of ± 0.5 degrees. Bishop, Henry and Smith [1971, Figure 6c] describe a cell that was about twice as finely tuned. In the monkey, Poggio and Fischer [1978] found four types of depth-sensitive cells in areas 17 and 18:

1. cells excited by and narrowly tuned to stimuli at the depth of the plane of fixation (that is, cells that responded to "features" located at the same depth as that given by the current alignment of the centers of the two eyes);

2. cells whose response was essentially the complement of (1);

3. *near* neurons, that were excited by stimuli in front of the fixation plane and were suppressed by those behind it; and

4. *far* neurons, the opposite of *near* neurons.

Some of the class (1) cells had a disparity tuning as sharp as 3 minutes of disparity, while some of the class (2) cells exhibited a total range of binocular interaction that could extend to more than ± 1 degree of disparity.

It is interesting to note the correlation between the cells described by Poggio and Fischer, and the pools hypothesis proposed by Richards [1970, 1971].

Although Hubel and Weisel [1970] reported a columnar grouping of cells representing a given stereoscopic depth relative to the surface of fixation, there is no evidence about the physiological connections among these cells. Almost all disparity-sensitive cells have, however, been reported to be inhibited by disparities lying outside the tuning range.

Finally, little is known about the spatial features to which disparity neurons are sensitive. Hubel and Weisel [1970] state that in the monkey, most binocular depth cells have vertically oriented, elongated receptive fields (which would tend to respond to vertically oriented "edges" in the visual field). Nelson *et al.* [1977] found that binocular neurons in the striate cortex of the cat are insensitive to differences in the orientations of slits or bars in the two eyes.

We mentioned earlier that one of the original motivations for the use of directional operators in the Marr-Poggio theory was the proposal that the computation was being performed by the simple cells of visual cortex. Practical problems and computational arguments led to a revising of the theory, and the directional operators were dropped in favor of non-directional ones. Since the simple cells can no longer be considered as performing the non-directional $\nabla^2 G$ convolution, it is of interest to consider what neural components do perform this operation. It has been proposed that the $\nabla^2 G$ convolutions are performed by the X and Y type ganglion cells of the retina, which have the required non-directional form [Marr and Ullman, 1980; Richter and Ullman, 1980].

2.9 Summary

The conclusion drawn by Marr and Poggio [1979] is that many of the psychophysical and neurophysiological findings cast doubt on the relevance of cooperative algorithms to the question of the fusion process in human stereo vision. Based on these findings, they developed a theory that was specifically intended to be consistent with the known psychological evidence. In this chapter, we have outlined that theory, the main points of which are summarized here.

We have shown that the stereo process consists of two major problems, the extraction of a description of the elements of an image corresponding to physically identifiable locations in the scene, and the determination of the corresponding descriptors from each processed image. The problem of extracting matchable descriptions of the images is solved by the Marr-Hildreth theory of edge detection. This consists of convolving each image with a set of filters of the form $\nabla^2 G$, where ∇^2 is the Laplacian and G is a Gaussian. For each size filter, the zero-crossings of the convolved image are localized. Matching takes place between zero-crossing segments of the same sign and roughly the same orientation in the two images, for a range of disparities up to about the width of the filter's central region. Because of the roughly bandpass nature of the filters, false targets pose only a simple problem within this range. This matching takes place for each filtered image, and the disparities obtained at a coarse filtering are used to align the images via vergence eye movements, thereby causing the finer filtered images to come into range of correspondence.

Note that a major consequence of this approach is that not every point in an image will receive an explicit match. This will turn out to be important when we discuss surface interpolation in Chapter 5.

CHAPTER 3

THE STEREO IMPLEMENTATION

An important factor in the development of any computational theory is the design and implementation of an explicit algorithm for that theory. There are several benefits from such a task. The act of implementation itself forces one to make all details of the theory explicit. This often uncovers previously overlooked difficulties which guide further refinement of the theory. A second benefit concerns the performance of the implementation. Any proposed model of a system must be testable. In this case, by testing pairs of stereo images, one can examine the performance of the implementation, and hence the adequacy of the theory itself. (This is provided, of course, that the implementation is an accurate representation of that theory.) In this manner, the performance of the implementation can be compared with human performance. If the algorithm differs strongly from known human performance, its suitability as a biological model is quickly brought into question (c.f. the analysis in Marr and Poggio, [1979] of the cooperative algorithm of Marr and Poggio, [1977b]).

This chapter describes an implementation of the Marr-Poggio stereo theory, written with particular emphasis on the matching process [Grimson, 1980a, 1980b, 1981a]. Later chapters will discuss the effect of the implementation on refining the theory and the analysis of its performance on several test cases.

The implementation is divided into five modules, roughly corresponding to the five steps of the Marr-Poggio theory. These modules are shown in Figure 3.1, and each is described in turn.

3.1 Input

Two aspects of the human stereo system that are embedded in the theory must be made explicit in the input to the algorithm. The first is the orientation of the eyes with respect to the scene, as eye movements will be critical for obtaining fine disparity information. The second is the change in resolution of analysis of the image with increasing eccentricity, (the quantitative aspects of this were incorporated in Wilson and Bergen's model [1979]).

To account for these effects, the algorithm maintains as its initial input a pair of image arrays, representing the right and left views of the entire scene visible to the viewer. This pair of arrays corresponds to the environment around the visual system; different portions of these arrays will be accessed as the positions

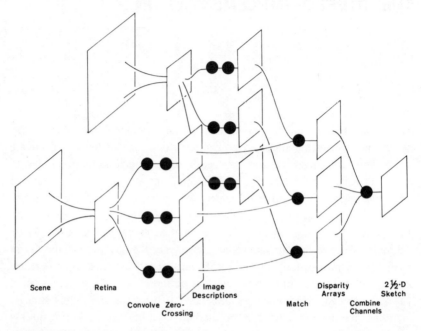

Scene   Retina   Image   Disparity   2½-D
                                         Descriptions   Arrays   Sketch
                   Convolve Zero-   Match   Combine
                             Crossing   Channels

Figure 3.1
Diagram of the Implementation. From the initial arrays of the scene, a retinal pair of
images are extracted. These subimages reflect the current eye orientations relative to
the scene and may be considered as the representation of the light intensities falling
on the retina. Each retinal image is convolved with a set of different sized filters of
the form $\nabla^2 G$, and the zero-crossings of the output are located. For each filter size,
the zero-crossing descriptions are matched, based on the sign and orientation of each
zero-crossing point. The disparity arrays created for each filter are combined into a
single disparity description, and information from the larger filters can be used to
verge the eyes, thereby bringing the smaller filters into a range of operation.

of the eyes change relative to the scene. To create this representation of the
scene, photographs of natural images were digitized on an Optronix Photoscan
System P1000. The sizes of these images are indicated in the legends. Grey-
level resolution is 8 bits, providing 256 intensity levels. For the random dot
patterns illustrated in this book the images were constructed by computer rather
than digitized from photographs.

For a given position of the eyes relative to the scene a representation of the
images on the two retinas is extracted by obtaining a second, smaller pair of
images from the arrays representing the whole scene. The matching process will
then take place on the array representing the retinal images. It is important
that the coordinate systems of those arrays coincide with the current positions

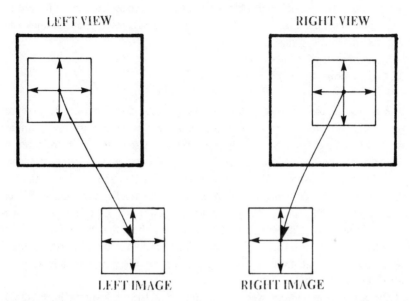

Figure 3.2
Mapping from the Scene Representations to the Retinal Representations. From each view of the scene, a subimage is extracted. The position of the subimages reflects the positions of the two optical axes.

of the eyes. Thus, different sections of the scenes will be mapped to the center (fovea) of the retinal images as the positions of the eyes are varied. Successively foveating sections of a scene allows the smallest channels to come into the range of correspondence. These sections of the scenes can be separately matched to a very fine level of disparity. Note that the portion of the scene image that is mapped into the retinal image may differ for the two eyes depending on the relative positions of the two optical axes (see Figure 3.2). In particular, there may be differences in vertical alignment as well as in horizontal alignment. A second factor should also be taken into account. The work of Wilson and Bergen [1979] and Wilson and Giese [1977] implies that the resolution of the earlier stages of the algorithm — the convolution and zero-crossings — scales linearly with eccentricity. This aspect has not been implemented and in our situation is not critical since the images analyzed correspond to small visual angles (on the order of 4° on a side).

At the completion of this stage, the program has created a representation of the images that has accounted for eye position and, if appropriate, for retinal scaling with eccentricity. For each pass of the algorithm the matching will take place on the representation of the retinal images, thereby implicitly assuming some particular eye positions. Once the matching has been completed, the disparity values obtained may be used to change the positions of the two optical axes, thus causing a new pair of retinal images to be extracted from the representations of the scene. The matching process may then proceed again.

3.2 Convolution

The retinal representations of the images must be transformed into a representation upon which the matcher can operate. We have already seen arguments in the previous chapter concerning the form and size of the filters required to perform this transformation. The present implementation uses four filters, each of which has the form of $\nabla^2 G$, the Laplacian of a Gaussian, with w values of $4, 9, 17$ and 35 image elements. These values are derived from the data of Wilson and Bergen [1979]. The coefficients of the filters were represented to a precision of 1 part in 2048. Coefficients of less than $\frac{1}{2048}$'th of the maximum value of the filter were set to zero. Thus, the truncation radius of the filter (the point at which all further filter values were treated as zero) was approximately $1.8w$, or equivalently, 5.08σ.

The actual convolutions were performed on a LISP machine constructed at the MIT Artificial Intelligence Laboratory using additional hardware specially designed for the purpose [Knight, et al. 1979]. Figures 3.3 and 3.4 illustrate some images and their convolutions with various sized filters.

At the completion of this stage of the algorithm, we have four filtered copies, corresponding to the different filter sizes, of each of the images.

3.3 Detection and Description of Zero-Crossings

In theory, the elements to be matched between images are (1) zero-crossings whose orientations are not horizontal, and (2) terminations. The exact definition and hence the detection of terminations is at present uncertain, however. Moreover, terminations are much rarer than zero-crossings. As a consequence, only zero-crossings are used in the present implementation.

Horizontally oriented segments of the zero-crossing contours may be ignored, since they do not have a well defined disparity. Thus, the detection of zero-crossings can be accomplished by scanning the convolved image horizontally for adjacent elements of opposite sign, or for three horizontally adjacent elements, the middle one of which is zero, the other two containing convolution values of opposite sign. This provides the position of zero-crossings to within an image element. Note that there is no theoretical limit on the accuracy with which the zero-crossings may be localized. For the purposes of matching, however, a resolution of one picture element suffices.

In addition to their location, the sign of the zero-crossings and a rough estimate of the local, two-dimensional orientation of pieces of the zero-crossing contour

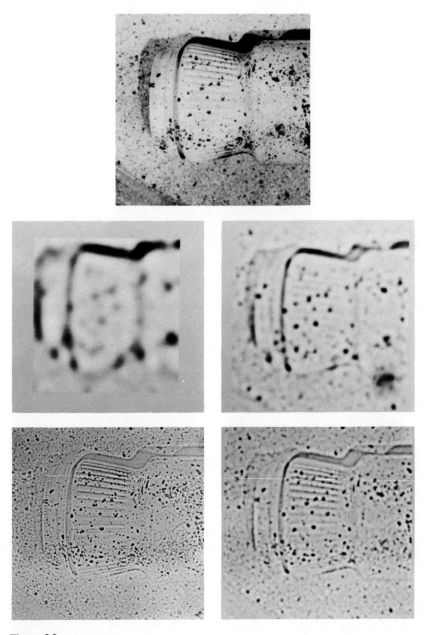

Figure 3.3
Examples of Convolutions. A natural image is illustrated at the top. Below are examples
of the convolved image, after application of different sized $\nabla^2 G$ operators, with central
diameters, w, of $36, 18, 9$ and 4 picture elements. The original image was 480 picture
elements on a side.

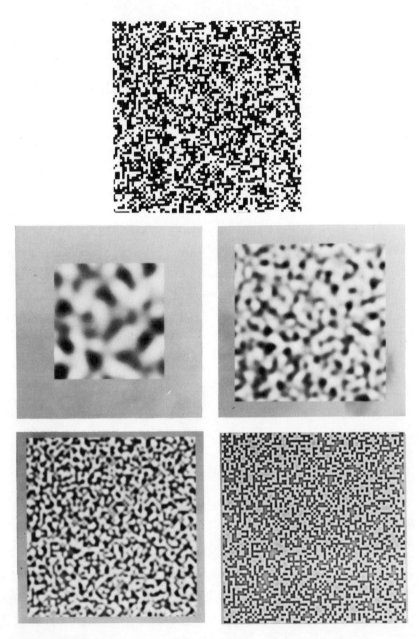

Figure 3.4
Examples of Convolutions. A random dot pattern is illustrated at the top. Below are examples of the convolved image, after application of different sized $\nabla^2 G$ operators, with central diameters, w, of $36, 18, 9$ and 4 picture elements. The original image was 320 picture elements on a side.

are recorded. Recall that the sign of a zero-crossing was determined by whether the convolution values change from positive to negative or negative to positive while scanning from left to right across the zero-crossing. In the present implementation the orientation at a point on a zero-crossing segment is computed as the direction of the gradient of the convolution values across that segment, and recorded in increments of 30 degrees. Figures 3.5 and 3.6 illustrate zero-crossings obtained in this way from the convolutions of Figures 3.3 and 3.4. Positive zero-crossings are shown white, and negative zero-crossings, black.

This zero-crossing description is computed for each image and for each size of filter.

3.4 Matching

The matcher implements the algorithm outlined in Chapter 2 (which is the second of the matching algorithms described by Marr and Poggio [1979, p.315]). For each size of filter, matching consists of 6 steps:

1. Fix the eye positions.
2. Locate a zero-crossing in one image.
3. Divide the region about the corresponding point in the second image into three pools.
4. Assign a match to the zero-crossing based on the potential matches within the pools.
5. Disambiguate any ambiguous matches.
6. Assign the disparity values to a buffer.

These steps may be repeated several times during the fusion of an image. Given positions for the eyes, these matching steps are performed, with the results stored in a buffer. These results can be used to refine the eye positions, causing a new set of retinal images to be extracted from the scene and another iteration of the matching steps.

The first step consists of fixing the two eye positions. The alignment between the two zero-crossing descriptions, corresponding to the positions of the eyes, is determined in two ways. The initial offsets of the descriptions are arbitrarily set to zero. Thereafter, the offsets of the two eyes are determined by accessing the current disparity values for a region and using these values to adjust the vergence of the eyes. In the current implementation, this is done by modifying the extraction of the retinal images from the images of the entire scene, as explained earlier.

Once the eye positions have been fixed, and the retinal images extracted, the zero-crossing descriptions are obtained as in Figures 3.5 and 3.6. For a zero-crossing description obtained from a particular filter size, the matching is performed by locating a zero-crossing in one image and then partitioning a region

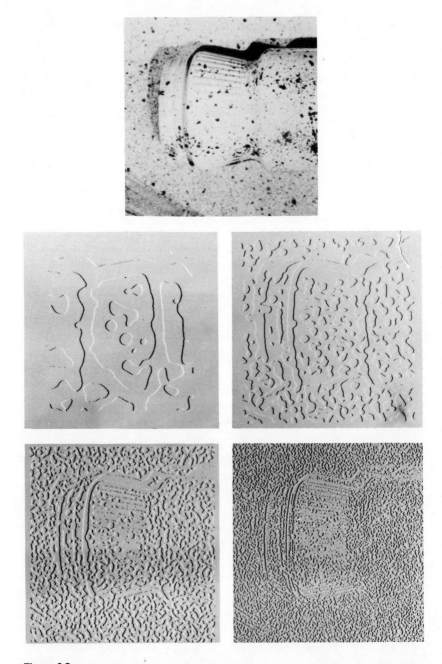

Figure 3.5
Examples of Zero-Crossings. A natural image is shown at the top. Below are examples of the horizontal zero-crossings, obtained from different sized $\nabla^2 G$ operators, with central diameters, w, of 36, 18, 9 and 4 picture elements. The positive zero-crossings are shown as white, the negative ones as black.

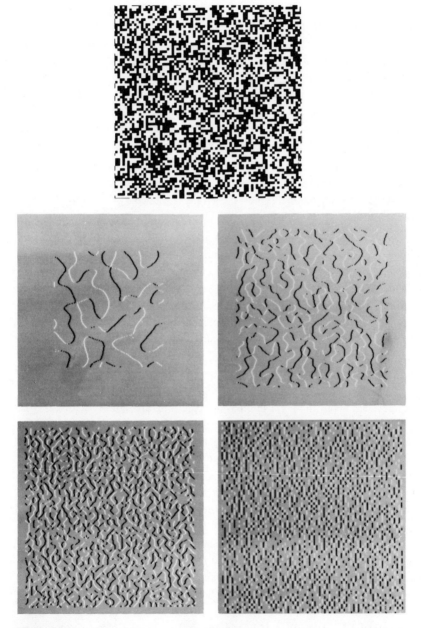

Figure 3.6
Examples of Zero-Crossings. A random dot pattern is shown at the top. Below are
examples of the horizontal zero-crossings, obtained from different sized $\nabla^2 G$ operators,
with central diameters, w, of 36, 18, 9 and 4 picture elements. The positive zero-
crossings are shown as white, the negative ones as black.

about the same location in the other image into three pools, two larger conver-gent and divergent regions, and a smaller one lying centrally between them. These pools form the region to be searched for a possible matching zero-crossing. Together these pools span a disparity range equal to $\sqrt{2}\,w_{2D}$ where w_{2D} is the diameter of the central region of the corresponding convolution filter. The simplest form for the pools is to require that they lie along the same horizontal line as the zero-crossing to be matched. This requirement can be relaxed to consider vertical disparities as well as the horizontal.

The following criteria are used for matching zero-crossings in the left and right filtered images, for each pool:

1. The zero-crossings must arise from convolutions with the same size filter.
2. The zero-crossings must have the same contrast sign.
3. The zero-crossing segments must have roughly the same orientation.

A match is assigned on the basis of the responses of the pools. If exactly one zero-crossing of the appropriate sign and orientation (within 30 degrees) is found within a pool, the location of that crossing is transmitted to the matcher. If two candidate zero-crossings are found within one pool (an unlikely event), the matcher is notified and no attempt is made to assign a match for the point in question. If the matcher finds a single zero-crossing in only one of the three pools, that match is accepted, and the disparity associated with the match is recorded in a buffer. If two or three of the pools contain a candidate match, the algorithm records that information for future disambiguation.

Once all possible unambiguous matches have been identified, an attempt is made to disambiguate double or triple matches. This is done by scanning a neighborhood about the point in question, recording the sign of the disparity of the unambiguous matches within that neighborhood. (The sign of the disparity refers to the sign of the pool from which the match comes: divergent, convergent or zero.) If the ambiguous point has a potential match of the same sign as the dominant type within the neighborhood, then that is chosen as the match (this is the "pulling" effect). Otherwise, the match at that point is left ambiguous.

It is possible that the region under consideration does not lie within the $\pm w$ disparity range examined by the matcher. This situation is detected and handled by the following operation. Consider the case in which the region does lie within the disparity range $\pm w$. Excluding the case of occluded points, every zero-crossing in the region will have at least one candidate match (the correct one) in the other filtered image. On the other hand, if the region lies beyond the disparity range $\pm w$, then the probability of a given zero-crossing having at least one candidate match will be less than 1. In fact, the probability of a zero-crossing having at least one candidate match in this case is roughly 0.7 (see section 2.5, also [Marr and Poggio, 1979]. In this event the matching algorithm is run for all the zero-crossings, for a given eye position. Any zero-crossing for which there is no match

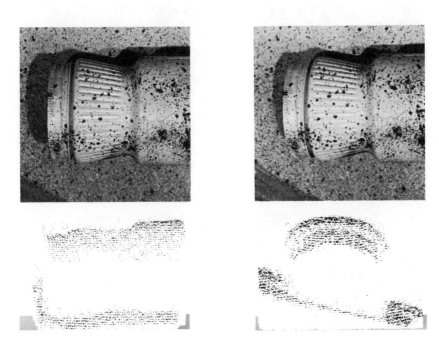

Figure 3.7
Example of a Disparity Map. The top pair of images is a stereo pair of a natural scene. In the bottom two images, two views of the disparity map are shown. A point (x, y) with disparity d is represented in a three-dimensional array as the point (x, y, d). This array is then viewed from two different angles, the left image corresponding to viewing the array from the lower edge of the original image, the right image corresponding to viewing the array from the left edge of the original image. For graphical convenience, the disparity values have been inverted.

is marked as such. If the percentage of matched points in any region is less than a threshold of 0.7 then the region is declared to be out of range, and no disparity values are accepted for that region.

The size of the regions used for checking the statistics of matching zero-crossings should be proportional to the density of the zero-crossings, in order to ensure a fixed confidence level. Typically, the regions were roughly 25 picture elements on a side, for a channel with filter size $w = 9$.

The overall effect of the matching process, as driven from the left image, is to assign disparity values to most of the zero-crossings obtained from the left image. Examples of the output appear in Figures 3.7 and 3.8. In each array, a zero-crossing at position (x, y) with associated disparity d has been placed in a three-

Figure 3.8
Example of a Disparity Map. The top pair of images is a stereo pair of a random
dot stereogram. The bottom image shows a view of the disparity array. For graphical
convenience, the disparity values have been inverted.

dimensional array with coordinate (x, y, d). For display purposes, the array is
shown in the figures as viewed from a point some distance away. The heights in
the figure correspond to the assigned disparities. (For graphical convenience, the
disparities have been inverted.)

On completing of this stage of the processing, a disparity array for each filter
size has been obtained. The disparity values are located only along the zero-
crossing contours obtained from that filter.

3.5 Vergence Control

The Marr-Poggio theory states that in order to obtain fine resolution disparity
information, it is necessary that the zero-crossings from the smallest channels be
assigned a match. Since the range of disparity over which a channel can obtain a
match is directly proportional to the size of the channel, this means that the eyes
must move to ensure that the corresponding zero-crossing descriptions from the
two images are within a matchable range. The disparity information required to
bring the smallest channels into their matchable range is provided by the larger
channels. That is, if a region of the image is declared to be out of range of fusion
by the smaller channels, one can frequently obtain a rough disparity value for that

region from the larger channels, and use this to verge the eyes. In this way, the smaller channels can be brought into a range of correspondence.

After the disparities from the different channels are combined, there is a mechanism for controlling vergence movements of the eyes. This mechanism operates by searching for regions of the image that have disparity values from the larger channels, but do not have disparity values for the smallest channel. The values from the large channel are used to provide a refinement to the current eye positions, thereby bringing the smaller channels into range of correspondence. Possible mechanisms for extracting the disparity value from a region of the image include using the peak value of a histogram of the disparities in that neighborhood, using the average of the local disparity values, or using the median of the local disparity values. In the current implementation, the search for such a region proceeds outwards from the fovea.

It should be noted here that although Marr and Poggio state that disparity information from the coarser channels can drive eye movements, they do not rule out that other information can also do this. In fact, they suggest in a later work [Marr and Poggio, 1980] that there may be other modules of the visual system that can initiate eye movements. Kidd et al. [1979] for example, found that certain types of texture boundaries can initiate eye movements. However, such effects are somewhat orthogonal to the question of the adequacy of the matching component of the Marr-Poggio theory, since they affect the input to the matcher, but not the actual performance of the matching algorithm itself.

3.6 The $2\frac{1}{2}$-Dimensional Sketch

Once the separate channels have performed their matching, the results are combined and stored in a buffer, called the $2\frac{1}{2}$-D sketch. There are several possible methods for accomplishing this. As far as the Marr-Poggio theory is concerned, the important point is that some type of storage of disparity information occurs, that there is some kind of buffer. Perhaps the strongest argument for this is the fact that up to 2 degrees of disparity can be held fused in the fovea, although the matching range for a single fixation of the eyes is only 30 minutes of arc.

I have considered two different possibilities for the way in which information from the different channels is combined. The method used in the current implementation will be described below. A more biologically feasible method will be outlined in the discussion.

One of the critical questions concerning the form of the $2\frac{1}{2}$-D sketch is whether its coordinates are consistent with those of the scene or those of the retinal images. For all the cases illustrated, the sketch was constructed by directly relating the coordinates of the sketch to the coordinates of the scene arrays. That is, as disparity information was obtained, it was stored in a buffer at the position corresponding to the position in the original scene from which the underlying zero-crossing came. Since disparity information about the scene is extracted from several eye positions, explicit information about the positions of the eyes is required in order to store this information into a buffer. This is probably inappropriate as a model of the human system, but it suffices for demonstrating the effectiveness of the matching module.

The actual mechanism for storing the disparity values requires some combination of the disparity maps obtained for each of the channels. Currently, the sketch is updated, for each region of the image, by writing in the disparity values from the smallest channel which is within range of fusion. Vergence movements are possible in order to bring smaller channels into a range of matching for some region. Further, for those regions of the image for which none of the channels can find matches, modification of the eye positions over a scale larger than that of the vergence movements is possible. By this method, one can attempt to bring those regions of the image into a range of fusion. There are several possibilities for the actual method of driving the vergence movements. Two of these were outlined in the previous section.

The final output of the algorithm consists of a representation of disparity values in the image, specified along zero-crossing segments from the smallest channel that was used to analyze that part of the scene.

3.7 Summary of the Process

The complete algorithm, as currently implemented, uses four filter sizes. Initially, the two views of the scene are mapped into a pair of working arrays. These arrays are convolved with each filter. The zero-crossings and their orientation are computed, for each channel. The initial alignments of the eyes determine the initial registration of the images. The matching of the descriptions from each channel is performed for this alignment. Any points with either ambiguous matchings or with no match are marked as such.

Next, the percentage of unmatched points is checked, for all square neighborhoods of a particular size. This size is chosen so as to ensure that the calculation of the matching statistics within that neighborhood is statistically sound. Only the disparity points of those regions whose percentage of unmatched points is below a certain threshold, are allowed to remain; all other points are removed. These values are stored in a buffer. At this stage, vergence movements may take place, using information from the larger channels to bring the smaller channels into a range where matching is possible. Further, if there are regions of the image which do not have disparity values for any channel, an eye movement may take place in an attempt to bring those portions of the image into a range where at least the largest filter can perform its matching.

Note that the matching process takes place independently for each of the four channels. Once the matching of each channel is complete, the results are combined into a single representation of the disparities.

The final output is a disparity map, with disparities assigned along most portions of the zero-crossing contours obtained from the smallest filters used. The accuracy of the disparities thus obtained depends on how accurately the zero-crossings have been localized, which may, of course, be to a resolution much finer than the initial array of intensity values that constitutes the image.

CHAPTER 4

ANALYSIS AND DEVELOPMENT

In the previous chapter, I described a specific algorithm derived from the Marr-Poggio theory, and its implementation in a computer program. Since Marr and Poggio's explicit concern was to develop a theory of the human stereo system, the implementation can be used to test the adequacy of their theory. This was done by comparing the results of running the program with the perception of human subjects on a range of stereoscopic images.

Besides examining the adequacy of the theory, the performance of the algorithm can also bring out aspects of the visual processing system that had not previously been noticed. Thus, the program itself plays an essential role in the overall task of deciding whether, and how closely, the algorithm it implements mirrors the human analysis of stereoscopic images.

4.1 Performance on Random Dot Patterns

Since random dot stereograms [Julesz 1960, 1971] contain no visual cues other than the stereoscopic ones, they are a useful tool for studying the stereo component of the human visual system in isolation. One test of the adequacy of the algorithm as representative of human stereo vision is to compare human perception with the performance of the algorithm on such patterns. Since random dot stereograms have known disparity values, these patterns can also be used to assess the correctness of the algorithm's performance.

Table 1 lists some of the matching statistics for various random dot patterns. These are illustrated in the figures and discussed below.

The first pattern consisted of a central square separated in depth from a second plane. The pattern had a dot density of 50%. The statistics of matching are labelled by the 50% Square row in Table 1 and its analysis was shown in Figure 3.7. Each dot was a square four image elements on a side. For the algorithm, this corresponds to a dot of approximately two minutes of visual arc. The total pattern was 320 image elements on a side. The central plane of the figure was shifted 12 image elements in one image relative to the other. The final disparity map assigned after the matching of the smallest channel had the following statistics: The number of zero-crossing points in the left description that were assigned a disparity was 11847. Of this total of 11847 disparity values, 11830 were exactly correct and an additional 14 deviated by one image element from the correct

TABLE OF MATCHES						
Pattern	Density	Total	Exact	One Pixel	Wrong	%Wrong
Square	50%	11847	11830	14	3	.03
Square	25%	9661	9632	22	7	.07
Square	10%	5286	5264	20	2	.04
Square	5%	3500	3498	0	2	.06
Wedding	50%	11162	11095	61	6	.06
Noise-w4	50%	2270	1909	346	15	.7
Noise-w9	50%	8683	6621	1868	194	2.
Noise-w4-1	50%	63	28	24	11	17.
Noise-w9-1	50%	8543	5194	2864	485	6.
90%Corr	50%	9545	9091	263	191	2.
80%Corr	50%	4343	4120	143	80	2.
70%Corr	50%	134	127	2	5	4.
Diag Corr	50%	6753	6325	271	157	2.

Table 1.

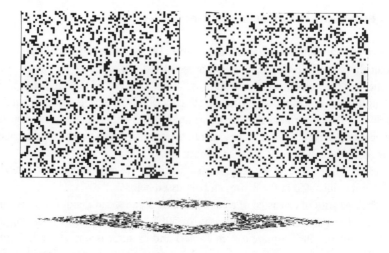

Figure 4.1
25% Density Random Dot Pattern. The top pair of images are a stereo pair of random dot patterns. The bottom image is a view of the disparity array. A point (x, y) with disparity d has been represented as the point (x, y, d). For graphical clarity, the disparities have been inverted. This three-dimensional array is viewed from some distance away in order to illustrate the disparities.

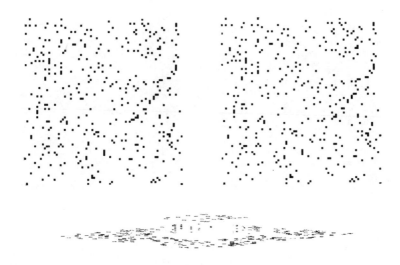

Figure 4.2
5% **Density Random Dot Pattern.** The top pair of images form a stereo pair. The bottom image is a view of the disparity array.

value. Approximately 0.03% of the matched points, or roughly 3 points in **10000** were incorrectly matched.

A similar test was run on patterns with a dot density of 25%, 10% and 5%. These are shown in Table 1 in the rows labelled 25% Square, 10% Square and 5% Square. The results are illustrated in Figures 4.1 and 4.2. For each of these cases, the number of incorrectly matched points was extremely low, their error rates lying around 0.05%. Those points which were assigned incorrect disparities all occurred at the border between the two planes, that is, along the discontinuity in disparity. This was also true for the 50% density case.

Figure 4.3 shows a more complex random dot pattern, consisting of a wedding cake, built from four different planar layers, each separated by 8 image elements, or 2 dot widths. The matching statistics are shown in Table 1 in the row labelled Wedding. In this case, the number of zero-crossing points assigned a disparity was 11162. Of these points, 11095 were assigned a disparity value which was exactly correct, and an additional 61 deviated from the correct value by one image element. Approximately 0.06% of the points, all occurring at the boundaries between the planes, were incorrectly matched. A second complex pattern, a spiral staircase with a range of continuously varying disparities, is illustrated in Figure 4.4.

There are a number of special cases of random dot patterns which have been used to test various aspects of the human visual system. The algorithm was also tested on several of these stereograms. These cases are outlined below. Again, the

Figure 4.3
Wedding Cake Pattern. The object consists of four layered planes, in the form of a wedding cake.

Figure 4.4
Spiral Staircase Pattern. The object is a spiral staircase, with a range of continuously varying disparities.

Figure 4.5
Blurred Stereogram. One of the images of a 50% random dot pattern has been altered
by convolving it with a Gaussian. Fusion is still obtained, although the disparity values
are not as sharp as in the original case.

Figure 4.6
Stereogram with Filtered Noise. High pass filtered noise has been added to one of
the images. Virtually no disparity values are obtained for the smallest channel. The
disparity map in the figure is that of the next largest channel.

Figure 4.7
Stereogram with Filtered Noise. The top disparity map represents the $w = 9$ channel.
The lower disparity map represents the $w = 4$ channel.

performance of the algorithm is compared with the performance of humans with good stereo vision.

It is known that if one or both of the images of a random dot stereogram are blurred, fusion of the stereogram is still possible [Julesz 1971, p.96]. To test the algorithm in this case, the left half of a 50% density pattern was blurred by convolving it with a Gaussian filter. This is illustrated in Figure 4.5. The disparity values obtained in this case were not as exact as in the case where these was no blurring. Rather, there was a distribution of disparities about the known correct values. As a result, the percentage of points that might be considered incorrect (more than one image element deviation from the correct value) rose to 6%. The qualitative performance of the algorithm was still correct, however, representing two planes separated in depth. It is interesting to note that slight distribution of disparity values about those corresponding to the original planes is consistent with the human perception of a pair of slightly warped planes. For larger filters, there was little difference between the performance of the algorithm on this stereogram and its performance on stereograms which have not been blurred.

Figure 4.8
Compressed Stereogram. One of the images has been compressed in the horizontal direction. Fusion is still obtained, although now the planes appear to be slightly slanted.

Julesz and Miller [1975] showed that fusion is also possible in the presence of some types of masking noise. In particular, if the spectrum of the noise is sufficiently far from the spectrum of the pattern, fusion of the pattern is still possible. Within the framework of the Marr-Poggio theory, this is equivalent to stating that if one introduces noise whose spectrum is such that it interferes with one of the stereo channels, fusion is still possible among the other channels, provided that the noise does not have a substantial spectral component overlapping other channels as well. The algorithm was tested on this case by high pass filtering a second random dot pattern to create the noise, and adding the noise to one image. In the cases illustrated in Figures 4.6 and 4.7, the spectrum of the noise was designed to interfere maximally with the smallest channel. In the case of the patterns labelled in Table 1 by Noise-$w4$ and Noise-$w9$, the noise was added such that the maximum magnitude of the noise was equal to the maximum magnitude of the original image. Noise-$w4$ illustrates the performance of the smallest channel. Noise-$w9$ illustrates the performance of the next larger channel. It can be seen that for this case, some fusion is still possible in the smallest channel, although it is patchy. The next larger channel also obtains fusion. In both cases, the accuracy of the disparity values is reduced from the normal case. This is to be expected, since the introduction of noise tends to displace the positions of the zero-crossings. In the cases labelled in Table 1 by Noise-$w4$-1 and Noise-$w9$-1, the noise was added such that the maximum magnitude was twice that of

Figure 4.9
Decorrelated Stereogram. In one of the images, 10% of the dots have been decorrelated
at random. Fusion is still obtained.

the maximum magnitude of the original image. Here, matching in the smallest
channel is almost completely eliminated (Noise-$w4$-1), yet matching in the next
larger channel is only marginally affected (Noise-$w9$-1).

The implementation was also tested on the case of adding low pass filtered
noise to a random dot pattern, with results similar to that of adding high pass
filtered noise. Here, the larger channels are unable to obtain a good matching,
while the smaller channels are relatively unaffected.

If one of the images of a random dot pattern is compressed in the horizontal
direction, the human stereo system is still able to achieve fusion [Julesz 1971,
p.213]. The algorithm was tested on this case, and the results are shown in Figure
4.8. It can be seen that the program still obtains a reasonably good match. The
planes are now slightly slanted, which again agrees with human perception.

If some of the dots of a pattern are decorrelated, it is still possible for a human
observer to achieve some kind of fusion [Julesz 1971, p.88]. Two different types
of decorrelation were tested. In the first type, increasing percentages of the dots
were decorrelated in the left image at random. In particular, the cases of 10%,
20% and 30% decorrelation were tried, and are illustrated in Figures 4.9 and
4.10. For the 10% case, (Table entry 90% Corr) it can be seen that the algorithm
was still able to obtain a good matching of the two planes, although the total
number of zero-crossings assigned a disparity decreased, and the percentage of
incorrectly matched points increased. When the percentage of decorrelated dots
was increased to 20% (Table entry 80% Corr), the number of matched points

Figure 4.10
Decorrelated Stereogram. In one of the images, 20% of the dots have been decorrelated at random. Fusion is still obtained, although in this case, there are many regions of the image where no disparity values are assigned.

decreased again, although the percentage of those incorrectly matched remained about the same. Finally, when the percentage of decorrelated dots was increased to 30% (Table entry 70% Corr), the algorithm found virtually no section of the image which could be fused.

The failure of the algorithm to match the 30% decorrelated pattern is caused by the component of the algorithm which checks that each region of the image is within range of correspondence. Recall that in order to distinguish between the case of two images beyond range of fusion (for the current eye positions) which will have only randomly matching zero-crossings, and the case of two images within range of fusion, the theory requires that the percentage of unmatched points be less than approximately 0.3. For the case of the pattern with 30% decorrelation, each region of the image will, on the average, have roughly 30% of its zero-crossings with no match and the algorithm will decide that the region is out of matching range. Thus, the algorithm cannot distinguish a correctly matched region of a degraded pattern from the matches that would be made between two random patterns. Hence, no disparities will be accepted for the region. It is interesting to note that many human subjects can achieve some kind of fusion up to about 20% decorrelation, the fusion becoming weaker as the decorrelation increases. For patterns with 30% decorrelation, the fusion is usually eliminated.

One can also decorrelate the pattern by breaking up all white triplets along one set of diagonals, and all black triplets along the other set of diagonals [Julesz

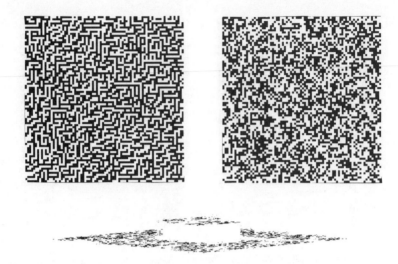

Figure 4.11
Diagonally Decorrelated Stereogram. One of the images has been decorrelated in the
following manner. Along all the diagonals in one direction, any white triples have been
broken by the insertion of a black dot. Along the diagonals in the other direction,
any black triples have been broken by the insertion of a white dot. Fusion is still
obtained.

1971, p.87]. The Table entry Diag Corr indicates the matching statistics for this
case. Again, it can be seen that the program still obtains a good match, as do
human observers. The performance of the algorithm is illustrated in Figure 4.11.
This is a particularly fascinating example, since at first glance it would appear
extremely unlikely that the two patterns could be fused. Yet the program is quite
consistent with human perception on this case, obtaining a good matching of the
two images.

4.2 Natural Images

The algorithm was also tested on some natural images. In these cases, an exact
evaluation of the performance of the algorithm is difficult, although a qualitative
comparison is possible.

Figure 4.12 is a stereo pair of images from a scene of a basketball game. From
the disparity map, it can be seen qualitatively that the arm of the foremost player
is much closer to the viewer than his torso, and that his torso, in turn, is closer to
the viewer than the basket, which is closer than the backboard. At the extreme
right of the image, there is a second arm, also positioned between the foremost
player and the basket.

Figure 4.12
A Natural Stereogram. The stereo images are of a scene of a basketball game. The disparity map is represented in such a manner that the width of the black bars, terminated by a white dot, correspond to the disparity of the point. It can be seen that the disparity values are all qualitatively correct, with the arm of the foremost player emerging from the background of the basket and the wall. The images were 480 pixels on a side.

Figure 4.13 is a stereo pair of images of a sculpture by Henry Moore. As in the basketball scene, the disparity map obtained by the algorithm is in qualitative agreement with the objects in the scene. Here, the trees in the background are found to lie at a depth far removed from the sculpture. Further, the general shape of the sculpture is captured by the algorithm, consisting of a roughly cylindrical piece in the lower left, lying in front of a doughnut-shaped piece. There is a second roughly cylindrical shape, in the upper right portion of the scene, which also has disparity values placing it in front of the doughnut-shaped piece.

Figure 4.13
A Natural Stereogram. The images are of a sculpture by Henry Moore. The disparity array is represented as in Figure 4.12. It can be seen that the disparity values obtained by the program roughly correspond to the shape of the surface. The images were 320 pixels on a side.

As a final example, we illustrate that the process of creating surface representations from images is not strictly a terrestial process. This is demonstrated in Figure 4.14, which consists of a stereo pair of images of the Martian surface, taken by the Viking lander. To better illustrate the disparities, the values obtained by the stereo algorithm have been interpolated locally.

Although the range of disparity between the horizon and the foreground is extremely large in these images (on the order of 200 picture elements) the algorithm is still able to perform the correspondence. Further, note that the interpolated depth representation contains of a number of sharp breaks in depth, corresponding to a series of hillocks, or dunes, each of which occludes portions of those behind it. This may seem somewhat surprising, since the monocular images give

Figure 4.14
The Martian Surface The top pair of figures are a stereo pair of images of the Martian surface, taken by the Viking lander. The bottom figure is a disparity map in which the disparity values have been locally interpolated to enhance the display. It can be seen that the disparity values contain a series of roughly planar regions with large separations in depth between them. Although the stereo images give the monocular impression of a single planar surface, stereoscopic fusion reveals that the image consists of a series of dunes occluding one another — a perception which is consistent with the disparity map obtained by the algorithm.

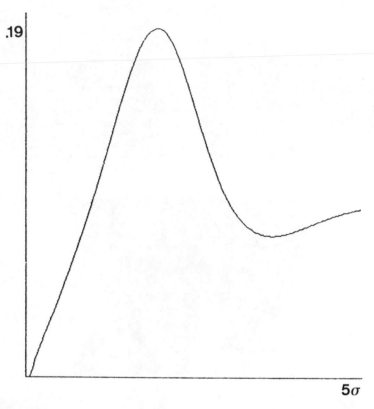

Figure 4.15
Probability Distribution of First Zero-Crossing. This is a graph of the probability of reaching a zero-crossing within a certain distance, given a zero-crossing at the origin. In this case, the zero-crossing will have opposite sign.

the impression of a uniform plain running off into the horizon. Interestingly, a fusion of the stereo pair will reveal that the algorithm is correct, as the actual surface does consist of a series of dunes.

4.3 Statistics

In Section 2.5, we saw that the Marr-Poggio theory essentially avoided the false targets problem by appropriately choosing the size of the neighborhood over which the matcher seeks a correspondence. In the original theory, the size of the neighborhood for each filter was choosen to be $\pm w$ (where w is the extent of the central negative region of the filter) with the expectation that false targets will occur in at most 50% of the cases. This size for the neighborhood was

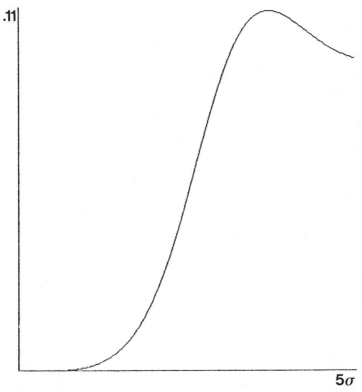

.11

5σ

Figure 4.16
Probability Distribution of Second Zero-Crossing. This is a graph of the probability
of reaching a second zero-crossing within a certain distance, given a zero-crossing at
the origin. The second zero-crossing will have the same sign as the zero-crossing at
the origin.

obtained from the statistical characterestics of the filters proposed in the theory.
In this case, the filters were directionally sensitive, with one-dimensional cross-
sections which are a difference of two Gaussian functions, and which essentially
perform a directional second differentiation of the smoothed image. In Chapter 2,
however, we employed directionally insensitive second-order filters, whose form
is the Laplacian of a Gaussian, a modification to the original Marr-Poggio theory.
These filters are used to obtain the zero-crossing descriptions. In addition, the
orientation (or directionality) of the zero-crossings is used as a matching criterion
after the descriptions have been obtained. It thus becomes of interest to check
whether a proper accounting of the use of non-oriented filters will make statistical
predictions consistent with empirically observed statistics.

TABLE OF STATISTICS				
parameter	without orientation, expected	without orientation, empirical	with orientation, expected	with orientation, empirical
average distance between zero-crossings of same sign	5.29σ	5.24σ	15.87σ	18.56σ
probability of candidates in at most one pool	$>.35$	.38	$>.78$	.81
probability of candidates in two pools	$<.64$	.60	$<.21$	.19
probability of candidates in all three pools	$<.01$	.02	$<.01$	.001
given a candidate near zero, probability of no other candidates	$>.81$	.75	$>.94$	.93

Table 2.

For the case of non-oriented filters, the derivation of the statisitical distribution of zero-crossings is very similar to that used by Marr and Poggio [1979], and is found in Appendix I. The probability distributions of intervals between zero-crossings are shown in Figures 4.15 and 4.16.

In this case, the expected worst case behavior of multiple zero-crossings within a particular range of matching is different than that predicted by Marr and Poggio for oriented filters. In particular, the predicted density of zero-crossings is some-what higher than in the Marr-Poggio case. At first glance, this would seem to suggest that the situation is worse than that given by the Marr-Poggio analysis. The use of orientation as a matching criterion, however, has yet to be included. To do this, some estimate of the distribution of orientation of zero-crossings is needed. The matching algorithm segments the orientation distribution into blocks of 30 degrees. The simplest estimate is given by assuming that the orientations are uniformly distributed, in which case, the probabilities given by the statistical analysis should be adjusted by a factor of $\frac{1}{6}$. However, there is no real justification for assuming that the orientations will be uniformly distributed. In fact, the distribution tends to be more strongly weighted towards vertical orientations. Hence, rather than adjusting by a factor of $\frac{1}{6}$, a more conservative factor of $\frac{1}{3}$ will be used.

A table comparing predicted and empirical statistics of the distribution of similar zero-crossings is shown in Table 2. A number of interesting comparisons can be made from this. First, consider the case in which orientation is not used as a matching criterion. The number of multiple targets predicted by Rice's formula (which specifies the probability distribution of separations between zero-crossings,see Appendix I) agrees well with the empirical statistics found in practice. For example, if the size of the matching neighborhood is taken as $\pm 2.044\sigma$, Rice's formula predicts a worst case probability of 0.36 for double targets. The empirical statistics in this case are 0.33. If the range is extended to $\pm 2.36\sigma$, Rice's formula predicts a worst case probability of 0.49 and the empirical statistics are 0.44. For a range of $\pm 2.84\sigma$, the prediction probability is 0.65 and the empirical statistic is 0.62.

Second, the use of orientation as a matching criterion can greatly improve the problem of false targets. For example, let w_{1D} be the width of the central negative region of the one-dimensional projection of the $\nabla^2 G$ operator. This is related to the central diameter w_{2D} of the two-dimensional operator by

$$w_{2D} = \sqrt{2}\,w_{1D}$$

and these are related to the space constant σ of the operator by

$$w_{2D} = 2\sqrt{2}\,\sigma.$$

If the matching range has the value $\pm w_{1D}$, then using orientation to within 30 degrees as a matching criterion reduces the percentage of false targets to 0.091. Even for a matching range of $\pm w_{2D}$, the percentage of false targets rises only to 0.20.

This raises an interesting possibility concerning the range of the matching neighborhood. In the original theory, Marr and Poggio [1979] considered the possiblity of avoiding the false targets problem almost entirely by reducing the probability of its occurence, while maintaining a range of matching consistent with estimates of the size of Panum's area. According to their analysis, however, if the matching range is so restricted as to reduce the probability of false targets to less than 0.05, then the range is smaller than estimates of Panum's area by a factor of 2. If the range of matching is adjusted to account for the size of Panum's area, then the probability of false targets rises to 0.50, making it necessary to introduce a disambiguation mechanism to resolve the false targets problem.

Given the statistical analysis derived above, one can propose a matching mechanism in which the zero-crossings are obtained from non-oriented filters and the orientation of the zero-crossing is used as a criterion for matching. In this case, matching over a range consistent with Panum's area will result in very few false targets (on the order of 0.10), and there is no need to introduce a disambiguation mechanism.

4.4 Discussion

We have indicated earlier that one reason for implementing a computational theory is that it provides an opportunity to test the theory's adequacy. We have seen that the performance of the implementation coincides well with that of human subjects over a broad range of random dot test cases obtained from the literature, including defocussing, compression, and the introduction of various kinds of masking noise to one image of a random dot stereo pair.

A second reason for implementing a computational theory is that the implementation serves as a useful feedback device for the theory, indicating errors or omissions in the theory, as well as indicating areas whose difficulty had not been previously appreciated. Throughout the course of the development of the stereo implementation, a number of interesting observations were made. Some of these indicated equivalent methods of implementation which had interesting properties with regard to alternative theories of the process. Others served to correct assumptions made by the theory. Still other observations arose at surprising places, where no difficulty was expected in the implementation process. In many of these cases, a solution to the problem led to decisions of wide ranging effect; examples are the use of zero-crossings and non-oriented filters. Thus, an implementation problem can instigate major changes in the theory. Without the act of implementation, such effects might not have been found. These observations are discussed in the following sections.

4.4.1 Pool Responses

The neighborhood over which a search for a matching zero-crossing is conducted is broken into three pools, corresponding to convergent, divergent and zero disparity. In the present implementation, the pools are used to deal with the ambiguous case of two matching zero-crossings, while the disparity values associated with a match are represented to within an image element. A second possibility is to use the pools not only to disambiguate multiple matches, but also to assign a disparity to a match. Thus, a single disparity value, equal to the disparity value of the midpoint of the pool, would be assigned for a matching zero-crossing lying anywhere within the pool. In this scheme, only three possible disparities could be assigned to a zero-crossing: zero, corresponding to the middle pool; or $\frac{\pm w}{2}$, corresponding to the divergent or convergent pools.

Under this type of scheme, the role of a finely tuned zero pool becomes quite important. In the current implementation, in which disparity values are assigned exactly, there is no obvious need for a zero-tuned pool — it is not really necessary for the disambiguation of multiple matches. However, if each pool can only assign a constant disparity value, then a finely tuned zero pool is very useful in providing fine disparity values, since the narrowness of the pool, as compared to the convergent and divergent pools, will provide finer information.

Interestingly, computer experiments show that either scheme will work. In the case of a single disparity value for each pool, the disparities assigned by the smallest channel are within an image element of those obtained using exact disparities for each match. This modification was tried on both natural images and random dot patterns, and suggests that the accuracy with which the pools represent the match is not a critical factor for the actual matching process.

4.4.2 Matching Errors

Points that were incorrectly matched in the test cases all lie along depth discontinuities. The reason is that at any depth discontinuity, there will be an occluded region which is present in one image, but not the other. Any zero-crossings within that region cannot have a correct matching zero-crossing in the other image. There is, however, a non-zero probability of such a zero-crossing being matched incorrectly to a random zero-crossing in the other image. In principle, the algorithm detects occluded regions by using the statistics of the number of unmatched zero-crossings to mark all zero-crossing matches in the region as unknown. However, only a portion of a region which contains a depth discontinuity will have been matched incorrectly. Zero-crossings in the rest of the region will have a unique match. Thus, when the statistical check on the number of unmatched points is performed, it is possible for the entire region to be considered in range, and thus all matches, including the incorrect ones of the occluded region, will be accepted. For the random dot patterns considered at the beginning of this chapter, the percentage of zero-crossings assigned an incorrect disparity due to this type of error was less than 1%.

4.4.3 Depth Discontinuities

It is interesting to comment on the effect of depth discontinuities for the different sized filters. For random dot patterns, the zero-crossings obtained from the larger filters tend to outline blobs or clusters of dots. Thus in general, the positions of the zero-crossings do not correspond to single elements of the underlying image. For example, suppose the dot pattern consists of one plane separated in depth from a second plane. In such a case, one might well find a zero-crossing contour such that zero-crossing points at one end of the contour correspond to dots on the first plane, and zero-crossing points at the other end of the contour correspond to dots on the second plane. Such zero-crossings will be assigned disparities that reflect, to within the resolution of the channel, the structure of the image. The zero-crossings lying between the two ends of the contour will, however, receive disparities that smoothly vary from one extreme to the other. Consequently, the largest channel would see a smooth hump rather than a plane separated in depth from a second plane.

For the smaller filter this does not occur since the zero-crossing contours tend to outline individual dots or connected groups of dots. Thus the disparities assigned are such that the dots tend to belong to one plane or the other and the final disparity map is one of two separated planes.

To achieve perfect results from stereo, it is probably necessary to include in the $2\frac{1}{2}$-D sketch a way of dealing competently with discontinuities. In a later section, we shall discuss this issue. In this connection, it is interesting to point out that when one looks at a 5% random-dot stereogram portraying a square in front of its background, one sees vivid subjective contours at its boundary, although the output of the matcher does not account for this.

4.4.4 Constraint Checking

An integral part of most computational theories, proposed as models of aspects of the human visual system, is the use of computational constraints based on assumptions about the physical world [Marr and Poggio, 1979, Marr and Hildreth, 1980, Ullman, 1979a]. An interesting point of comparison between algorithms for various visual processes concerns whether or not these algorithms check that the constraints imposed by the theory are satisfied. For example, Ullman's rigidity constraint in the analysis of structure from motion is explicitly checked by his algorithm. For the Marr-Poggio stereo theory, two constraints were used, uniqueness and continuity of disparity values. It is curious that in the algorithm used to solve the stereo problem, the continuity constraint is explicitly checked while the uniqueness constraint is not. Uniqueness of disparity is required in just one direction of matching, since only those zero-crossing segments of the left image that have exactly one match in the right image are accepted. However, it may be the case that more than one element of the right image could be matched to an element of the left image. In the analogous situation, matching from the right image to the left, the same is true. Note that one could easily alter the algorithm to include the checking of uniqueness, thereby retaining only those disparity values corresponding to zero-crossing segments with a unique disparity value when matched from both images. However, evidence from Braddick [1978], discussed in the next section, indicates that this is not the case. Hence, in the Marr-Poggio stereo theory, although both the requirement of uniqueness and continuity are presumed, only one of these two constraints is explicitly checked by the algorithm. The other constraint is probably not checked because it is physically very unlikely to be violated.

4.4.5 From Which Image Do We Match?

Although the Marr-Poggio matcher is designed to match from one image into the other, there is no inherent reason why the matching process cannot be driven from both eyes independently. In fact, there may be some evidence that this is so, as is shown by the following experiment by Braddick [1978] on an extension to Panum's limiting case. First, a sparse random dot pattern was constructed. From this pattern, a partner was created by displacing the entire pattern by slight amounts to both the left and the right. Thus, for each dot in the right image, there corresponded two dots in the left image, one with a small displacement to the left, and the other with a small displacement to the right. The perception obtained by viewing such a random dot stereogram is one of two superimposed planes.

Suppose the matching process were driven from only one image, for example, from the right image to the left. In this case, the implementation would not be able to account for Braddick's results, since all the zero-crossings would have two possible candidates. However, suppose that the matching process were driven independently from both the right and left images, an unambiguous match from either side being accepted. In this case, although every zero-crossing in the right image would have an ambiguous match, the program would obtain a unique match for each zero-crossing in the left image.

Braddick's case has been tested with the program, allowing it the match from both images and accept any disparity found in either direction. The results are shown in Figure 4.17. It can be seen that the results of the implementation are that of two transparent planes, as in human perception.

An interesting conjecture is that there may be half stereo blind people who can see two planes when the images are presented such that the double image is in one eye, and who see none or one fuzzy plane when the double image is in the other eye.

4.4.6 Representations

There are a number of questions concerning the form of the $2\frac{1}{2}$-D sketch, which have yet to be firmly answered. Some of these problems, and the results of experimentation with the implementation as it relates to them, are indicated below.

The first critical question concerns whether the sketch uses the coordinates of the scene or of the working arrays. In the first case, the coordinates of the sketch would be directly related to the coordinates of the arrays of the entire scene. The advantage of this is that since disparity information about the scene is extracted from several eye positions, the representation of the disparities over the entire scene can be readily updated. However, this advantage also raises a difficulty. In order to store this information into a buffer whose coordinate system is determined by the image of the entire scene, explicit information about the positions

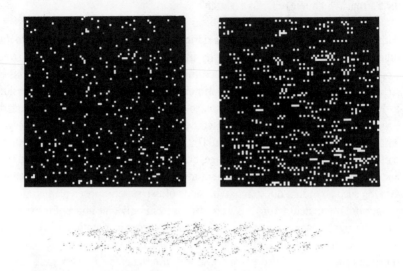

Figure 4.17
Panum's Special Case. The perception of the stereo pair is of a transparent plane above a second plane. The disparity map produced by the algorithm agrees with this.

of the eyes is required. This is fine computationally, but in the human visual system, this information may not be available to the stereo process.

In the second case, no such problem arises. Here, the coordinates of the sketch are directly related to the coordinates of the retinal images. Such a system is called retinocentric, as it reflects the current positions of the eyes. It does not require explicit knowledge of the eye positions relative to some fixed coordinate system within the scene, and thus it seems to be the most natural representation. But this then raises the question of how information about disparities in the scene are maintained across eye movements.

The second question concerns the role of resolution. Different sections of the images are analyzed at different resolutions for a given position of the optical axes. Consequently, the amount of buffer space required to store the disparity will vary widely in the visual field, being much greater for the fovea than for the periphery. This again suggests the use of a retinocentric representation, because if one used a frame that had already allowed for eye-movements, it would require foveal resolution everywhere. Not only does such a buffer waste space, but it does not agree with our own experience as perceivers. If it were so, one should be able to build up a perceptual impression of the world that was everywhere as detailed as it is at the center of the gaze, and this is clearly not the case.

The final point about the $2\frac{1}{2}$-D sketch is that it is intended as an intermediate representation of the current scene. It is important for such a representation to

Figure 4.18
Single Fixation Example. The top images are a random dot wedding cake. The disparity map is that obtained by combining the different sized channels for a single fixation of the eyes. In this case, the eyes were fixated at the level of the bottom, outermost plane. It can be seen that the disparity values for the bottom plane are very sharp, since at this level the smallest channels are able to make the correspondences. For the region in the center of the image, the disparity values are much sparser and less accurate; at this level, only the larger channels are within range of correspondence. The reader may check this perception by viewing the stereogram, while fixating only on the bottom plane.

pass on its information to higher level processes as quickly as possible. Thus, it probably cannot wait for a representation to be built up over several positions of the eyes. Rather, it must be refreshed for each eye position.

All of these factors combine to suggest a refinement to the implementation, as outlined above. In particular, a retinocentric representation should be used in order to represent disparities with decreasing resolution as eccentricity increases.

For the cases illustrated in this book, the $2\frac{1}{2}$-D sketch was created by storing fine resolution disparity values into a representation with a coordinate system identical to that of the scene. As we have argued above, a second alternative is to store values from all channels into a retinocentric representation, using disparity values from the smaller channels where available, and the coarser disparities from the larger channels elsewhere. In this way, a disparity representation for a single fixation of the eyes may be constructed, with disparity resolution varying across the retina. Such a method of creating the $2\frac{1}{2}$-D sketch has been tested on the implementation, and is indicated in Figure 4.18.

4.4.7 Random Dot Patterns versus Natural Images

In the first part of this chapter, we have seen that the algorithm performs well on a wide range of random dot patterns, and is consistent with human perception on that set of patterns. We have also seen that the algorithm can perform well on some natural images. However, there are some differences between using random dot patterns as input and using natural images as input that can result in a difference in performance on natural images.

First, random dot patterns consist of synthesized intensity values, whereas the intensity values of natural images incorporate many factors of the imaging process. This can serve to add "noise" to the intensity values, and in turn can affect the positions and orientations of the zero-crossings. Second, the vertical alignment of random dot patterns is a trivial matter, while for natural images, the vertical alignment is important. When random dot stereograms are synthesized, it is simple to ensure that there is exact vertical alignment between the elements. However, in natural images, this is not the case. Even if the two images of a natural scene are aligned vertically with respect to some object in the scene, the process of projection may cause other regions of the scene to be slightly misaligned vertically.

The algorithm can be modified to account for this vertical deviation by allowing both horizontal and vertical alignment of the images to be controlled. That is, when the positions of the eyes are specified to the algorithm, they include a vertical as well as a horizontal displacement relative to one another. For example, suppose that the disparity values from one of the larger channels specify a particular horizontal alignment of the eyes. The algorithm will make this adjustment and match the zero-crossing descriptions of the smaller channels accordingly. If it is the case that the smaller channels do not obtain a match, it may be due to a slight vertical misalignment. Since we know from the larger channel that the images are in rough alignment, we can maintain this horizontal alignment while altering the vertical alignment. The matching is repeated for this new alignment, and the process continued over some range of vertical disparities until the smaller channel is able to obtain a match. In all the cases tested on the implementation, the total range of vertical deviation across the image was small, on the order of 3 or 4 image elements, and the algorithm was able to obtain a correct match by means of the above process.

4.4.8 The Algorithm Applied to Natural Images

In the first part of this chapter, we examined the performance of the Marr-Poggio algorithm on a wide range of random dot patterns, and indicated that its performance was consistent with that of human perception. The results of testing the implementation on the broad range of images demonstrates that the matching module is acceptable as an independent module. In particular, the agreement between the performance of the algorithm and that of human observers on the many random dot patterns demonstrates that the matching module is acceptable, since in these cases, all other visual cues have been isolated from the matcher.

With natural images, we have seen that the algorithm also seems to perform well. However, there are situations in which the algorithm can return disparity values inconsistent with other information in the image. We need to determine whether this reflects a basic error in the theory or its implementation, or whether there are other aspects of the visual process interacting with stereo which have not been accounted for in this implementation.

With natural images, it is reasonable to expect that other visual modules may affect the input to the matcher and that they may also alter the output of the matcher. For example, the evidence of Kidd, Frisby and Mayhew [1979] concerning the ability of texture boundaries to drive vergence eye movements indicates that other visual information besides disparity may alter the position of the eyes, and thus the input to the matcher. However, it does not necessarily imply that the theory of the matcher itself is incorrect.

The performance of the implementation supports this point. In general, the matching algorithm performs well on natural images. Occasionally, a natural image provides some difficulty for the implementation, however. A particular example of this occurs in the image of Figure 4.19. Here, the regular pattern of the windows provides a strong false targets problem. In running the implementation, the following behavior was observed. If the initial vergence position was at the depth of the building, the zero-crossings corresponding to the windows were all assigned a correct disparity. If, however, the initial vergence position was at the depth of the trees in front of the building, the windows were assigned an incorrect disparity, due to the regular pattern of zero-crossings associated with them. Clearly, this seems wrong. But does this mean the implementation is also wrong? Curiously, if one fuses the zero-crossing descriptions without eye movements, human observers have the same problem: if the eyes are fixated at the level of the building, all is well; if the eyes are fixated at the level of the trees, the windows are incorrectly matched. I would argue that this implies that the implementation, and hence the theory of the matching process is in fact correct. Given a particular set of zero-crossings, the module finds any acceptable match and writes it into a buffer. When the output of this buffer is sent to the $2\frac{1}{2}$-D sketch, it must be made consistent with other sources of information feeding the $2\frac{1}{2}$-D sketch. In this case, it is possible that some later processing module is capable of altering the disparity values, based on other information unavailable to the stereo process, and the correct depth is written into the $2\frac{1}{2}$-D sketch.

Thus, I would suggest that future refinements to the Marr-Poggio theory must account for the interactions of other aspects of visual information processing on the input and output of the matching module.

Figure 4.19
A Natural False Targets Problem. The zero-crossings corresponding to the windows of the furthest building form a regular pattern which accentuates the false target problem. The performance of the algorithm on these images is critically dependent on the positions of the eyes relative to the scene. If the fixation point is at the level of the building, the correct matching of the images takes place. If the fixation point is at the level of the trees in front of the building, then a "wallpaper" effect takes place, and the windows are matched incorrectly. Psychophysical experiments indicate that humans may have the same difficulty.

4.4.9 Parallel versus Serial

One final note concerns a possible confusion about the implementation of the algorithm. The description of the implementation of the Marr-Poggio algorithm was essentially a serial one, stating that the coarsest filters were run first, matching was performed and the resulting disparity information was then used to run the next finer filter. In this manner, the computation is viewed as proceeding in a serial manner from coarse to fine filters. Of course, the computer implementation also proceeds in such a serial manner. This is not to imply, however, that the human visual system is also required to proceed in a serial manner. While it is that case that disparity information may be required in order to bring finer filters into range of operation, it is certainly feasible that all levels of filters operate in

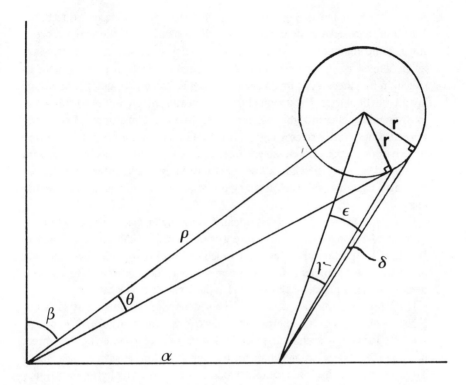

Figure 4.20
Geometry of Edge Effects. The angle δ measures the angular error in disparity associated with matching the occluding boundaries in both eyes.

parallel. Thus, it is quite possible that at any stage, all filters perform their matching in parallel, and disparity information from any filter is accepted. If a vergence movement is performed, the correspondence computation takes place again in all filters and disparity information from any filter is accepted. Thus, although the description of the algorithm given previously is a serial one, there is no intrinsic reason why the computation, either in the human visual system or a machine, cannot proceed in a parallel manner.

4.5 Edge Effects

The initial motivation for the use of zero-crossings stemmed from the desire to match only those locations on a surface which gave rise to image properties that could be localized physically. Thus, surface scratches, texture markings, sharp reflectance changes all were characterized by strong local changes in intensity.

Such changes in intensity give rise to a zero-crossing in a second directional derivative, and serve as descriptors that will be matched by the stereo process. It is not apparent, however, that there is an isomorphism between zero-crossings in the convolved image and those object features whose position we want to match. In fact, there is one major counter-example, namely occluding contours, or boundaries of objects. The design of the zero-crossing detector does not allow one to distinguish between zero-crossings caused by surface markings (photometric zero-crossings) and zero-crossings caused by changes in the gross shape of the surface (topographic zero-crossings). Instead, it assumes that all zero-crossings are relevant. One must therefore ask whether one will be badly misled by allowing the stereo algorithm to match topographic zero-crossings as well as photometric ones.

Consider a featureless cylinder, oriented vertically in space. The edges of the cylinder will in most situations cause a zero-crossing in the convolved image. However, the portion of the cylinder which will project to such a zero-crossing in the two eyes is different. It would seem that one does not want to match such descriptors since they do not correspond to the same physical location.

Let us examine this case carefully. The geometry of the situation is shown in Figure 4.20. We wish to determine the angle δ as a function of ρ, β, θ, and α, since δ corresponds to the difference in disparity between matching the correct point on the cylinder and matching the occluding contours as seen in each image. Trigonometric manipulation yields the following expressions, where $\epsilon = \gamma + \delta$,

$$\tan \epsilon = \frac{r}{\sqrt{a^2 + \rho^2 - r^2 - 2a\rho \sin \beta}}$$

$$\tan \gamma = \frac{r[\sqrt{\rho^2 - r^2} - a \sin(\beta + \theta)]}{(\rho^2 + a^2 - r^2) - 2a\sqrt{\rho^2 - r^2}\sin(\beta + \theta) + ra\cos(\beta + \theta)}$$

$$\tan \delta = \frac{\tan \epsilon - \tan \gamma}{1 + \tan \epsilon \tan \gamma}$$

Consider the special case of the cylinder being centered between the eyes, as shown in Figure 4.21, where the above expressions simplify. Note that in this case:

$$\sin \beta = \frac{a}{2\rho}$$

$$\cos \beta = \frac{\sqrt{4\rho^2 - a^2}}{2\rho}$$

$$\sin \theta = \frac{\sqrt{\rho^2 - r^2}}{\rho}$$

$$\cos \theta = \frac{r}{\rho}$$

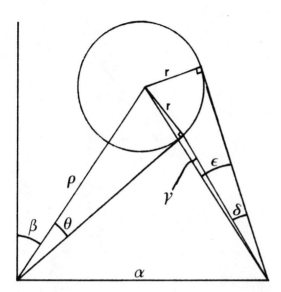

Figure 4.21
Special Case of Object Centered Between The Eyes.

so that the following expressions hold:

$$\tan \epsilon = \frac{r}{\sqrt{\rho^2 - r^2}}$$

$$\tan \gamma = \frac{r\left\{ \sqrt{\rho^2 - r^2}(2\rho^2 - a^2) - ra\sqrt{4\rho^2 - a^2} \right\}}{2\rho^2(\rho^2 - r^2) - ra\sqrt{\rho^2 - r^2}\sqrt{4\rho^2 - a^2} + a^2 r^2}$$

$$\tan \delta = \frac{ra^2}{2\rho^2\sqrt{\rho^2 - r^2} - ra\sqrt{4\rho^2 - a^2}}$$

If r and ρ are represented in units of the interocular distance a, say $r = aa$ and $\rho = ba$, then algebraic manipulation yields:

$$a = \frac{2b^3}{\sqrt{\left(\cot \delta + \sqrt{4b^2 - 1}\right)^2 + 4b^4}}.$$

Given some minimum acceptable angular error, for example $\delta < 0.5'$, one may graph the maximum allowed radius r of the cylinder as a function of the

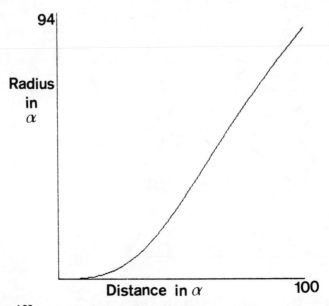

Figure 4.22
Graph of Effects of Matching Occluding Contours. The curve indicates the maximum radius of the cylinder, as a function of its distance from the viewer, which will cause an error in disparity of less than 0.5′ of arc.

distance from the viewer, ρ. This particular case is graphed in Figure 4.22. For almost all likely situations, the error in disparity associated with matching the occluding contours of a cylindrical object is negligible. At a distance from one eye of 1 interocular unit, the maximum radius is 0.0003 interocular units, a very tight constraint. For a distance of 10 interocular units (roughly 2 feet), however, the maximum radius is 0.29 interocular units (roughly 0.75 inches). This translates into cylinders of a diameter of roughly twice the width of a thumb, viewed at arm's length. In general, except for very small distances, the stereo algorithm will not introduce unacceptable errors in disparity when matching the zero-crossings corresponding to occluding boundaries.

There is an alternative method for estimating the error involved in matching occluding contours. Consider the geometry illustrated in Figure 4.23. The distance δ measures the error in the shape of the cylinder that would result from matching the occluding contours. Trigonometric manipulation yields the following expressions:

$$\cos\frac{\phi}{2} = \frac{d}{\sqrt{\frac{a^2}{4} + d^2}} = \frac{r}{r + \delta}.$$

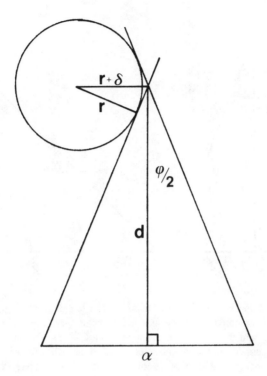

Figure 4.23
Geometry of Matching Occluding Contours. The distance δ, as a function of d and r, measures the error in the perceived shape of the cylinder that would result from matching the occluding contours.

Thus,

$$\frac{\delta}{r} = \frac{\sqrt{\frac{a^2}{4} + d^2} - d}{d}$$

and this is approximated by

$$\frac{\delta}{r} \approx \frac{-d + d(1 + \frac{a^2}{8d^2})}{d} \approx \frac{a^2}{8d^2}.$$

Thus, the error in the perceived shape of the cylinder relative to its size is very small for cylinders separated from the viewer by distances larger than one interocular unit.

This result implies that the error in depth associated with matching occluding contours is very minor, except for situations of very small separation from the viewer. Thus, it is acceptable to allow the matching of topographic as well as photometric zero-crossings.

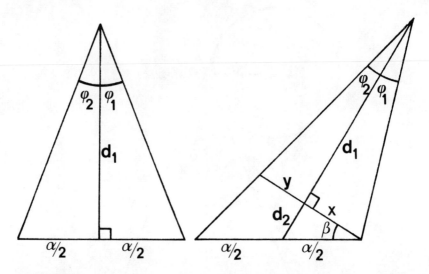

Figure 4.24
The Geometry of the Computation of Distance. The left diagram shows the simplest case of an object centered along the axis between the eyes. The interocular distance is denoted by α, and the disparity is given by $\phi = \phi_1 + \phi_2$. The distance of interest is d_1, as a function of the interocular separation α and the disparity ϕ. The right diagram shows the general case of an object lying off axis. Here, the distance of interest is $d = d_1 + d_2$ as a function of the disparity $\phi = \phi_1 + \phi_2$, the interocular separation α, and the off axis angle β.

4.6 Relating Disparity to Surface Shape

Since my ultimate goal is to describe the surface structure of objects in the scene, it is necessary to convert the disparity information into a form that more directly relates to the surface shape. There are two obvious transformations of disparity: depth or distance, and surface orientation. Again, the term *depth* will refer to the subjective distance to the object as perceived by the viewer, while *distance* refers to the objective physical distance from the viewer to the object. The surface orientation of a point is defined as the orientation of the vector which is normal to the surface at that point, relative to some coordinate system.

4.6.1 Exact Distance

The geometrical situation involved in computing distance for a coordinate system centered between the eyes is illustrated in Figure 4.24. Two cases are shown: the simplest case of an object centered between the eyes, and the more complex case of an object off axis. The interocular distance is denoted by a, and the disparity by $\phi = \phi_1 + \phi_2$.

In the simplest case, $\phi_1 = \phi_2$, and

$$d_1 = \frac{a}{2} \cot \phi_1$$

$$= \frac{a}{2} \cot \frac{\phi}{2}.$$

In the general case,

$$d_2 = \frac{a}{2} \sin \beta$$

and

$$x = \frac{a}{2} \cos \beta.$$

The law of sines implies that

$$x + y = \frac{a \cos(\phi_2 + \beta)}{\cos \phi_2} = a(\cos \beta - \sin \beta \tan \phi_2).$$

Thus

$$y = \frac{a}{2}(\cos \beta - 2 \sin \beta \tan \phi_2).$$

As a consequence,

$$\tan \phi_1 = \frac{a \cos \beta}{2d_1}$$

$$\tan \phi_2 = \frac{a \cos \beta}{2d_1 + 2a \sin \beta}.$$

Thus,

$$\tan \phi = \frac{\tan \phi_1 + \tan \phi_2}{1 - \tan \phi_1 \tan \phi_2} = \frac{a \cos \beta (4d_1 + 2a \sin \beta)}{4d_1^2 + 4d_1 a \sin \beta - a^2 \cos^2 \beta}.$$

Trigonometric and algebraic manipulation yields

$$d_1 = \frac{a}{2}\left(\cos \beta \cot \phi - \sin \beta + \sqrt{1 + \cos^2 \beta \cot^2 \phi} \right).$$

Hence,

$$d = d_1 + d_2 = \frac{a}{2}\left(\cos \beta \cot \phi + \csc \phi \sqrt{1 - \sin^2 \beta \cos^2 \phi} \right).$$

Note that if $\beta = 0$, then this expression reduces to

$$d = \frac{a}{2}(\cot \phi + \csc \phi),$$

and $\cot \phi + \csc \phi = \cot \frac{\phi}{2}$, so that the expression correctly reduces to the simple case.

To compute d exactly, it is necessary to know not only the disparity ϕ, but also the interocular distance a and the angle β. To what does this angle refer? Let us consider as our basic coordinate system, a system spanned by an axis passing through both eyes, an axis perpendicular to this and pointing "straight up" and an axis perpendicular to both of these and pointing "straight ahead". This coordinate system may have its origin centered either at one of the eyes, or midway between them.

In measuring exact disparity, there are two angular factors involved. One is the angular position of the imaging system relative to the coordinate frame, given by the position of the optic axis. In the case of the eye, this is the angle of the ray from the center of the fovea through the center of the lens, relative to a coordinate system, and this angle describes the gross orientation of the imaging system relative to the scene. The second angular factor is the relative retinal displacement of two corresponding image positions, given some pair of optic axes for the two eyes. This angular factor describes the relative disparity of a point, relative to the current fixation point (specified by the intersection of the two optic axes).

In order to determine the angle β, one needs to know the values of both these factors. While the retinal disparity will be measured by the stereo algorithm, we also need to know the actual camera angles, that is the exact angular position of the eyes, relative to the coordinate system. For a general imaging system, this is not a problem. However, for the human system, one must consider whether the system has access to these angles. For example, does the human system read the tensions on the eye muscles in such a way as to extract the optical axis angles relative to a fixed coordinate frame? Furthermore, one must also know the interocular separation, and one must again ask whether there is any evidence that this value is actually accessible to the human system.

4.6.2 Relative Distance

Rather than attempting to measure the distance exactly, one may instead simply attempt to measure the distance relative to some fixed point. The distance is given by

$$d = \frac{a}{2}\left(\cos\beta\cot\phi + \csc\phi\sqrt{1 - \sin^2\beta\cos^2\phi}\right).$$

If the objects being viewed are assumed not to lie too far off axis, then β is small. (Note that this assumption is reasonable because if an object lies too far off axis, only one eye will be able to view it.) In this case, the distance expression reduces to the approximation:

$$d \approx \frac{a}{2}\cot\frac{\phi}{2}.$$

Thus,

$$d + \Delta d \approx \frac{a}{2} \cot \frac{\phi + \Delta \phi}{2}$$

and

$$\frac{\Delta d}{d} \approx \cot \frac{\phi + \Delta \phi}{2} \tan \frac{\phi}{2} - 1.$$

By employing a series expansion for the cot and tan functions, the above expression reduces to

$$\frac{\Delta d}{d} \approx \frac{-\Delta \phi}{\phi + \Delta \phi} \left(1 + \frac{2\phi^2 \Delta \phi + \phi(\Delta \phi)^2}{12} + \cdots \right).$$

We know that the change in disparity $\Delta \phi$ must be less than 2° [Marr and Poggio, 1979]. Further, if any object is assumed to lie at least 10 centimeters from the viewer, then the disparity ϕ must be less than 34°. These two factors combined yield an estimate for the maximum error in relative depth of less than 6%. Hence, the approximation

$$\frac{\Delta d}{d} \approx \frac{-\Delta \phi}{\phi + \Delta \phi}.$$

Thus, we see that even to determine relative depth, it is still necessary to have some estimate of the actual disparity to the point of fixation, as well as the relative disparities at nearby points in the image. The interocular distance no longer plays a role, however.

Of course, for the general case of practical imaging systems, the accessibility of the camera angles and the separation of the cameras is not a major concern, since these parameters can easily be measured.

4.6.3 Surface Orientation

Another possible method of representing surface shape is to use surface orientation for small patches of the surface. One can, of course, compute surface orientation from depth values, but here the problem of computing surface orientation directly from disparity is considered. The geometry of the computation of surface orientation is illustrated in Figure 4.25.

In this system, the vector corresponding to a particular point is given by

$$\mathbf{r} = d\{\cos \psi \cos \theta, \cos \psi \sin \theta, \sin \psi\}$$

or

$$\mathbf{r} = d\mathbf{v}.$$

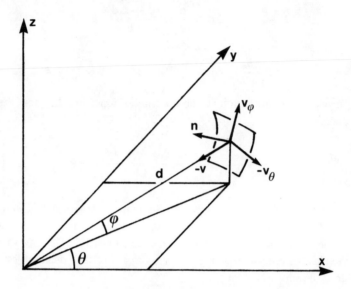

Figure 4.25
The Geometry of the Computation of Surface Orientation. The vector **r** describes the distance to a surface point in space, as a function of θ, ψ and the distance d. The surface normal at the point is denoted by **n** and can be related to a new coordinate system spanned by the view vector, and its partial derivatives with respect to ψ and θ.

The partial derivatives of this vector are

$$\mathbf{r}_\theta = d_\theta \mathbf{v} + d \cos \psi \mathbf{v}_\theta$$

$$\mathbf{r}_\psi = d_\psi \mathbf{v} + d \mathbf{v}_\psi$$

where

$$\mathbf{v} = \{\cos \psi \cos \theta, \cos \psi \sin \theta, \sin \psi\}$$

$$\mathbf{v}_\theta = \{-\sin \theta, \cos \theta, 0\}$$

$$\mathbf{v}_\psi = \{-\sin \psi \cos \theta, -\sin \psi \sin \theta, \cos \psi\}$$

The normal vector at this point is given by the cross product of the two partial derivatives

$$d d_\psi \cos \psi \mathbf{v}_\psi + d d_\theta \mathbf{v}_\theta - d^2 \cos \psi \mathbf{v}.$$

If this vector is related to a coordinate system spanned by the view vector and its partial derivatives, with unit coordinate vectors $-\mathbf{v}_\theta$, $\mathbf{v}_\psi$, and $-\mathbf{v}$, then the normal is given in this system by

$$N = \left\{ -dd_\theta, dd_\psi \cos \psi, d^2 \cos \psi \right\}$$

The unit normal is given by

$$n = \frac{\{-d_\theta, d_\psi \cos \psi, d \cos \psi\}}{\sqrt{d_\theta^2 + \cos^2 \psi (d_\psi^2 + d^2)}}.$$

By rotating the original axis system about the x axis, one can set $\psi = 0$. Thus, the expression for the unit normal becomes

$$n = \frac{\left\{ -\frac{d_\theta}{d}, \frac{d_\psi}{d}, 1 \right\}}{\sqrt{\frac{d_\theta}{d}^2 + \frac{d_\psi}{d}^2 + 1}}.$$

From our previous analysis of the case of relative depth, we know that

$$\frac{d_\theta}{d} \approx -\frac{\phi_\theta}{\phi + \phi_\theta}$$

$$\frac{d_\psi}{d} \approx -\frac{\phi_\psi}{\phi + \phi_\psi}.$$

Finally, if changes in distance are assumed to be small relative to the actual distance, $d_\theta \ll d, d_\psi \ll d$, then the unit normal may be approximated by

$$n \approx \left\{ \frac{\phi_\theta}{\phi + \phi_\theta}, -\frac{\phi_\psi}{\phi + \phi_\psi}, 1 \right\},$$

where ϕ_θ and ϕ_ψ are the partial derivatives of disparity in the directions of the two coordinate axes.

It is apparent from these calculations that if one wishes to compute local surface orientation directly from disparity, one must be able to compute the partial derivatives of disparity. But since the Marr-Poggio stereo algorithm explicitly determines disparity only along zero-crossing contours, one is confronted with the task of determining derivatives from a sparse array. Provided the disparity array is not too sparse, this can be done. Perhaps the easiest method is to determine the local gradient of the disparity about a point by a least-squares planar fit. This would allow one in most situations to determine ϕ_θ and ϕ_ψ, and hence the local surface orientation.

4.7 Summary

In this chapter, we have seen examples of the stereo algorithm applied to stereo pairs from the psychological literature and to stereo pairs of natural images. The correlation between the performance of the algorithm and the perception of human observers supports the adequacy of the Marr-Poggio algorithm as a model of the human stereo system. We also rederived the statistical distribution of distances between zero-crossings and showed how the assumptions underlying the design of the stereo matcher are validated. Finally, we discussed some of the problems and extensions associated with the stereo algorithm.

CHAPTER 5

THE CONSTRAINTS ON INTERPOLATION

In the first part of this book, we presented a computational theory of stereo vision. This theory provided a method for computing explicit surface values, such as distance or relative distance, at a particular set of points in the image, namely the zero-crossing contours of the Primal Sketch. At other locations of the image, no explicit surface information is computed.

Other components of the early visual system may also compute surface information only at scattered locations in the image; an example is the computation of structure from motion. In a computational theory developed by Ullman [1979a], motion analysis is considered as a two stage process. The first stage is the solution of a correspondence problem similar to that of stereopsis. In the case of motion, the images are taken at different points in time, rather than from different points in space. The second stage is the computation of the three-dimensional structure of the corresponding elements. The heart of the computation is identical to that of stereopsis; that is, we perform the following steps:

1. locate a point in one image,
2. locate the corresponding point in the next image, and
3. determine the structure of the associated object from this correspondence.

Although the algorithms by which the stereo and motion correspondences are computed may differ, the same computational arguments apply for choosing the basic elements to be matched. Ullman suggests that the motion correspondence problem utilizes Primal Sketch elements, such as edge and line segments, and that the subsequent structure-from-motion computation derives surface information only at the locations of these primitive elements.

Hence, both the stereo and the motion modules of the human early visual system compute explicit surface information only along specific contours in the images. Is such a representation of surface shape sufficient?

In this chapter, we will argue that such a representation is not sufficient for many purposes. We then turn to the problem of determining what surfaces could fit through the known points and how to distinguish between the infinite class of possible surfaces. In particular we will rely on the information implicitly carried in the positions of the zero-crossings — a surface cannot change in a radical manner between known zero-crossings, otherwise it would in general give rise to additional zero-crossings not represented in the Primal Sketch. We call this the *surface consistency constraint* [Grimson, 1980b, 1981b], and refer to it informally as *no news is good news*. In later chapters, this constraint will be used to compute the best surface to interpolate between the known data.

5.1 Motivating the Interpolation Process

We will first discuss the issue of how specific and explicit a surface representation is created. To within a particular resolution, the output of the stereo algorithm constitutes a complete representation of a surface. The point of interest is whether the human system requires and constructs a more specific, finer resolution representation of surfaces. The question of the sufficiency of the representation will be addressed from several viewpoints.

5.1.1 Psychophysics

For the human visual system, one must consider the question of the sufficiency of the stereo or motion output from a psychophysical standpoint. In other words, does there exist any experimental evidence that could determine the form of the representation? Although the question of two-dimensional interpolation of subjective contours has been studied in the psychological literature, the question of three-dimensional interpolation of subjective surfaces has had less attention (see, however, Gulick and Lawson, [1976], Lawson and Gulick [1967]).

Some initial psychophysical evidence is available, however. Figure 5.1 illustrates a sparse, 5% density random dot stereogram. The impression obtained upon viewing this stereogram is one of two distinct planes, sharply separated in depth. Yet, by the Marr-Poggio theory, explicit disparity information is available only along the edges of the dots, which cover a very small portion of the total area. Hence, it would seem, on the basis of this stereogram, that some type of filling-in, or interpolation of surface information, is taking place in the visual system. Particularly noteworthy in this case are the strong subjective contours between the two planes (see also, Lawson and Gulick [1967]).

The role of the interpolation process can be investigated in more detail by the method illustrated in Figure 5.2. The object in this stereogram is a half cylinder, lying below a reference plane. The density of the dots which lie on the cylinder fades gradually from 10% to zero in the center of the image. In this manner, a gap is created in the cylinder, without any sharp changes in dot density (and thus without any suggestion of an object occluding the cylinder). For most viewers, this stereogram yields the perception of a complete cylinder, thereby indicating again that some type of interpolation is taking place. Moreover, one can carefully test the attributes of the interpolation process by inserting a stereoscopic probe (a small pointer added to the cylinder scene which can be moved in depth relative to the perceived stereogram) into the center of the blank region. Consider, for example, the two interpolation schemes illustrated in Figure 5.2(c). For the first

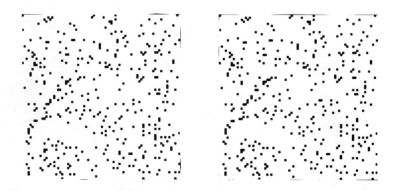

Figure 5.1
A Sparse Random Dot Stereogram. Although explicit disparity is only available at the edges of the dots, a vivid impression of two planar surfaces is obtained.

case, interpolation of the surface is strictly linear between the known disparity values, corresponding to a planar truncation of the cylinder, between the lowest visible points. This is inconsistent with the perception of the stereogram; when a psychophysical probe is inserted at a depth corresponding to this imaginary plane, it is perceived as lying above the surface of the cylinder. In the second case, interpolation of the surface is a linear extension of the tangents of the surface through the bottom-most visible points, corresponding to the planar extension of the cylinder, terminating in a sharp intersection of the planes. Again, this is inconsistent with the perception of the stereogram; when a psychophysical probe is inserted at a depth corresponding to the intersection of the two planes, it is perceived to lie below the surface of a now transparent cylinder. Thus, an upper and a lower bound on where the surface appears to lie has been established. When the probe is placed in positions intermediate to the previous two, the situation is less clear. For most positions, the probe appears roughly to lie on the surface of the cylinder, with the strongest perception occurring when the probe lies exactly on the cylinder.

One can also test the interpolation process along other sections of the cylinder, for example, by leaving gaps along the shoulder of the cylinder, rather than at its lowest point. Similar results to those described above are obtained in this case. The conclusion I draw from this experiment is that some type of interpolation is taking place. It may be rather imprecise, although it does seem roughly to preserve the curvature of the object involved. Note that the linear and tangential extensions of the disparities, both of which were seen to be incorrect, potentially introduce sharp discontinuities in the surface orientation of the surface. This observation will become important in the development of the constraints on the interpolation, discussed in section 5.6.

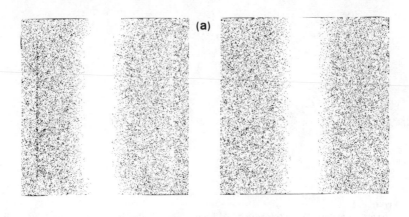

(a)

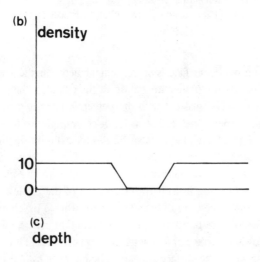

(b) density

10
0

(c)
depth

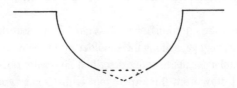

Figure 5.2
The Half Cylinder. The pair of images in (*a*) is a random dot stereogram of a
half cylinder. The diagram in figure (*b*) shows the dot density used to create the
stereogram. The diagram in figure (*c*) shows the depth values of a cross-section of
the stereogram. The dotted lines indicate the perception which would be expected for
linear interpolation (1) and tangential interpolation (2). The actual perception is of a
smooth cylinder.

5.1.2 Computational Needs

From a computational standpoint, the efficacy of a representation must be judged relative to its utility. In other words, is a representation of surface values along zero-crossing contours sufficient for the purposes of the $2\frac{1}{2}$-D Sketch? This can be answered by considering what further stages of processing must be applied to the representation. The purpose of the $2\frac{1}{2}$-D Sketch is to make surface information, as well as contours of surface discontinuity, explicit in a viewer-centered representation, with the intention of later extracting volumetric descriptions of objects in the scene [Marr and Nishihara, 1978]. Although not necessarily compelling, it can be argued that the extraction of such volumetric descriptions would be enhanced by the creation of an input representation which contained explicit surface information everywhere. Due to the discrete resolution of the visual system, this implies that on a grid representation of the scene, an explicit surface value should be represented at each grid point.

5.1.3 Applications

Two motivations for converting the output of the stereo or motion systems to a complete representation have been presented, both relating directly to the human visual system. A third, more general, motivation can be added. There are many applications, such as high-altitude photomapping, hand-eye coordination systems, industrial robotics, and inspection of manufactured parts, where it is useful to create a complete specification of the visible surfaces of a scene. Thus, for general image processing systems, it is of interest to determine a method of interpolating the output of the Marr-Poggio stereo algorithm, or the output of the Ullman structure from motion algorithm, in order to obtain a complete representation of surface information.

5.2 The Interpolation Problem

There are two aspects of the problem of creating complete depth specifications. The more general aspect is the strictly mathematical question of surface reconstruction, independent of its relevance to the human visual system. Suppose one is given a visual process that determines surface information at points corresponding to relevant changes in the images. In general, there will be many possible surfaces consistent with these initial surface points, but we would obviously like to compute a single surface. Mathematically, one approach to this problem is to ask: can one assign a probability density function to the set of possible surfaces, which measures the inconsistency of each surface with all available information? If so, can an algorithm for finding the surface be constructed that optimizes this probability by finding the least inconsistent surface?

The ultimate objective, however, is to understand and model the human visual system. Hence, we need to ask whether a particular algorithm is applicable to the human system, and whether there is any corroborating evidence that such an algorithm in fact exists in the human system. To deal with this issue, we shall again rely on Marr's paradigm of early visual processing. In this context, the key point of the paradigm is that the computational theory, and an algorithm developed to solve it, may be considered as independent. That is, the computational theory deals with the theoretical questions of what information processing computations are inherent to the task, independent of the specific algorithm used to solve them. There may be several algorithms that will actually perform a given computation. Some will be more suited to the biological constraints of the human visual system than others. However, it is important to stress that such considerations arise at the level of designing an algorithm to solve a computational problem, and not at the level of the computational theory itself.

We will first develop the computational theory, based on the mathematical problem of choosing which surface is most consistent with the visual information. Secondary to this, the development of algorithms to solve the computational problem and the relevance of such algorithms to the human visual system will be considered.

5.3 The Computational Constraint

We now consider the computational constraints involved in the process of creating complete surface specifications. The basic input to the interpolation process consists of the zero-crossings of the convolved image, with depth information computed along zero-crossing contours.

Suppose one were to attempt to construct a complete surface description based only on the surface information known along the zero-crossings. An infinite number of surfaces would consistently fit the boundary conditions provided by these surface values. Yet there must be some way of deciding which surface, or at least which small family of surfaces, could give rise to the zero-crossing descriptions. This means that there must be some additional information available from the visual process which, when taken into account, will identify a class of nearly indistinguishable surfaces that represent the visible surfaces of the scene.

In order to determine what information is available from the visual process, one must first carefully consider the process by which the zero-crossing contours are generated. We have already relied on the fact that sudden changes in the reflectance of a surface, caused, for example, by surface scratches or texture markings, will give rise to zero-crossings in the convolved image. Sudden or sharp changes in the shape of the surface will under most circumstances also give rise to zero-crossings. This fact will be used to constrain the possible shapes of surfaces that could produce particular surface values along the zero-crossing contours.

We illustrate the basic argument with an example. Suppose one is given a closed zero-crossing contour, within which there are no other zero-crossings. An example would be a circular contour, along which the depth is constant. There are many surfaces which could fit this set of boundary conditions. One such surface is a flat disk. One could, however, also fit other smooth surfaces to this set of boundary conditions. For example, the highly convoluted surface formed by $\sin\left(x^2 + y^2\right)^{\frac{1}{2}}$ would be consistent with the known disparity values (see Figure 5.3). Yet in principle, such a rapidly varying surface should give rise to other zero-crossings. This follows from the observation that if the surface orientation undergoes a periodic variation, then it is likely that the irradiance values will also undergo such a variation. Since the only zero-crossings are at the borders of the object, this implies that the surface $\sin\left(x^2 + y^2\right)^{\frac{1}{2}}$ is not a valid representative surface for this set of boundary conditions.

Hence, the hypothesis, which will be evaluated in the following sections, is that the set of zero-crossing contours contains implicit information about the surface as well as explicit information. If one can determine a set of conditions on the surface shape that cause inflections in the irradiance values, then one may be able to determine a likely surface structure, given a set of boundary conditions along the zero-crossing contours.

5.4 No News is Good News

In general, any one of a multitude of widely varying surfaces could fit the boundary conditions imposed along the zero-crossings. The intention in this section is to show that to be completely consistent with the imaging process, such surfaces must meet both explicit conditions and implicit conditions. The explicit conditions are given by the depth or surface orientation values along the zero-crossing contours. The implicit conditions are that the surface must not impose any zero-crossing contours other than those which appear in the convolved image. This implicit condition leads to the *surface consistency constraint* [Grimson, 1981b], namely:

The absence of zero-crossings constrains the possible surface shapes.

Just as the presence of a zero-crossing tells us that some physical property is changing at a given location, the absence of a zero-crossing tells us the opposite, that no physical property is changing, and in particular that the surface topography is not changing in a radical manner. We informally refer to this constraint as *no news is good news*, since it says that the surface cannot change radically without informing us of this fact by means of zero-crossings.

In order to make explicit any constraints on the shape of the surface for locations in the image not associated with a zero-crossing, we will carefully examine the factors which influence irradiance (or intensity) in the image. These factors

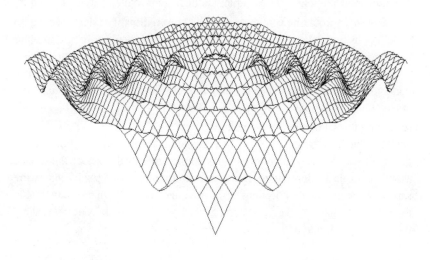

Figure 5.3
Possible Surfaces Fitting Depth Values at Zero-Crossings. Given boundary conditions of a circular zero-crossing contour, along which the depth is constant, there are many possible surfaces which could fit the known depth points. Two examples are a flat disk, and the highly convoluted surface formed by $\sin\left(x^2 + y^2\right)^{\frac{1}{2}}$, shown here.

will be expressed in the image irradiance equation, which describes the manner in which a particular irradiance (or intensity) is formed at a point in the image. Two goals are kept in mind. The first is to determine what surface conditions will cause a local change in irradiance, and the second is to combine this constraint with the input from the visual processes, such as stereo or structure from motion, in order to design an algorithm for interpolating surface information. Many factors are involved in the formation of image irradiances. As a consequence, changes in any of those factors can cause a change in the image irradiances, and give rise to a zero-crossing in the convolved image. We are interested in showing that factors such as surface shape cannot be changing in a radical manner in regions in which there are no zero-crossings.

The basic result, corresponding to the intuitive argument given above, is that the probability of a zero-crossing occurring, in regions where the illumination is roughly constant and the surface material does not change, is a monotonic function of the variation in the orientation of the surface normal. This means that the probability of a zero-crossing increases as the variation in surface orientation increases. By inverting this argument, we will show that the best surface to fit the known data is that which minimizes the variation in surface orientation since this surface is most consistent with the zero-crossings in the convolved image.

The remainder of this chapter is a technical proof of this result. Readers uninterested in the details of the proof may safely skip the rest of this chapter without sacrificing the flow of the argument.

5.5 Image Formation

In order to examine the process of zero-crossing formation, a review of the factors involved in the formation of an image will be presented. One factor is the geometry of the projection from the scene to the image. Another is the manner in which image irradiance values at a point are formed. The analysis of these processes has been undertaken by several investigators. In this section, we rely on the work of Horn [1975, 1977], Horn and Sjoberg [1979], and Woodham [1978].

5.5.1 From the Object to the Image

Consider the projection of a surface point onto the image plane as illustrated in Figure 5.4. It is convenient to think of the image plane as being in front of the lens rather than behind it, in order to avoid inversion of the image. Position the lens at the origin and the image plane perpendicular to the z axis. The focal length of the lens, that is, the distance between the view point and the image plane, will be represented by f.

The proportionality of similar triangles yields

$$\frac{u}{f} = \frac{x}{z+d} \qquad \frac{v}{f} = \frac{y}{z+d}$$

so that

$$u = \left(\frac{f}{z+d}\right)x \qquad v = \left(\frac{f}{z+d}\right)y.$$

These equations define the standard *perspective projection*, determining an image point (u, v) corresponding to an object point (x, y, z). If the size of the objects in the scene is small compared to the viewing distance, then for all surface points

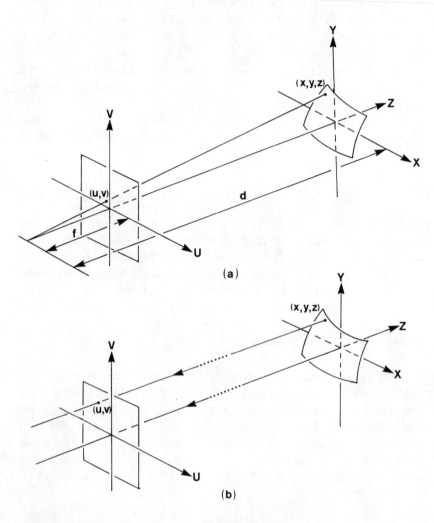

Figure 5.4
The Image Projection. Figure (*a*) shows a perspective projection. The focal length is given by *f* and the distance from the object coordinate origin to the center of the lens is given by *d*. The image plane is placed in front of the lens to avoid image inversion. Figure (*b*) shows an orthographic projection. This occurs in the case of objects that are small relative to the viewing distance, where the focal length *f* is infinite, causing all rays from the object to the image plane to be parallel. (Redrawn from Woodham, [1978]).

(x, y, z), z is nearly constant and the equations become, after scaling,

$$u = x \qquad v = y.$$

These equations define the standard *orthographic projection*, and thus determine where a point on a surface will appear in the image. Note that in the case of orthographic projection, all rays from the surface to the image plane are parallel, so the use of separate image coordinates is somewhat redundant. Thus, the image coordinates and object coordinates can be referred to interchangeably.

5.5.2 Grey-Level Formation

It is now necessary to determine what irradiance value will be associated with a particular image location. A careful analysis of this process may be found in [Horn, 1970, 1975; Nicodemus, et al., 1977; Woodham, 1978; Horn and Sjoberg, 1979]. In this section, we outline the major points of the grey level formation process. In summary, there are three factors governing the irradiance recorded at any position in the image:

1. the amount of radiant flux striking a surface,
2. the percentage of incident flux reflected by the surface material (as opposed to the percentage absorbed), and
3. the distribution of that reflected flux as a function of direction.

It will be seen that a sharp change in each of these factors will give rise to a zero-crossing in the convolved image. Further, in regions where both the incident illumination and absorption characteristics of the surface material are roughly constant, an equation relating the recorded irradiances to the shape of the surface will be derived. This image irradiance equation will be used in later sections to verify our surface consistency constraint. We now turn to a more detailed examination of these statements.

The apparent "brightness" recorded by an imaging device is a measurement of *image irradiance* E, the radiant flux striking a unit area of the receptive field. The flux reaching a small portion of the receptive field will be exclusively a function of a corresponding small surface element on some object in the scene, provided the imaging system is properly focused. We want to specify the factors that determine the image irradiance at a point in the image, as a function of the corresponding surface element.

Consider a source of illumination with intensity I in the direction of a surface patch of area dA. Further assume that this patch is oriented with its surface normal making angle θ with the line connecting the patch to the source. The patch will be foreshortened relative to the source, and will appear as a smaller patch of area $dA \cdot \cos\theta$ oriented perpendicular to the source. The solid angle spanned by the patch is thus

$$dw = dA \cdot \frac{\cos\theta}{r^2}.$$

The radiant flux intercepted by this patch is then

$$d\Phi = I \cdot dw = I \cdot dA \cdot \frac{\cos\theta}{r^2}.$$

Thus, the irradiance of the surface (the incident flux density) is simply

$$E = \frac{d\Phi}{dA} = I \cdot \frac{\cos\theta}{r^2}.$$

This specifies the amount of light striking a surface from a source. It is dependent on the initial illumination intensity I as well as the orientation of the surface relative to the source θ, and the distance to the source r.

The apparent "brightness" of a surface element thus depends on its orientation relative to the viewer and the light sources. A smooth opaque non-planar object will give rise to a shaded image, in which brightness varies spatially, even in cases where the object is illuminated evenly and where the object is covered by a uniform surface layer. Thus, the flux emitted from a surface patch toward an imaging device must be measured as the *radiance*, the flux emitted per unit *foreshortened* surface area per unit solid angle, or equivalently, the flux emitted per unit surface area per unit *projected* solid angle.

What happens next? When a ray of light strikes a surface it may be absorbed, transmitted, reflected or undergo some combination therein. We are concerned with the percentage of incident flux which is reflected, and more particularly with the percentage of flux reflected in a given direction (such as toward the viewer). The amount of flux absorbed depends on the surface material, and the percentage of incident flux which is reflected is usually represented by a factor called *albedo*, denoted ρ. The behavior of the reflected flux is determined by the *surface microstructure*, those surface features too small to be resolved by the imaging system. For notational purposes the effects of surface microstructure will be referred to as *photometric*, while the effects of the surface topography, or gross surface shape, will be referred to as *topographic*.

The surface microstructure can affect the reflected flux in a variety of ways. Horn and Sjoberg [1979] sketch three examples. If the surface is flat and the underlying material homogeneous, the reflected ray will lie in the plane formed by the incident ray and the surface normal and will make an angle with the local normal equal to the angle between the incident ray and the local normal. Materials with this type of microstructure are referred to as "specular", "metallic" or "dielectric". If the surface is not perfectly flat on a microscopic scale, it will scatter parallel incident rays in many directions. If the deviations of the local surface normal are small, most of the rays will lie near the direction for ideal specular reflection. The perceived surface is referred to as "shiny" or "glossy". Finally, if the surface layer is not homogeneous on a microscopic scale, the light rays which penetrate the surface will be scattered by refraction and reflection at boundaries between regions with differing refractive indices. The scattered rays may reemerge near the point of entry in many directions. Such surfaces are said to have a "diffuse", "flat" or "matte" reflection. Thus, the distribution of reflected light in each case depends on the direction of incident rays and the details of the microstructure of the surface.

To specify the effects of the surface microstructure on the exitant flux density, we need to define a reflectance function associated with a surface. The *Bidirectional Reflectance-Distribution Function* (BRDF) introduced by Nicodemus et al. [1977] specifies reflectance in terms of incident- and reflected-beam geometry (see Figure 5.5). In other words, it specifies how bright a surface element will appear when illuminated from a given direction and viewed from a second given direction.

The BRDF is defined as the ratio of reflected radiance dL_r in the direction of the viewer to the irradiance dE_i from the direction of a portion of the source:

$$f_r(\theta_i, \phi_i; \theta_r, \phi_r) = \frac{dL_r(\theta_i, \phi_i; \theta_r, \phi_r; E_i)}{dE_i(\theta_i, \phi_i)}$$

where θ and ϕ indicate a direction, the subscript i denotes quantities associated with incident radiant flux and the subscript r denotes quantities associated with reflected radiant flux. Note that the angles as indicated in Figure 5.5 are given within a surface-specific coordinate system, with one axis along the local normal to the surface and another defining an arbitrary reference direction in the local tangent plane. Directions are specified by polar angle (θ) measured from the local normal and azimuth angle (ϕ) measured counter-clockwise from the reference direction in the surface. The reflectance function describes the reflective properties of a surface independent of any particular illumination geometry.

We have determined that the scene radiance (or reflected flux density) is a function of the intensity of the source I, its distance from the object r, the orientation of the surface relative to the viewer (θ_n, ϕ_n), the orientation of the source relative to the surface (θ_i, ϕ_i), the albedo of the surface material ρ and the microstructure of the surface material, as described by the BRDF f_r.

At this point, we have considered what happens to light rays which strike a surface patch and are reflected. We must finally consider the relationship between the amount of flux reflected by a surface patch towards the image sensor, and the amount of flux recorded by the sensor. Horn and Sjoberg, [1979] show that if the imaging device is properly focussed, and the lens is small relative to its distance from the object, then image irradiance is proportional to scene radiance. This means that the irradiances recorded by the sensor will be directly proportional

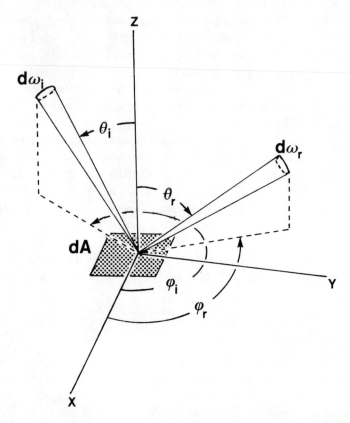

Figure 5.5
Beam Geometry. Four angles are needed to specify the Bidirectional Reflectance-Distribution Function. These are the polar angle θ_i and the azimuth angle ϕ_i of the incident beam, and the polar angle θ_r and the azimuth angle ϕ_r of the reflected beam. (Redrawn from Horn and Sjoberg, [1979]).

to the flux reflected by a surface element. Thus we see that, ignoring scale constants, the image irradiance is a function of the six factors $I, r, (\theta_n, \phi_n), (\theta_i, \phi_i), \rho$ and f_r. We shall now show how a series of simple assumptions can simplify this dependence.

Most surfaces have the property that the reflectance is not changed by rotating a surface element about its normal (exceptions are diffraction gratings, irridescent plumage and "tiger's eye"). Such surfaces are referred to as *isotropic*. If a surface possesses this property, we can greatly simplify the beam geometry, as shown in Figure 5.6. In this case, only three angles are needed to determine reflectance.

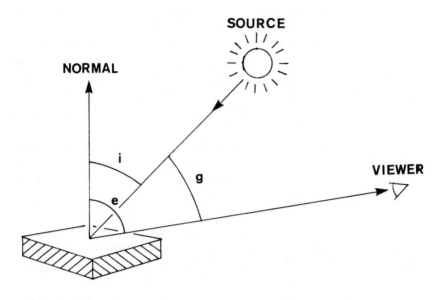

Figure 5.6
The Imaging Geometry. The incident angle i is the angle between the incident ray and surface normal. The view angle e is the angle between the emergent ray and the surface normal. The phase angle g is the angle between the incident and emergent rays. (Redrawn from Woodham, [1978]).

The angle between the local surface normal and the incident ray is called the incident angle and is denoted by i. The angle between the local surface normal and the emitted ray is called the view angle and is denoted by e. The angle between the incident and emitted rays is called the phase angle and is denoted by g. In the following, we shall assume that the surfaces are isotropic. This reduces the image irradiance to a function of I, r, i, e, g and ρ.

We know that the incident flux density follows an inverse-square reduction as a function of distance. If two surfaces lie at very different depths, and all other factors are roughly equal, this inverse-square dependence will cause a noticeable difference in the irradiances associated with the different surfaces. If the projections of the two surfaces are adjacent in the image, the different irradiances will give rise to a zero-crossing in the convolved image. This is to be expected, since the Marr-Hildreth theory of edge detection was based on the requirement of detecting changes in the image corresponding to changes in some physical property of the surfaces. In this case, the changing physical property is object continuity.

Given that these situations will cause a zero-crossing, we can restrict our attention to regions of the image between the borders of the objects. Thus we can assume that the source is distant relative to the surfaces. This has two consequences. The first is that each surface receives roughly uniform illumination. This implies that the I/r^2 term is roughly constant and may be ignored in what follows. The second is that the angle between the viewer direction and the source direction will be roughly constant over all surfaces, that is, the phase angle g is roughly constant.

If the surface material changes, there will frequently be an associated change in the albedo. If all other factors are roughly equal, this will cause a change in the irradiances and there will be a corresponding zero-crossing in the convolved image. This is again expected from the Marr-Hildreth theory of edge detection: a changing physical property of the surface should correspond to a zero-crossing in the convolved image. In general we shall restrict our attention to regions of the surfaces between such material changes, so that the albedo ρ is roughly constant. In these regions, we can consider the image irradiances to be a function of i, e and ρ (ignoring scale constants).

If we assume that the source is distant enough and small enough to be treated as a point source, then we can simplify the geometry further by reducing the angles i and e to a specification of the local surface normal, in the following manner. Consider a Cartesian coordinate system with z-axis aligned with the line of sight, and x-axis some arbitrary direction in the plane normal to the line of sight. Suppose the surface is specified in the coordinate system by $z = f(x, y)$. Elementary calculus states that the vectors

$$\left\{ 1, 0, \frac{\partial z}{\partial x} \right\} \qquad \left\{ 0, 1, \frac{\partial z}{\partial y} \right\}$$

are tangent to the surface at a given point. The cross product

$$\left\{ \frac{\partial z}{\partial x}, \frac{\partial z}{\partial y}, -1 \right\}$$

is normal to the tangent plane, and hence to the surface. Defining

$$p = \frac{\partial z}{\partial x} \qquad q = \frac{\partial z}{\partial y}$$

the normal vector becomes $\{p, q, -1\}$. The quantity (p, q) is usually referred to as the *gradient* and the space of all points (p, q) is referred to as *gradient space*.

In this case, the angles i and e can be straightforwardly transformed into the normal components p and q. Since we are considering the case of a distant point source, its direction relative to the surface can be represented by a direction vector $\{p_s, q_s, -1\}$. A straightforward calculation shows that the angles i and e are given by:

$$\cos(i) = \frac{1 + pp_s + qq_s}{\sqrt{1 + p^2 + q^2}\sqrt{1 + p_s^2 + q_s^2}}$$

$$\cos(e) = \frac{1}{\sqrt{1 + p^2 + q^2}}.$$

Extended sources (sources whose size relative to their separation from the scene cannot be treated as a point source, for example, fluorescent lights in a normal sized room) can be frequently treated by superposition of point sources, or as being equivalent to an appropriately chosen point source [Silver, 1980]. Thus, the irradiance reduces to a function of p, q and ρ.

Finally, if we assume that the objects are distant relative to the viewer, the image projection may be treated as orthographic. In this case, the coordinate system of the image and the coordinate system of the scene can be treated as identical so that we obtain the *image irradiance equation:*

$$E(x, y) = \rho(x, y)R\big(p(x, y), q(x, y)\big)$$

where $E(x, y)$ is the image irradiance recorded at a point in the image, ρ is the albedo associated with the surface intersecting the ray from (x, y) and $R(p, q)$ is the reflectance map [Horn, 1970, 1975, Horn and Sjoberg, 1979, Horn and Bachman, 1977]. Note that the reflectance map R differs from the reflectance function f_r. The reflectance function describes the amount of flux reflected in a particular direction, given an incident flux from a second given direction. The reflectance map combines the effects of the reflectance function in the case of uniform illumination and isotropic surface material with the illumination geometry and the image sensor's view point. In the case of constant albedo the image irradiance equation reduces to the partial differential equation [Horn, 1970, 1975; Horn and Sjoberg, 1979]:

$$E(x, y) = R\big(p(x, y), q(x, y)\big).$$

These two equations describe the manner in which an image irradiance (or grey-level) is obtained at a particular point in the image.

5.6 The Interpolation Theorem

We have seen that zero-crossings can arise from many factors. We shall restrict our attention to regions in which illumination is constant, albedo is roughly constant and surface material is isotropic. Our intention is to show that in such cases, if the surface topography changes radically, the image irradiances must also change radically. We will then be able to use the contrapositive statement — if the image irradiances do not change radically, then the surface topography also does not change. Note that if the albedo or the illumination is not constant over the region, we cannot make this statement. That is, there could be situations in which the surface topography does change radically without causing a corresponding change in the image irradiances, because one of the other factors, such as the albedo, is also changing in such a manner as to mask out the effects of the change in topography. These situations are fortunately very rare, since they require a precise meshing of the effects of the changing albedo with the changing surface topography and in general are highly dependent on the viewer position and illuminant direction. Thus, a small change in the viewer position will usually decouple the conflicting effects of albedo and surface shape, and the change in topography will give rise to a zero-crossing. (In other words, it is generally difficult to paint a radically curved surface so as to appear flat from all viewpoints. The opposite is not true, of course. One can easily paint a flat surface to appear curved.)

The concern here is whether there can be zero-crossings corresponding to topographic rather than photometric changes in an object, for example, the radial sine surface of Figure 5.3. Indeed, if the albedo is roughly constant, the form of the equations indicates that there may be topographic effects that could also cause sharp changes in irradiance. The surface conditions under which such a change in irradiance can occur are important, since the absence of zero-crossings in a region would then imply the absence of such surface conditions for that region. It is precisely these restrictions on surface shape which will allow one to determine a surface consistent with the depth values along the zero-crossing contours. The basic problem is, under what conditions does bending of the surface force an inflection in the irradiance array? This question will be answered in the following sections by considering specific cases.

There are two points to note, before beginning the mathematical details. The first concerns the role of the Gaussian filter in constructing the primal sketch representations upon which the correspondence is computed. The Gaussian performs a smoothing of the image, thereby isolating irradiance changes at a particular scale. At the same time, it removes some of the noise problems which arise from using a discrete grid to represent the image. In what follows, we shall concentrate on the differential operator (∇^2) and its role in the creation of the zero-crossings. The effect of the Gaussian will not be considered in any detail. Hence, the surface reconstruction will not account for minor surface fluctuations on the scale of the grid resolution. This is not a major problem. (Equivalently, the problem may be considered as one of applying the Laplacian ∇^2 to the image $G * E$. The reconstruction will be based on this image information.)

The second point concerns the use of the Laplacian operator ∇^2 as opposed to directional derivatives. The mathematical arguments which follow are based on the consideration of zero-crossings of the convolution of a directional second-order differential operator with the image, $(\mathbf{v} \cdot \nabla) * E$. We have already seen that the Marr-Hildreth theory of edge detection is based on the use of zero-crossings of the image convolved with the Laplacian, $\nabla^2 * E$. This difference is not critical, for the following two reasons. Marr and Hildreth show that under some simple assumptions, the zero-crossings obtained by either operator are identical. In particular, the *condition of linear variation* [Marr and Hildreth, 1980] states that: *the irradiance variation near and parallel to a line of zero-crossings should locally be linear*. If this condition is assumed to be true then it can be shown [Marr and Hildreth, 1980, Appendix A] that the zero-crossings obtained with the Laplacian are identical to those obtained using directional derivatives. Thus, in those situations for which the condition of linear variation is valid, no difference is obtained. In the case where the condition of linear variation does not hold, the difference in the zero-crossings of the operators lies in their position, not in the existence of such zero-crossings. For example, at a corner (which frequently carries strong visual information), both $\nabla^2 * E$ and $(\mathbf{v} \cdot \nabla) * E$ will give rise to zero-crossings. The only difference will be in the exact position of the zero-crossings. We shall see that such variation in position is of negligible consequence to the reconstruction process. Hence, it will be assumed that the arguments developed in the next section, based on the zero-crossings of a directional second derivative will also generally apply to the zero-crossings of the Laplacian.

Finally, in what follows, the functions ρ, R and f are assumed to have continuous second order partial derivatives. Throughout, it is assumed that the albedo effects can be ignored relative to the topographic ones, that is, the albedo factor may be considered roughly constant and will therefore not affect any study of derivatives. Without loss of generality, one may assume that $\rho = 1$ and ignore the albedo in what follows.

5.6.1 General Argument

The basic hypothesis is that in order for a surface to be consistent with a given set of zero-crossings, not only must it give rise to a zero-crossing in the convolved irradiances at those points, but it must also *not* give rise to zero-crossings anywhere else. Under most situations, this restriction would require that the surface not change in a radical manner between zero-crossing contours. (For example, the surface shown in Figure 5.3 is not consistent with the boundary conditions of a circular zero-crossing contour of uniform depth). It is difficult to prove this assertion in general, since the image formation equation includes terms dependent on the imaging process and on the light source geometry, as well as factors dependent on the photometric properties of the surface itself. However, under some fairly weak assumptions concerning the relative strengths of photometric and topographic changes, and the form of the reflectance function, we will prove the *surface consistency theorem*, describing the probability of a zero-crossing as a function of the shape of the surface. The importance of this theorem is that it leads to a method for measuring the probability of a particular surface being

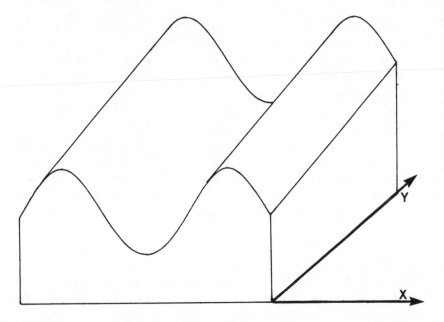

Figure 5.7
An Example of a Developable Surface. The component of the surface orientation in the y direction is constant for this region of the surface, so that the only variations in surface orientation take place in the x direction.

inconsistent with the zero-crossing information. This in turn suggests that it will be possible to derive a method for determining the best possible surface to fit the known information.

5.6.2 A One-Dimensional Example

To illustrate the scope of the surface consistency theorem, we shall consider first the one-dimensional case of a developable surface, before proving the general theorem concerning arbitrary surfaces. Note that the Laplacian is orientation independent, so that without loss of generality, one may rotate the coordinate system of the image to suit our needs. One may assume that the surface has the form $f(x, y)$ such that $f_y(x, y) = q(x, y) = c$, in the local region under consideration. Hence, the partial derivatives of q vanish, as do any partial derivatives of p involving y. A sample surface is shown in Figure 5.7 (similar surfaces have been studied by Stevens [1979]).

Suppose that a one-dimensional slice in the x direction of the surface contains at least two inflection points. Figure 5.8 indicates a sample surface and its derivatives. Since q is assumed constant, the derivatives of the image irradiance equation are given by:

$$\nabla^2 E = \left(\nabla^2 \rho\right)R + 2\rho_x R_p p_x + \rho\left(R_{pp} p_x^2 + R_p p_{xx}\right).$$

(Note that except where explicitly stated otherwise, we shall use a subscript to denote a partial derivative, so that, for example, $p_x = \partial p/\partial x$.) In this situation of a developable surface, we can prove the following result.

Theorem 0: Consider a portion of a second differentiable, developable surface oriented along the y axis such that $f_y(x, y) = q = c$, for some constant c. If the following conditions are true:

1. *The surface portion contains exactly two inflection points in the x direction, at x_1 and x_2,*
2. *At the points x_1 and x_2, normalized changes in albedo are dominated by normalized changes in reflectance,*

$$\left|\frac{\nabla^2 \rho}{\rho}\right| < \left|\frac{R_p p_{xx}}{R}\right|,$$

3. *The reflectance map R does not pass through an extremum in this region of the surface,*
4. *The reflectance map R is not constant over this region of the surface,*
5. *The albedo ρ is non-zero,*

then there exists a point $x_1 < x' < x_2$ such that $\nabla^2 E(x') = 0$.

Proof: The signum function is defined by:

$$sgn(x) = \begin{cases} 1 & \text{if } x > 0 \\ -1 & \text{if } x < 0 \\ 0 & \text{if } x = 0 \end{cases}$$

From the derivatives of the image equation,

$$\nabla^2 I = (\nabla^2 A)R + 2A_x R_p p_x + A\left(R_{pp} p_x^2 + R_p p_{xx}\right).$$

At the inflection points x_1 and x_2, $p_x(x_i) = 0$. Hence, evaluation of the equation yields

$$\nabla^2 I(x_i) = \nabla^2 A(x_i) R(p(x_i)) + A(x_i) R_p(p(x_i)) p_{xx}(x_i) \quad \text{for } i = 1, 2.$$

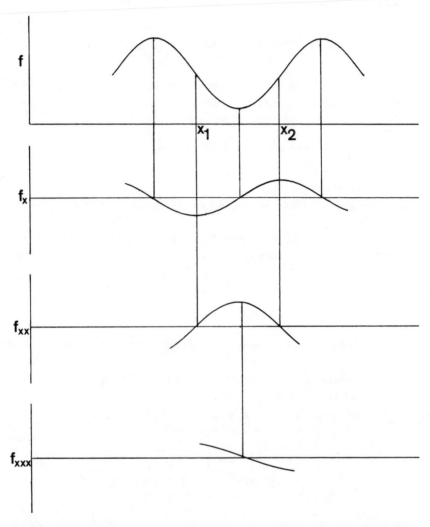

Figure 5.8
One-Dimensional Example. The top figure illustrates a slice of the surface, containing two inflection points. The second figure illustrates the first derivative of the surface function. The two inflection points of the surface correspond to extrema in the first derivative. The third figure illustrates the second derivative of the surface function. The two inflections in the surface correspond to zero-crossings in the second derivative. The bottom figure illustrates the third derivative of the surface function. Between the points corresponding to the two inflection points of the surface, the third derivative contains a zero-crossing.

Condition (2) implies that the albedo changes are negligible in this region, so that the first term may be ignored,

$$sgn(\nabla^2 I(x_i)) = sgn(A(x_i)R_p(p(x_i))p_{xx}(x_i)).$$

Condition (5) implies that $sgn(A) = 1$. Observing that

$$sgn(xy) = sgn(x)\, sgn(y),$$

the sign of the convolved intensity function at the surface inflection points is given by

$$sgn(\nabla^2 I(x_i)) = sgn(R_p(p(x_i))p_{xx}(x_i)).$$

Condition (3) implies that R_p does not change sign in this region of the surface and hence

$$sgn(R_p(p(x_1))) = sgn(R_p(p(x_2))).$$

Note that $p_x = 0$ at x_1, x_2. The fact that there are exactly two inflections on the surface implies that $p_x \not\equiv 0$ over the neighborhood (x_1, x_2). Thus,

$$sgn(p_{xx}(x_1)) \neq sgn(p_{xx}(x_2)),$$

and thus

$$sgn(\nabla^2 I(x_1)) \neq sgn(\nabla^2 I(x_2)).$$

The second differentiability of the surface implies that there exists a point $x' \in (x_1, x_2)$ such that $\nabla^2 I(x') = 0$. ∎

The contrapositive of this theorem states something important about the possible surfaces which can fit the known depth information. Specifically, given the conditions of the theorem, if there is a set of known depth points to which a surface is to be fit, there cannot be two or more inflections in the surface between any two zero-crossing points. If there were, there would have to be an additional zero-crossing there as well.

Corollary 0.1: Suppose one is given a set of known depth points at a set of zero-crossings, along a developable surface. If the albedo A is non-zero and the reflectance R is not constant for this region of the surface, then the surface cannot contain two or more inflection points between any pair of adjacent zero-crossings. ∎

There are many ways of extending this result. Some are indicated in Appendix II. The most important extension is to consider general surfaces, rather than developable ones. We make this extension in the following sections.

5.6.3 The Analytic Argument

Consider a surface f, and take a planar slice of the surface, normal to the image plane, along some direction (given for example by the angle α between the x axis and the direction of the slice). This is illustrated in Figure 5.9. At each point along the resulting curve C, one may associate a surface orientation, or gradient, given by a pair of partial derivatives, $p(x, y) = \partial f(x, y)/\partial x$, and $q(x, y) = \partial f(x, y)/\partial y$. Thus, one may construct a two-dimensional space spanned by a coordinate system with axes given by p and q, the gradient space introduced by Huffman [1971] and used by Mackworth [1973], and by Horn [1977] to relate the geometry of image projections to the radiometry of image formation. The curve obtained by the planar intersection of the surface transforms into a new, parametric curve in gradient space:

$$N_f(t) = \{p(t), q(t), -1\}$$

In fact, this curve corresponds to the mapping of the normal to the surface, as one moves along the planar slice; the subscript f is used to indicate that this is the normal to the surface f.

Because the albedo is roughly constant, the image irradiances are determined by the reflectance factor $R(p, q)$. Thus, the irradiances may be related to Horn's reflectance map, in which one considers the surface defined by $R(p, q)$ in gradient space. Hence, the curve C on the original surface will map onto a curve N_f in gradient space and this may be projected onto the surface $R(p, q)$ to obtain a new curve $C'(t)$. At each point t along the parametric curve, the corresponding irradiance is given by $R(p(t), q(t))$, (scaled by the constant ρ, which we will ignore without loss of generality).

We are interested in the conditions on the original surface and the reflectance surface that will cause a zero-crossing in the second directional derivative of the image irradiances. (Recall that by reflectance surface, we mean the reflectance map $R(p, q)$ considered as a surface in gradient space.) The following lemma shows that if the normal to the reflectance surface is orthogonal to the variation in the normal to the actual surface at two different points, then there must be a zero-crossing in the convolved irradiances.

Before proving this result analytically, I will sketch a more intuitive geometric argument. The basic point is to consider what conditions will cause the first directional derivative of the irradiances to become zero. Once those conditions have been determined, an appeal to Rolle's theorem will allow us to relate the same conditions to the existence of a zero-crossing.

Tracing along a curve on the surface f, we can observe the surface orientation of f at each point on the curve. This allows us to transform the curve on the surface to a parametric curve N_f in gradient space. Superimposed on this space is the reflectance map R which can be considered as a surface in gradient space. The irradiance corresponding to a point on the original curve is given by projecting the parametric curve N_f onto the surface R. There are two vectors of interest in this space. The first is the normal to the reflectance surface N_f and the second is the

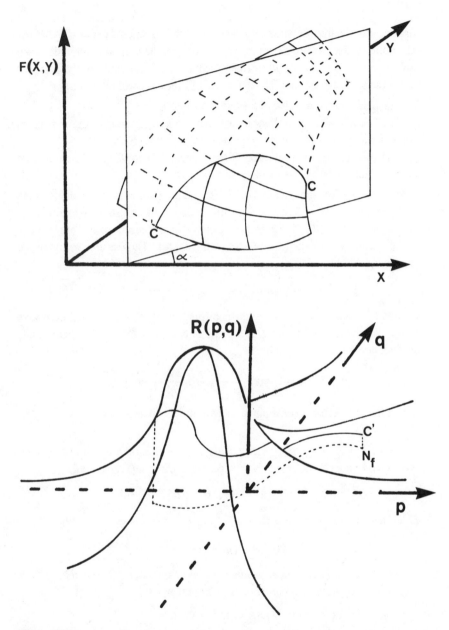

Figure 5.9
The Generation of Image Irradiance. The curve C is generated by taking the intersection of a plane normal to the image plane with the surface. The direction of the plane is given by the angle α it makes with the x-axis. By taking the surface normal at each point, this curve C can be mapped into gradient space, resulting in a parametric curve N_f. Furthermore, this curve can be projected onto the reflectance map R (which defines a surface on p-q space) to obtain a parametric curve C' along which the irradiance is given by the corresponding value of R.

parametric derivative (or parametric tangent) of the parametric curve, $d\mathbf{N}_f/dt$. At each point on the parametric curve, we may project the normal to the reflectance surface onto the p-q plane and consider the parametric derivative of the curve, as well as the projected normal. The derivative of irradiance will be zero if:

1. The parametric derivative of the curve $\mathbf{N}_f$ is zero.
2. The normal to the reflectance surface has no component in the p-q plane, (corresponding to an extremum in the reflectance surface R).
3. The two vectors, the projection of the reflectance normal and the parametric tangent of the p-q curve, are orthogonal.

We now prove the lemma analytically. To aid in the discussion, we define some useful notation. Let $\mathbf{v}$ be a vector in three-space with direction cosines $\cos a_x$, $\cos a_y$, and $\cos a_z$ (the direction cosines refer to the cosine of the angle made by the vector and the coordinate axes of the space). Thus, a unit vector in the direction of $\mathbf{v}$ is denoted by

$$\mathbf{v} = \cos a_x\,\mathbf{i} + \cos a_y\,\mathbf{j} + \cos a_z\,\mathbf{k}$$

where $\mathbf{i}, \mathbf{j}, \mathbf{k}$ are unit vectors along the coordinate axes. The directional derivative of $\Phi(\mathbf{r})$, a function of a vector $\mathbf{r}$, is the rate of change of Φ with distance s along the direction $\mathbf{v}$ and is denoted by

$$(\mathbf{v} \cdot \nabla)\Phi = \cos a_x\frac{\partial \Phi}{\partial x} + \cos a_y\frac{\partial \Phi}{\partial y} + \cos a_z\frac{\partial \Phi}{\partial z}.$$

If the direction vector is constrained to lie in the x-y plane, then $\cos a_z = 0$ and $\cos a_y = \sin a_x$.

Lemma 1: Consider a planar slice of the surface f, normal to the image plane, whose direction vector is given by $\mathbf{v}$ with associated direction cosine $\cos a$,

$$\mathbf{v}(a) = \{\cos a,\, \sin a\}.$$

This defines a parametric normal curve

$$\mathbf{N}_f(t) = \{p(t),\, q(t),\, -1\}.$$

Assume the surface f and the reflectance surface R are twice differentiable. If there exists two points t_1, t_2 such that at these points either

$$(1a) \quad (\mathbf{v} \cdot \nabla)p\big|_{t_i} = 0,\ (\mathbf{v} \cdot \nabla)q\big|_{t_i} = 0$$

$$(1b) \quad \frac{\partial R}{\partial p} = 0,\ \frac{\partial R}{\partial q} = 0$$

$$\text{or}\ (2) \quad \mathbf{N}_R\ \textit{is nontrivially orthogonal to}\ (\mathbf{v} \cdot \nabla)\mathbf{N}_f$$

and such that $(\mathbf{v} \cdot \nabla)p, (\mathbf{v} \cdot \nabla)q, \partial R/\partial p, \partial R/\partial q$ are not all identically zero, then there exists some point t' such that $t_1 < t' < t_2$ and $(\mathbf{v} \cdot \nabla)^2 E(t') = 0$. That is, there exists a zero-crossing in the second directional derivative of the irradiances.

Proof: From the image equations, one derives

$$(\mathbf{v} \cdot \nabla)E = \mathbf{N}_R \cdot (\mathbf{v} \cdot \nabla)\mathbf{N}_f,$$

where

$$\mathbf{N}_R = \left\{ \frac{\partial R}{\partial p}, \frac{\partial R}{\partial q}, -1 \right\}$$

$$(\mathbf{v} \cdot \nabla)\mathbf{N}_f = \{(\mathbf{v} \cdot \nabla)p, (\mathbf{v} \cdot \nabla)q, 0\}.$$

If there are two points, t_1, t_2 such that condition (1a), (1b), or (2) holds, then

$$(\mathbf{v} \cdot \nabla)E(t_1) = 0$$

$$(\mathbf{v} \cdot \nabla)E(t_2) = 0.$$

By the second differentiability of the surface f and the reflectance surface R, and by Rolle's theorem, there exists some t' such that $t_1 < t' < t_2$ and such that $(\mathbf{v} \cdot \nabla)^2 E(t') = 0$. We need only show that this is a non-trivial zero-crossing. Since the components of $\mathbf{N}_R$ and $(\mathbf{v} \cdot \nabla)\mathbf{N}_f$ are not identically zero, neither is $(\mathbf{v} \cdot \nabla)E$. As a consequence, it is possible without loss of generality to choose t_1 and t_2 to be adjacent points along this direction at which the first directional derivative of the irradiance vanishes. That is, since the function is not uniformly zero, we can distinguish those points at which the first directional derivative vanishes. It is straightforward to choose t_1 and t_2 to be adjacent, so that there is no other point t_3 with $t_1 < t_3 < t_2$ such that the first directional derivative vanishes at t_3 as well. Hence, by Rolle's theorem, there is a non-trivial zero-crossing in the second directional derivative of the irradiance function $E(t)$. ∎

In order to understand the scope of this lemma, we consider some applications of it to simple surfaces. Consider first the one-dimensional case of a developable surface, oriented parallel to the y axis. More specifically, consider a surface of the form $f(x, y)$ such that $\partial f(x, y)/\partial y = q(x, y) = c$. The following corollaries hold:

Corollary: Consider a developable surface, oriented parallel to the y axis. If there are two points t_1, t_2 such that $(\mathbf{v} \cdot \nabla)p(t_i) = 0$ (that is, there are two inflections in the slice of the surface, along the direction $\mathbf{v}$ of the slice) then there exists some point t' such that $t_1 < t' < t_2$ and such that $(\mathbf{v} \cdot \nabla)^2 E(t') = 0$ (there exists a zero-crossing in the convolved image).

Proof: Since by definition, $q = c$, we know that $(\mathbf{v} \cdot \nabla)q = 0$. But then the existence of two points such that $(\mathbf{v} \cdot \nabla)p = 0$ implies that at those points, $(\mathbf{v} \cdot \nabla)\mathbf{N}_f$ is zero. Hence, the lemma applies, and there is a zero-crossing in the second directional derivative of the irradiances. ∎

Corollary: Consider a developable surface, oriented parallel to the y axis. If there is a point t_1 such that $(\mathbf{v} \cdot \nabla)p(t_1) = 0$ and a point t_2 such that $\partial R/\partial p =$

$0, \partial R / \partial q = 0$ *(for example, the reflectance surface passes through an extremum)* *then there exists some point* t' *such that* t' *lies between* t_1 *and* t_2 *and such that* $(v \cdot \nabla)^2 E(t') = 0$ — *there exists a zero-crossing in the convolved image.*

Proof: As before, at the point t_1 we know that $(v \cdot \nabla) N_f$ is zero. At the point t_2, the first two components of the reflectance normal N_R vanish. Hence, the lemma applies, and there is a zero-crossing in the second directional derivative of the irradiances. ∎

More specific proofs of these corollaries may be found in Appendix I.

Lemma 1 gives a set of sufficient conditions for the existence of a zero-crossing. The most important condition is (2), which states that the normal to the reflectance surface should be non-trivially orthogonal to the directional derivative of the normal to the actual surface. We now need an estimate for when this can occur. Clearly, this estimate will depend on the shape of the reflectance surface as well as the shape of the actual surface. Since we will not in general be able to determine the exact form of the reflectance surface R and since we are interested in the relationship between the existence of zero-crossings and the shape of the actual surface, we will have to make some assumptions about the form of the reflectance surface. In particular, we show that if the reflectance map is isotropic and that its normal is uniformly distributed, then an explicit expression for the probability of a zero-crossing can be derived. We will consider the relevance of these assumptions after we have derived the expression.

The next question to consider is how to relate changes in the shapes of general surfaces to the existence of zero-crossings. As before, let v be some unit direction vector, with associated direction cosine $\cos \alpha$. We know that

$$(v \cdot \nabla) E = (v \cdot \nabla) N_f \cdot N_R.$$

Consider some point on the surface (x_0, y_0), with associated gradient (p_0, q_0). For each direction v consider the intersection of the surface with a plane, normal to the image plane, which passes through the point (x_0, y_0) in the direction of $v(\alpha)$. Such an intersection defines a curve, and hence defines a directional variation in the surface normal, given by

$$(v \cdot \nabla) N_f.$$

Associated with this vector variation is a direction, denoted by the unit directional vector

$$w(\alpha) = \frac{(v \cdot \nabla) N_f}{|(v \cdot \nabla) N_f|}$$

where $w(\alpha)$ defines a directional cosine angle β such that

$$w(\beta(\alpha)) = \{\cos \beta(\alpha), \sin \beta(\alpha)\}.$$

The following lemma derives a specific expression for the probability of the first directional derivative of the irradiance vanishing at some point.

Lemma 2: Consider any point (x_0, y_0) with associated normal

$$N_f = \{p_0, q_0, -1\}.$$

Assume that the reflectance surface R is isotropic (the reflectance at a point on the surface is not altered by rotating the surface about its normal at that point), twice differentiable and that its normal, given by

$$N_R = \left\{ \frac{\partial R}{\partial p}, \frac{\partial R}{\partial q}, -1 \right\}$$

is uniformly distributed. If the vector components

$$\frac{\partial R}{\partial p}, \quad \frac{\partial R}{\partial q}, \quad (v \cdot \nabla)p, \quad (v \cdot \nabla)q$$

are not identically zero, then the probability that there exists some direction v such that

$$(v \cdot \nabla)E(x_0, y_0) = 0$$

is given by

$$\frac{\left| \{ \frac{\pi}{2} - \beta(\alpha): \quad 0 \leq \alpha < \pi \} \right|}{\pi}$$

Proof: For each direction v with associated directional cosine angle α, $0 \leq \alpha < \pi$, take a planar slice of the surface through (x_0, y_0) and consider the surface normal $N_f(p_0, q_0)$. For each angle α and associated direction vector v, the variation in the normal is given by

$$(v \cdot \nabla)N_f.$$

Since R is isotropic, the reflectance normal at this point is constant over all values of α and is given by

$$N_R(p_0, q_0) = \left\{ \frac{\partial R(p_0, q_0)}{\partial p}, \frac{\partial R(p_0, q_0)}{\partial q}, -1 \right\}.$$

By Lemma 1, we know that $(v \cdot \nabla)E = 0$ if $(v \cdot \nabla)N_f$ is orthogonal to N_R, or equivalently, if $w \cdot N_R = 0$. Now, for each value of the angle α, the associated direction vector w defines a new directional angle β. The range of directional angles assumed by w is

$$\{\beta(\alpha): \quad 0 \leq \alpha < \pi\}.$$

The range of directional angles orthogonal to this set is, of course,

$$\left\{\frac{\pi}{2} - \beta(a): \quad 0 \leq a < \pi\right\}.$$

In order for $(\mathbf{v} \cdot \nabla)E$ to vanish, there must be some direction $\beta(a)$ in this set for which $\mathbf{w}(\beta(a))$ is orthogonal to $\mathbf{N}_R$. By normalizing over the entire possible range of directional angles, we see that since $\mathbf{N}_R$ is uniformly distributed, the probability that $\mathbf{N}_R$ is orthogonal to some $\mathbf{w}(\beta(a))$ is given by

$$\frac{\left|\left\{\frac{\pi}{2} - \beta(a): \quad 0 \leq a < \pi\right\}\right|}{\pi}$$

and the proof is complete. ∎

Thus, we are set to prove the main result relating the shape of a surface to the probability of a zero-crossing occuring. Lemma 1 gives us a set of sufficient conditions for the existence of a zero-crossing. Lemma 2 derives an expression for measuring the probability of the major condition of this set occuring. We can now combine both lemmas to obtain the probability of a zero-crossing occurring for some region of a surface.

Theorem 1 (Surface Consistency Theorem): Consider some region of a surface

$$\left\{f(x, y): \quad (x, y) \in \mathcal{R} \subset E^2\right\}.$$

If the reflectance surface R is isotropic, and its normal $\mathbf{N}_R$ is uniformly distributed, then the probability of a zero-crossing in $(\mathbf{v} \cdot \nabla)^2 E$ for some direction $\mathbf{v}$, with associated directional angle a, is a monotonic function of the variation in $\mathbf{N}_f$ over the region $\mathcal{R}$,

$$Z(\mathcal{R}) \equiv \rho_2\left(\{(p(x, y), q(x, y)): (x, y) \in \mathcal{R}\}\right) \times$$

$$\times \int\int_{\mathcal{R}} \left|\left\{\cos^{-1}(\mathbf{w}(\beta(a)) \cdot \mathbf{x}): 0 \leq a < \pi\right\}\right| dx dy$$

where $\mathbf{w}$ is the unit direction vector,

$$\mathbf{w}(\beta(a)) = \frac{(\mathbf{v} \cdot \nabla)\mathbf{N}_f}{|(\mathbf{v} \cdot \nabla)\mathbf{N}_f|}$$

$\mathbf{x}$ *is a unit vector in the x direction, and ρ_2 is the normal two-dimensional Euclidean metric.*

Proof: By Lemma 1, we know that the probability of a zero-crossing in the second directional derivative of the irradiance function is directly related to the probability that $(\mathbf{v} \cdot \nabla)E = 0$ at a point within $\mathfrak{R}$. In fact, if there are two points within the region $\mathfrak{R}$ such that $(\mathbf{v} \cdot \nabla)E = 0$, and such that the directions associated with the directional derivatives align with the direction of the line joining the two points, then we know that there is a zero-crossing in $(\mathbf{v} \cdot \nabla)^2 E$.

Over the region $\mathfrak{R}$, the density of points such that $\partial R/\partial p = 0, \partial R/\partial q = 0$ is proportional to the range of p-q space spanned by $\mathfrak{R}$,

$$\rho_2(\{(p(x,y), q(x,y)){:}(x,y) \in \mathfrak{R}\}).$$

To see this, note that due to the uniform distribution of $\mathbf{N}_R$, the points at which the vector vanishes have an equal chance of being located at any point in the p-q space. Clearly, the probability of such a point corresponding to a point in $\mathfrak{R}$ is directly related to the size of the p-q neighborhood spanned by $\mathfrak{R}$.

At any point in $\mathfrak{R}$, the probability of

$$\mathbf{N}_R \cdot (\mathbf{v} \cdot \nabla)\mathbf{N}_f = 0$$

is known, by Lemma 2, to be proportional to

$$\left| \left\{ \cos^{-1} \left(\mathbf{w}(\beta(\alpha)) \cdot \mathbf{x} \right){:}0 \leq \alpha < \pi \right\} \right|.$$

Thus, over the region $\mathfrak{R}$, the density of points such that the two vectors are orthogonal is proportional to

$$\int\int_{\mathfrak{R}} \left| \left\{ \cos^{-1} \left(\mathbf{w}(\beta(\alpha)) \cdot \mathbf{x} \right){:}0 \leq \alpha < \pi \right\} \right| dx\,dy.$$

As stated, if there are two points in $\mathfrak{R}$ such that the first partial derivative of irradiance vanishes, and such that the direction associated with the directional derivatives coincides with the direction of the line joining the two points, then we know that there must be a zero-crossing in the second directional derivative of the irradiance function. Clearly, the probability of this occurring is monotonically related, in general, to the density of points at which either

$$\frac{\partial R}{\partial p} = 0, \quad \frac{\partial R}{\partial q} = 0$$

or

$$\mathbf{N}_R \cdot (\mathbf{v} \cdot \nabla)\mathbf{N}_f = 0.$$

Thus, the probability of a zero-crossing in the region $\mathfrak{R}$ is a monotonic function of $Z(\mathfrak{R})$. ∎

Corollary 1.1: Given a region $\Re$ of the image, and given a surface f consistent with the known depth values at the given zero-crossings, the probability of the surface f being inconsistent with the zero-crossings is a monotonic function of $Z(\Re)$.

Proof: We are given the region $\Re$, which contains some zero-crossings with known depth values, and a surface f which fits those known depth values. For any subregion of $\Re$ with no zero-crossings, we know that Theorem 1 applies. Since there are no zero-crossings in this subregion, the probability of the surface f being inconsistent with the zero-crossing information is clearly proportional to the probability of an additional zero-crossing being forced by the shape of f. Hence, by Theorem 1, the probability of surface inconsistency is a monotonic function of $Z(\Re)$. ∎

This corollary suggests that to find the least inconsistent surface, relative to some set of boundary conditions, it is necessary to find the surface which minimizes this functional $Z(\Re)$, or at least which minimizes some measure which is monotonically related to this functional. Note that both terms in the expression of the above theorem are directly related to the variation in the surface normal N_f.

Two assumptions were made in the statement of the surface consistency theorem. One was that the reflectance surface R is isotropic, the other, that its normal N_R is uniformly distributed. What do these assumptions imply about the imaging situation? The assumption of an isotropic reflectance function is minor. It is equivalent to assuming that the reflectance is not altered by rotating a surface patch about its normal. While there are materials which violate this assumption (diffraction gratings, irridescent plumage, "tiger's eye"), most surface materials do satisfy the assumption. The assumption of a uniform distribution of the reflectance normal is stronger. Although a stronger version of the surface consistency theorem can be proved by weakening this assumption, we can also justify the assumption by an appeal to the "general position" principle of viewer geometry and illuminant geometry. The notion of general position requires that all properties of the observed image irradiances be roughly independent of the specific viewer position or illuminant position. In other words, a small movement of the viewer or the illuminant should not grossly affect the properties of the image irradiances. In terms of the reflectance surface, a slight alteration of the viewer position or illuminant position will generally result in a translation (and possibly a scaling) of the reflectance surface R relative to the p-q coordinate system. Within the proof of the theorem, the assumption of uniform distribution is used to argue that at any point in the image, the reflectance normal N_R is equally likely to be found in any direction. By applying the principle of general position, we can loosely argue that the illuminant is equally likely to be in any of a range of positions and that the viewer is equally likely to be in any of a range of positions. As a consequence, the reflectance normal corresponding to a point in the image is equally likely to be found in any direction, and hence is uniformly distributed.

5.7 Examples

To illustrate these results, we show how inflections in the surface can cause zero-crossings in the convolved image, for different light source positions. Figures 5.10, 5.11, 5.12 and 5.13 show examples of a one-dimensional slice of a developable surface, with a Lambertian reflectance function (a perfectly diffuse surface which reflects flux uniformly in all directions), and the irradiance values obtained for different positions of a point light source. Figure 5.10 indicates the sample surfaces and the rough positions of the light sources for the different examples. Figures 5.11, 5.12 and 5.13 indicate sample surfaces and the corresponding irradiance profiles for different positions of the light source, as indicated in Figure 5.10. The positions in the irradiance function which would give rise to a zero-crossing in the convolved image are indicated.

5.8 Summary

In this chapter, we motivated the need for interpolating the results of the stereo algorithm to create complete surface descriptions. This was done by considering psychophysical evidence as well as considering computational arguments. Determining which surface to fit to the known stereo data is at first sight difficult, since any one of a widely varying family of surfaces could be used. We saw, however, that most of these surfaces can be discarded as possible interpolations, since they contain rapid fluctuations in surface orientation and these fluctuations should give rise to additional zero-crossings, not contained in the stereo data. Such zero-crossings would, of course, be inconsistent with the imaging data, and hence such a surface is considered to be unacceptable as a possible interpolation of the known data. Thus, we proved that the *surface consistency constraint* restricts the problem:

The absence of zero-crossings constrains the possible surface shapes

To make this constraint precise, we outlined the physics of image formation and outlined a derivation of Horn's image irradiance equation. We then showed that this expression accounts for the zero-crossings of the Marr-Hildreth edge detection algorithm in the case of surface boundaries, surface markings, texture changes, and so forth. The equations further suggest that even in regions where the physical factors causing the previous types of zero-crossings are constant, there may still be zero-crossings, due to a change in surface shape. We used this fact to prove the *surface consistency theorem* which relates the probability of a zero-crossing in the second derivative of an image to the variation in the original surface. In the next chapter, we shall use these results to formulate a computational theory of surface interpolation.

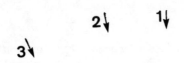

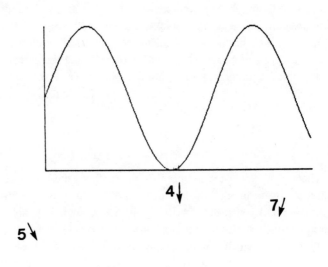

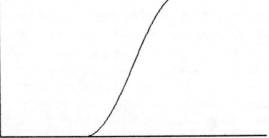

Figure 5.10
Examples of One-Dimensional Surfaces. The top figure shows one surface and the arrows indicate the rough orientations of the light source. The numbers refer to the irradiance profiles in Figure 5.11. The bottom figure shows a second surface, with a set of rough orientations of the light source. The numbers refer to the profiles of Figures 5.12 and 5.13.

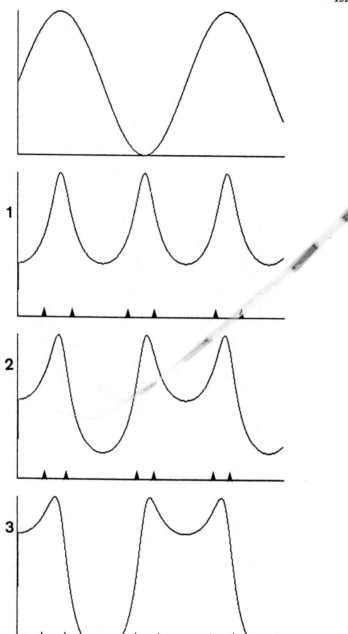

Figure 5.11
Examples of a Surface with Two Inflections. The top figure shows a slice of a surface. The bottom three figures indicate irradiance profiles for different positions of the light source. Note that in all cases, there are six irradiance inflections. In case 3, the irradiances also undergo a self-shadowing, where the irradiance value is zero. The positions in the irradiance function which would give rise to a zero-crossing in the convolved image are indicated.

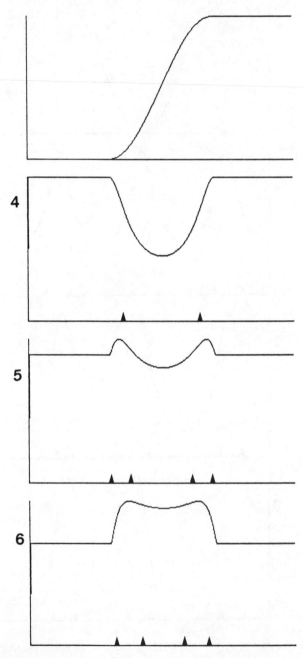

Figure 5.12
Examples of a Surface with One Inflection. The top figure shows a slice of a surface. The bottom three figures indicate irradiance profiles for different positions of the light source. The positions in the irradiance function which would give rise to a zero-crossing in the convolved image are indicated.

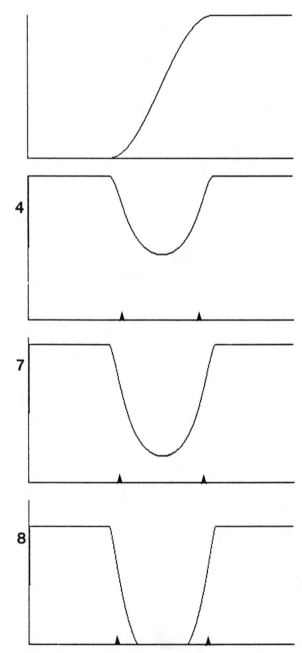

Figure 5.13
Examples of a Surface with One Inflection. The top figure shows a slice of a surface. The bottom three figures indicate irradiance profiles for different positions of the light source. Note that in case 8, the irradiance profile undergoes a self-shadowing. The positions in the irradiance function which would give rise to a zero-crossing in the convolved image are indicated.

CHAPTER 6

THE COMPUTATIONAL PROBLEM

We are now ready to considmrthe computational problem associated with the task of constructing complete surface specifications consistent with the information contained in the zero-crossings. The modules of early visual processing, such as stereo or structure-from-motion, provide explicit information about the shapes of the surfaces at specific locations in the images, corresponding to the zero-crossings of the convolved images. The surface consistency theorem of the previous chapter indicates implicit information about the shapes of the surfaces between the zero-crossings. Specifically, the *surface consistency constraint* states that between known depth values, the surface cannot change in a radical manner, since such changes would usually give rise to additional zero-crossings. In this chapter, these two factors will be combined, to obtain a complete surface specification.

6.1 The Surface Consistency Constraint

Suppose we are given a set of known depth points. We want a method for finding a surface to fit through these points that is "most consistent" with the surface consistency constraint. We will find the most consistent surface in two ways. In the *surface interpolation* problem we construct a surface that exactly fits the set of known points. The problem can be relaxed somewhat into a *surface approximation* problem, by only requiring that the surface approximately fit the known data and be smooth in some sense.

Given the initial boundary conditions of the known depth values along the zero-crossing contours, there is an infinite set of possible surfaces that fit through those points. We need to be able to compare members of this set of all possible surfaces fitting through those points, to determine which surface is more consistent. If we can do this, then the "most consistent" surface can be found by comparing all possible surfaces. A traditional method for comparing surfaces is to assign a real number to each surface. Then, in order to compare the surfaces, one need only compare the corresponding real numbers. The assignment of real numbers to possible surfaces is accomplished by defining a functional, mapping the space of possible surfaces into the real numbers, $\Theta: X \mapsto \Re$. This functional should be such that the more consistent the surface, the smaller the real number assigned to it. This means that the functional should invoke the surface consistency constraint, by capturing the essence of the surface consistency theorem. In this case, the most consistent surface will be the surface that is minimal under the functional. Background information about the use of functionals is contained in Appendix III. For further details, see, for example, Rudin [1973].

The key mathematical difficulty is to guarantee the *existence* and *uniqueness* of a solution. In other words, we need to guarantee that there is at least one surface which minimizes the surface consistency constraint, and to guarantee that any other surface passing through the known points, for which the functional measure of surface consistency has the same value, is indistinguishable from the first surface. This issue is not just a mathematical nicety, however, but is essential to the solution of many computational problems. Suppose we devise an iterative algorithm to solve some problem. What happens if we cannot guarantee the existence of a solution? The iterative process could be set off to solve an equation and never converge to an answer — clearly an undesirable state. Further, suppose a solution exists but is not guaranteed to be unique. Then an iterative process might converge to one solution when started from one initial point, and converge to another solution when started from a different initial point. Although small variations in the different solutions might be acceptable, the solutions should not differ in a manner inconsistent with our intuition about the problem. Thus, in the case of visual surface interpolation, the real trick is to find a functional which accurately measures the variation in surface orientation, as well as guarantees the existence of a unique best surface (or a family of indistinguishable surfaces).

How can we guarantee the existence and uniqueness of a solution? In our particular case of surface interpolation, we will be using the calculus of variations to determine a system of equations which the most consistent surface must satisfy, by applying the calculus to the situation of fitting a thin plate through a set of known points. While this system of equations characterizes the minimal surface, it does not guarantee uniqueness. The form of the boundary conditions (the set of known points) will determine the size of the family of minimal surfaces. Unfortunately, determining the types of input for which a unique solution exists is generally very hard. Instead, we will exploit a general case of the mathematical existence of a solution with the weakest possible conditions on the functional. That is, we will determine a weak set of conditions on the functional that are needed to ensure that a unique most consistent surface, or at least a unique family of surfaces that are most consistent, will exist. We will show that if the functional is an inner-product on a Hilbert space of possible surfaces, then a unique most consistent surface will exist. (A Hilbert space is an extension of normal Euclidean space — basically a vector space in which a dot product operation exists, so that we can relate the vectors to the real line, and in which functions are usually used in place of the normal notion of vector.)

In general, it is extremely difficult to find a functional that measures surface consistency and satisfies the conditions of an inner-product. Hence, we will show that if the functional is a semi-inner product on a semi-Hilbert space of possible surfaces, then the most consistent surface is unique up to possibly an element of the null space of the functional. The null space is simply the set of surfaces that cannot be distinguished by the functional from the surface which is zero everywhere. In this way, the family of most consistent surfaces can be found. Based on the form of the null space, we can determine whether or not the differences in minimal surfaces are intuitively indistinguishable, and what conditions on the known boundary values will guarantee a unique minimal surface, from this family.

Having derived conditions on the functional, we need to show that there is such a functional. Our intuitive notion is to find a functional that measures variation in surface orientation over an area of the surface. Although the condition of a semi-inner product is a mathematical requirement needed to guarantee a solution, it does not restrict in an unreasonable way the kinds of surfaces we consider, and gives rise to at least two very natural functionals, both of which can be derived from the calculus of variations: one measures the integral of the square Laplacian applied to the surface and the other measures the quadratic variation of the local x and y components of the surface orientation. Besides the mathematical justifications, we will also show practical and intuitive reasons in support of such functionals.

Given that there are at least two possible functionals, are there others? We will show that if we require a functional that is:

1. a monotonic function of the variation in surface orientation,
2. a semi-inner product, and
3. rotationally symmetric,

then there is a vector space of possible functionals, spanned by the square Laplacian and the quadratic variation. In other words, there is a family of possible functionals, given by all linear combinations of these two basic functionals.

Given that there is more than one possible functional, how do they differ? Using the calculus of variations, and some results from mathematical physics, we will show that the surfaces which minimize these functionals will be roughly identical in the interior of a region and will differ only along the boundaries of a region. As well, the null spaces of the functionals will differ, implying different families of most consistent surfaces corresponding to each functional. We know that the minimal surface is unique up to possibly an element of the null space. Since we require that the solution surface either be unique, or a member of an indistinguishable family of solutions, the size of the null space is important in judging the value of a functional. Based on this, we argue that the quadratic variation is to be preferred over the square Laplacian. If we require that the surface pass through the known points, we can show that the form of the stereo data will force a unique most consistent surface for the case of quadratic variation, while this is unlikely for functionals such as the square Laplacian.

Thus, we assert on mathematical grounds that the best functional is one which measures quadratic variation in surface orientation, and the most consistent surface to fit to the stereo data is that which passes through the known points and minimizes the quadratic variation. In the rest of this chapter, we present these facts in technical detail. For readers uninterested in the technical discussion that follows, a formal statement of the interpolation problem is found in the last section of this chapter. In Chapter 8, we will see examples of the types of minimal surfaces obtained under quadratic variation and the square Laplacian. It will be seen that the mathematical distinction in size of null space has a practical consequence, as the types of surfaces which minimize the square Laplacian will be seen to be inconsistent with our intuitive notion of the best surface to fit to the known points, while the surface which minimize the quadratic variation will be seen to be much more consistent with our intuitive notion of the best surface.

6.1.1 The Problem is Well-Defined

If surfaces are to be compared, by using a functional from the space of surfaces to the real numbers, with the purpose of finding the surface that best satisfies the surface consistency constraint, it is necessary to ensure that such a goal is attainable. What conditions on the form of the functional, or on the structure of the space of functions, are needed to guarantee the existence of such a "best" surface? One key constraint on the functional is given by the following theorem. The main point of the theorem is that in order to ensure that the problem is well-defined the functional should have the characteristics of a semi-norm.

Theorem 2: Suppose there exists a complete semi-norm Θ on a space of functions H, and that Θ satisfies the parallelogram law (for definition, see proof of theorem). Then, every nonempty closed convex set $E \subset H$ contains a unique element v of minimal norm, up to an element of the null space. Thus, the family of minimal functions is

$$\{v + s \mid s \in S\}$$

where

$$S = \{v - w \mid w \in E\} \cap \mathcal{N}$$

and $\mathcal{N}$ is the null space of the functional

$$\mathcal{N} = \{u \mid \Theta(u) = 0\}.$$

Proof: [See for example Rudin, 1973]. Any space with a semi-norm defined on it can be associated with an equivalent normed space. Let W be a subspace of a vector space H. For every $v \in H$, let $\pi(v)$ be the coset of W that contains v,

$$\pi(v) = \{v + u: u \in W\}.$$

These cosets are elements of a vector space H/W called the quotient space of H modulo W. In this space, addition is defined by

$$\pi(v) + \pi(w) = \pi(v + w)$$

and scalar multiplication is defined by

$$a\pi(v) = \pi(av).$$

The origin of the space H/W is $\pi(0) = W$. Thus, π is a linear map of H onto H/W with W as its null space.

Now consider the semi-norm Θ on the vector space H. Let

$$\mathcal{N} = \{v: \Theta(v) = 0\}.$$

This can easily be shown to be a subspace of H. Let π be the quotient map from H onto $H/\mathcal{N}$, and define a mapping $\Theta':H/\mathcal{N} \mapsto \Re$,

$$\Theta'(\pi(v)) = \Theta(v).$$

If $\pi(v) = \pi(w)$ then $\Theta(v - w) = 0$. Since $|\Theta(v) - \Theta(w)| \leq \Theta(v - w)$, then $\Theta'(\pi(v)) = \Theta'(\pi(w))$ and Θ' is well defined on $H/\mathcal{N}$. It is straightforward to show that Θ' is a norm on $H/\mathcal{N}$.

Now we can prove the statement of the theorem. The set E, a subset of H, can be transformed into a set E' in the quotient space $H/\mathcal{N}$ while preserving the convexity and closure properties.

The parallelogram law states

$$\left[\Theta'(v + w)\right]^2 + \left[\Theta'(v - w)\right]^2 = 2\left[\Theta'(v)\right]^2 + 2\left[\Theta'(w)\right]^2.$$

Let

$$d = \inf\left\{\Theta'(v):v \in E'\right\}.$$

Choose a sequence $v_n \in E'$ such that $\Theta'(v_n) \mapsto d$. By the convexity of E', we know that $\frac{1}{2}(v_n + v_m) \in E'$ and so $\left[\Theta'(v_n + v_m)\right]^2 \geq 4d^2$. If v and w are replaced in the definition of the parallelogram law by v_n and v_m, then the right hand side tends to $4d^2$. But $\left[\Theta'(v_n + v_m)\right]^2 \geq 4d^2$, so one must have $\left[\Theta'(v_n - v_m)\right]^2 \mapsto 0$ to preserve the equality. Thus, $\{v_n\}$ is a Cauchy sequence in $H/\mathcal{N}$. Since the norm is complete, the sequence must converge to some $v \in E'$, with $\Theta'(v) = d$.

To prove the uniqueness, if $v, w \in E'$ and $\Theta'(v) = d, \Theta'(w) = d$ then the sequence $\{v, w, v, w, \ldots\}$ must converge, as we just saw. Thus $v = w$ and the element is unique.

We have proven that under the norm Θ' on the quotient space $H/\mathcal{N}$, the set E' has a unique minimal element. Hence, the structure of the quotient space implies that under the semi-norm Θ on the space H, the set E has a unique minimal element v, up to possibly an element of the null space $\mathcal{N}$. In other words, the family of minimal elements is

$$\{v + s \mid s \in S\}$$

where

$$S = \{v - w \mid w \in E\} \cap \mathcal{N}.$$

∎

This theorem specifies one set of mathematical criteria needed to ensure that there exists a unique minimal element. Thus, if the surface consistency constraint could be specified by a functional that satisfied the conditions of a complete semi-norm, obeying the parallelogram law, it might be possible to show that there is a unique coset of "most consistent" surfaces. We would really prefer to be guaranteed a unique surface, rather than some set of surfaces. One way to tighten the result of the theorem is to require that the functional is a norm.

Corollary 2.1: If Θ is a complete norm on a space of functions H, which satisfies the parallelogram law, then every nonempty closed convex set $E \subset H$ contains a unique element v of minimal norm.

Proof: If the functional is a norm, the null space is the trivial null space, and the result holds uniquely. ∎

The theorem can be rephrased in terms of the surface interpolation problem as follows.

Corollary 2.2: Let the set of known points be given by

$$\{(x_i, y_i) \mid i = 1, \ldots, N\}$$

where the associated depth value is F_i. Let $\mathcal{F}$ be a vector space of "possible" functions on $\Re^2$ and let

$$U = \{f \in \mathcal{F} \mid f(x_i, y_i) = F_i \quad i = 1, \ldots, N\}$$

so that U is the set of functions that interpolate the known data $\{F_i\}$. Let Θ be a semi-norm, which measures the "consistency" of a function $f \in X$, that is, we shall say that f is "better" than g if $\Theta(f) < \Theta(g)$. If Θ is a complete semi-norm and satisfies the parallelogram law, then there exists a unique (to within a function of the null space of Θ) function $s \in U$ that is least inconsistent and interpolates the data. Hence the interpolation problem is well-defined.

Proof: Clearly U is a convex set since for any $f, g \in U$,

$$[\lambda f + (1 - \lambda)g](x_i, y_i) = (\lambda + 1 - \lambda)F_i = F_i$$

for any data point (x_i, y_i). Furthermore, U is closed, since if $f_n \in U$ and $f_n \mapsto f$, then $f(x_i, y_i) = F_i$ and $f \in U$. Then the previous corollary states that U has a unique (to within an element of the null space) element of minimal norm, which is exactly the desired "most consistent" surface. ∎

This corollary is a translation of Theorem 2 into the problem of interest to us, finding the surface most consistent with the known data from the stereo algorithm. It specifies a set of conditions under which the interpolation problem is well-defined. Here, the notion of well-defined refers to finding a solution to the interpolation problem that is unique, and by unique we mean up to an element of the null space of the semi-norm. As a consequence, the scope and structure of the null space of any semi-norm chosen to incorporate the surface consistency constraint will be important in determining the utility of that semi-norm. In general, the smaller the null space, the tighter the constraint on the family of possible surfaces which can interpolate the known data. For example, if the possible variations in the least inconsistent surface were very large (due to the semi-norm having a large null space), then the utility of this semi-norm would have to be questioned. On the other hand, if the null space is small, and the resulting variations in possible least inconsistent surfaces were small, the semi-norm would have to be given serious consideration. We will see examples of possible functionals and their null spaces in Section 6.1.4.

Thus, Theorem 2 and Corollary 2.1 specify two different sets of sufficient, but not necessary, criteria for ensuring differing types of uniqueness. In both cases, the criteria applied directly to the structure of the functional. Of course, the real trick is to find a functional Θ which captures our intuition of variation in surface orientation and meets the requirements needed to guarantee a unique solution.

6.1.2 The Space of Functions

Theorem 2 describes a set of sufficient conditions for obtaining a unique family of minimal surfaces. The fundamental point is that we require a complete parallelogram semi-norm to ensure a unique solution. These conditions precisely define a semi-inner product, and hence the space of functions over which we seek a minimum must be a semi-Hilbert space. Definitions and details of Hilbert spaces are given in Appendix III.

Corollary 2.3: If $\mathcal{F}$ is a semi-Hilbert space of possible surfaces, and $\Theta(v) = \mu(v, v)^{\frac{1}{2}}$ is an inner product semi-norm, where $\mu(v, v)^{\frac{1}{2}}$ is the semi-inner product on the space $\mathcal{F}$, then there exists a unique surface in $\mathcal{F}$ (to within an element of the null space of the semi-norm) that minimizes the semi-norm Θ over all surfaces.

Proof: By the definition of Hilbert space, the semi-norm is complete. It is easy to show that it satisfies the parallelogram law from the definition of $\Theta(v) = \mu(v, v)^{\frac{1}{2}}$. Thus, if the space of functions is a semi-Hilbert space, then, by Theorem 2, the interpolation problem is guaranteed to have a unique minimal solution, to within an element of the null space. ∎

Corollary 2.4: If $\mathcal{F}$ is a Hilbert space of possible surfaces, and $\Theta(v) = \mu(v, v)^{\frac{1}{2}}$ is an inner product norm, where $\mu(v, v)^{\frac{1}{2}}$ is the inner product on the space $\mathcal{F}$, then there exists a unique surface in $\mathcal{F}$ that minimizes the norm Θ over all surfaces. ∎

6.1.3 The Form of the Functional

The major problem is to determine the functional Θ. The surface consistency theorem related the consistency of a surface to the probability that the variation in surface normal is orthogonal to the reflectance normal. In principle, the functional Θ should directly measure this probability, denoted by ρ. If one could construct such a probability function, then finding the surface that minimizes this probability of inconsistency between the surface and the image intensities would be equivalent to finding the least inconsistent surface. This would constitute an optimal solution to the problem. Without explicit knowledge of the surface material and light source positions, it is not possible to explicitly construct this function ρ.

All is not lost, however. Theorem 2 states that if the functional is a complete, parallelogram, semi-norm, then the problem has a well-defined solution. This forms the first constraint on the functional. The surface consistency theorem states that the functional should also measure surface inconsistency, which is seen to be a monotonic function of the variation in surface orientation. Thus, if a functional can be found that is a complete, parallelogram semi-norm, and that is a monotonic function of the variation in surface orientation, then this functional will constitute an acceptable measure of surface inconsistency. Any surface that is minimal under such a functional would then be an acceptable reconstruction of the original surface in space.

The problem may be considered in the following manner. With every point on the surface f, associate a pair of partial derivatives, $f_x = p, f_y = q$, and hence, an orientation. Each point on the surface may be mapped to a point in a space spanned by p and q axes, the gradient space [Huffman, 1971; Mackworth, 1973; Horn, 1977]. With each surface patch, one may then associate a neighborhood of p-q space by mapping the p and q values associated with each point on the surface into gradient space. This neighborhood will be referred to as the p-q neighborhood spanned by the surface patch.

The surface consistency constraint implies that the probability of a zero-crossing occuring within a patch of the surface is monotonically related to the size of the p-q neighborhood spanned by the surface patch. The surface consistency theorem embodies a specific method for measuring this probability. Note, however, that any functional that is also monotonically related to the size of the p-q neighborhood will suffice. This is important, since it is also necessary that the functional be a complete, parallelogram semi-norm. Thus, the problem reduces to specifiying such a complete, parallelogram semi-norm, which monotonically measures the surface consistency constraint by measuring a monotonic function of the size of the p-q neighborhood spanned by each surface patch. To find the most consistent surface, one need only find the surface that minimizes this functional over each patch. Note that the surface will be "most consistent" only relative to the functional. There may be several functionals that are complete, parallelogram, semi-norms and that are monotonic functions of the variation in surface orientation. Each will give rise to slightly different minimal surfaces.

Of course, there are some constraints on the minimization of the measure of the p-q neighborhood. For example, each surface patch cannot be minimized in isolation. To see this, consider a cylindrical (or one-dimensional) surface. Between any two adjacent zero-crossing points, the minimization of the variation in surface orientation (related to the size of the neighborhood in p-q space) would result in a single point in gradient space, corresponding to a planar surface between the known depth values. The problem with this simple method of reducing surface inconsistency is that it does not account for the interaction of surface patches. In particular, such a method would result in a piecewise planar surface approximation. For any three consecutive zero-crossing points, such a method would introduce a discontinuity in surface orientation at the middle zero-crossing. This is unacceptable since the surface is required to be twice differentiable. Thus, there are some constraints on the manner in which the neighborhoods in p-q space are minimized.

We are thus faced with the following problem. We know from the boundary conditions provided by the stereo algorithm that the surface must pass through a set of known depth points located at the zero-crossings of the convolved images. We further know that at all other points in the image, the surface cannot change in such a manner as to cause an additional zero-crossing. With each surface portion, we can associate a measure of the probability of that surface implying a zero-crossing in the convolved image intensities. Since between zero-crossings, there are no other zero-crossings, this gives a measure of the inconsistency of this particular surface portion. To choose the least inconsistent surface, we must reduce this probability, as measured over all portions of the surface.

6.1.4 Possible Functionals

In this section, possible functionals Θ are considered, seeking complete, parallelogram semi-inner products where possible, since this will guarantee that the solution is unique to within the null space. However, it is important to stress that there may be several viable alternatives. The computational theory argued that the functional should measure the "consistency" of the surface. The attempt here is to define a measure based on this. The measure should be in a form that allows the constraints on the problem to be easily expressed. Also, the measure should be a semi-inner product on a semi-Hilbert space, in order to ensure a unique solution. We begin by considering several candidates in light of these requirements.

Case 1: One Dimension

For ease of discussion, the case of a cylindrical or one-dimensional surface will be considered first. By a cylindrical (or developable) surface we mean a second differentiable surface oriented along the y axis such that $\partial f/\partial y = q = c$, for some constant c.

Example 1.1: The variation in the normal to the curve is clearly related to its curvature. One could thus consider using a functional that directly measures curvature and integrates this measure over an area of the surface. To ensure that the functional is positive, this suggests using a functional of the form:

$$\Theta_1(f) = \left\{ \int \kappa^2 \, ds \right\}^{\frac{1}{2}} = \left\{ \int \int \frac{f_{xx}^2}{\left(1+f_x^2\right)^{\frac{5}{2}}} \, dx \right\}^{\frac{1}{2}},$$

where κ is the curvature of the curve at a point. (Recall that the subscript here implies a partial derivative, so that $f_{xx}^2 = (\partial^2 f/\partial x^2)^2$.) Although this is perhaps the most "natural" definition of a functional, it is not a semi-norm, and hence it is considered to be unacceptable. To see why it is not a semi-norm, consider the following. If f is in the space of surfaces, then

$$\Theta_1(af) = \left\{ \int \frac{a^2 f_{xx}^2}{\left(1+a^2 f_x^2\right)^3} \, dx \right\}^{\frac{1}{2}}$$

$$= |a| \left\{ \int \frac{f_{xx}^2}{\left(1+a^2 f_x^2\right)^3} \, dx \right\}^{\frac{1}{2}}$$

$$\neq a\Theta_1(f).$$

This condition will be true only if $f_x \equiv 0$. While this is certainly far too restrictive a condition to place on the possible surfaces, it does suggest a possible alternative.

Example 1.2: A second choice is the quadratic variation of the gradient, which may be measured by:

$$\Theta_2(f) = \left\{ \int f_{xx}^2 \, dx \right\}^{\frac{1}{2}}$$

Note that it is a close approximation to the curvature of the curve, provided that the gradient f_x is small. Θ_2 is a semi-norm, so the surface that minimizes this norm will be unique to within an element of the null space of the semi-norm. The null space of Θ_2 is the set of all linear functions:

$$\mathcal{N} = \text{span}\{1, x\}$$

where

$$\text{span}\{v_1, \ldots, v_m\} = \{a_1 v_1 + \ldots + a_m v_m \mid a_1, \ldots, a_m \in \mathfrak{R}\}.$$

Not only does this form of the functional satisfy the mathematical criteria of a complete, parallelogram semi-norm, it has a strong relationship to the "natural" form $\Theta_1(f)$, since the restriction of small f_x is acceptable. Those cases in which f_x is not negligible correspond to situations in which the surface is rapidly curving away from the viewer. These situations are such that the curvature of the surface will cause it to be invisible in one eye — giving rise to occluding boundaries. In general, we can assume that the image does not consist solely of occluding boundaries, so that such occurrences will be rare in an image. Moreover, between such points, the surface will satisfy the restriction and the above semi-norm is well-suited to the interpolation problem.

Case 2: Two Dimensions

To each of the examples of the one-dimensional case, there is an analogous two-dimensional case.

Example 2.1: As in the one-dimensional case, one possibility is to measure the curvature of the surface. The curvature of a surface is usually measured in one of two ways.

For any point on the surface, consider the intersection of the surface with a plane containing the normal to the surface at that point. This intersection defines a curve, and the curvature of that curve can be measured as the arc-rate of rotation of its tangent. For any point, there are infinitely many normal sections, each defining a curve. As the normal section is rotated through 2π radians, all possible normal sections will be observed. There are two sections of particular interest, that which has the maximum curvature and that which has the minimum. It can be shown that the directions of the normal sections corresponding to these sections are orthogonal. These directions are the *principal directions* and the curvatures of the normal sections in these directions are the *principal curvatures*, denoted κ_a and κ_b. It can be shown that the curvature of any other normal section is defined by the principal curvatures.

There are two standard methods for describing the curvature of the surface, in terms of the principal curvatures. One is the first (or mean) curvature of the surface

$$J = \kappa_a + \kappa_b.$$

The other is the second or Gaussian curvature of the surface

$$K = \kappa_a \cdot \kappa_b.$$

For a surface defined by the vector $\{x, y, f(x, y)\}$, these curvatures are given by

$$J = \frac{\partial}{\partial x}\left(\frac{f_x}{\sqrt{1 + f_x^2 + f_y^2}}\right) + \frac{\partial}{\partial y}\left(\frac{f_y}{\sqrt{1 + f_x^2 + f_y^2}}\right)$$

and

$$K = \frac{f_{xx}f_{yy} - f_{xy}^2}{\left(1 + f_x^2 + f_y^2\right)^2}.$$

Thus, there are two possibilities for the functional. One is to measure the first (or mean) curvature of the surface,

$$\Theta_3(f) = \left\{\int\int J^2 \, dx dy\right\}^{\frac{1}{2}}$$

$$= \left\{\int\int \frac{\left(f_{xx}(1 + f_y^2) + f_{yy}(1 + f_x^2) - 2f_x f_y f_{xy}\right)^2}{\left(1 + f_x^2 + f_y^2\right)^3} \, dx dy\right\}^{\frac{1}{2}}.$$

As in the one-dimensional case, this is not a semi-norm, since

$$\Theta_3(af) = |a|\left\{\int\int \frac{\left(f_{xx}(1 + a^2 f_y^2) + f_{yy}(1 + a^2 f_x^2) - 2a f_x a f_y f_{xy}\right)^2}{\left(1 + a^2 f_x^2 + a^2 f_y^2\right)^3} \, dx dy\right\}^{\frac{1}{2}}.$$

$$\neq |a|\Theta_3(f).$$

However, if f_x and f_y are assumed to be small, then it is closely approximated by a semi-norm. In this case, consider

$$\Theta_4(f) = \left\{\int\int \left(\nabla^2 f\right)^2 dx dy\right\}^{\frac{1}{2}}.$$

This is a semi-norm, with null space consisting of all harmonic functions.

A second possibility for reducing curvature is to reduce the second or Gaussian curvature,

$$\Theta_5(f) = \left\{\int\int K^2 \, dx dy\right\}^{\frac{1}{2}}$$

By an argument similar to the above, it can be shown that this is not a semi-norm. Note that by using the above approximation of small f_x and f_y, we get the functional

$$\Theta_6(f) = \left\{ \int \int f_{xx}f_{yy} - f_{xy}^2 \, dx dy \right\}^{\frac{1}{2}}.$$

We will return to this form in Section 6.4.

Example 2.2: As in the one-dimensional case, one can also consider the quadratic variation. The quadratic variation in $p = f_x$ is given by

$$\int \int \left(p_x^2 + p_y^2 \right) dx dy$$

and the quadratic variation in $q = f_y$ is given by

$$\int \int \left(q_x^2 + q_y^2 \right) dx dy.$$

If the surface is twice continuously differentiable, then $p_y = q_x$, and by combining these two variations, one obtains the quadratic variation:

$$\Theta_7(f) = \left\{ \int \int \left(f_{xx}^2 + 2f_{xy}^2 + f_{yy}^2 \right) dx dy \right\}^{\frac{1}{2}}.$$

Again, as in the one-dimensional case, this is a complete semi-norm that satisfies the parallelogram law. Hence, the space of interpolation functions has an element of minimal norm, which is unique up to an element of the null space, where the null space is the set of all linear functions:

$$\mathcal{N} = \text{span}\{1, x, y\}.$$

Duchon (1975, 1976) refers to the surfaces that minimize this expression as *thin plate splines* since the expression Θ_7 relates to the energy in a thin plate forced to interpolate the data.

Note that it is also possible to measure the quadratic variation in surface orientation, rather than the quadratic variation in gradient. The quadratic variation in orientation is not a semi-norm, however.

6.2 Where Do We Stand?

We have seen that for the general surface interpolation problem, there are two sets of constraints on the possible functionals. One is that the functional must measure a monotonic function of the variation in surface orientation. The other is that the functional should satisfy the conditions of a complete parallelogram semi-norm, or equivalently, a semi-inner product. If the functional satisfies these conditions, then we know that there will be a unique family of surfaces that minimize this functional and hence form a family of best possible surfaces to fit through the known information. In the examples sketched above we saw that there are at least two possible candidates for this functional, namely the square Laplacian,

$$\Theta_4(f) = \left\{ \int \int \left(\nabla^2 f\right)^2 dx dy \right\}^{\frac{1}{2}}$$

and the quadratic variation,

$$\Theta_7(f) = \left\{ \int \int \left(f_{xx}^2 + 2f_{xy}^2 + f_{yy}^2\right) dx dy \right\}^{\frac{1}{2}}.$$

There are several points still to consider. Are there other possible functionals? How do the minimal solutions to these functionals differ? What criteria can be applied to determine which functional is best suited to our surface interpolation problem? What is the best functional under those criteria? In the remainder of this chapter, we shall consider these questions in detail. The point we shall develop is that the appropriate functional to apply is the quadratic variation, and thus the surface that minimizes this functional is most consistent with the imaging information.

6.3 Are There Other Functionals?

We have determined at least two functionals that meet our conditions. Are there other possible functionals, and if so, how do their minimal solutions differ from those of the square Laplacian and the quadratic variation?

To answer this question, we rely on a result of Brady and Horn [1981], which we sketch below. Recall that the basic conditions on the functional were that it measure a monotonic function of the variation in surface orientation, and that it be a semi-inner product. The first requirement suggests that the functional must involve terms that are functions of the second order partial derivatives of the surface, since such terms will be related to the variation in surface orientation. The second requirement is needed to ensure the uniqueness of the solution. Recall that $\mu(f, g)$ is a semi-inner product if

1. $\mu(f, g) = \mu(g, f)$,
2. $\mu(f + g, h) = \mu(f, h) + \mu(g, h)$,
3. $\mu(af, g) = a\mu(f, g)$,
4. $\mu(f, f) \geq 0$,

and that given a semi-inner product $\mu(f, g)$, one can define the desired functional by $\Theta(f) = \mu(f, f)^{\frac{1}{2}}$.

The difficult condition to satisfy is (3), which implies that the semi-inner product should not contain any constant terms. The conditions taken together imply that we should consider any quadratic form as a possible semi-inner product:

$$\mu(f, g) = \int\int \alpha f_{xx}g_{xx} + \beta f_{xy}g_{xy} + \gamma f_{yy}g_{yy} +$$

$$+\delta(f_{xx}g_{xy} + f_{xy}g_{xx}) + \epsilon(f_{xx}g_{yy} + f_{yy}g_{xx}) +$$

$$+\varsigma(f_{xy}g_{yy} + f_{yy}g_{xy}).$$

Thus, the corresponding functional will have the quadratic form:

$$\Theta(f) = \int\int \alpha f_{xx}^2 + \beta f_{xy}^2 + \gamma f_{yy}^2 + 2\delta f_{xx}f_{xy} + 2\epsilon f_{xx}f_{yy} + 2\varsigma f_{xy}f_{yy}.$$

The final condition we apply to the functional is that it be rotationally symmetric. This follows from the observation that if the input is rotated, the surface that fits the known data should not change in form, other than also being rotated.

Minimizing the quadratic form of the functional $\Theta(f)$ can be considered as finding the minimum over the integral of the function $(\Delta f)^T M \Delta f$ where Δf is the vector:

$$\Delta f = \begin{pmatrix} f_{xx} \\ f_{xy} \\ f_{yy} \end{pmatrix}$$

and M is the symmetric matrix

$$M = \begin{bmatrix} \alpha & \delta & \epsilon \\ \delta & \beta & \varsigma \\ \epsilon & \varsigma & \gamma \end{bmatrix}.$$

If R is a rotation matrix, then the condition of rotational symmetry is given by

$$(R\Delta f)^T M(R\Delta f) = \Delta f^T M \Delta f.$$

Vector algebra implies that we must have

$$R^T M R = M \quad \text{or} \quad R^T M = M R^{-1}.$$

Equating elements shows that the matrix M must have the form

$$M = \begin{bmatrix} \frac{\beta}{2} + \epsilon & 0 & \epsilon \\ 0 & \beta & 0 \\ \epsilon & 0 & \frac{\beta}{2} + \epsilon \end{bmatrix}.$$

There are two important consequences of this fact. The first is that the set of all possible functionals forms a vector space, since if M_1 and M_2 satisify the conditions, then so does $\sigma M_1 + \nu M_2$. The second is that this vector space of operators is spanned by the square Laplacian and the quadratic variation since:

$$
\begin{bmatrix}
\frac{\beta}{2}+\epsilon & 0 & \epsilon \\
0 & \beta & 0 \\
\epsilon & 0 & \frac{\beta}{2}+\epsilon
\end{bmatrix}
= \epsilon
\begin{bmatrix}
1 & 0 & 1 \\
0 & 0 & 0 \\
1 & 0 & 1
\end{bmatrix}
+ \frac{\beta}{2}
\begin{bmatrix}
1 & 0 & 0 \\
0 & 2 & 0 \\
0 & 0 & 1
\end{bmatrix}.
$$

The first term of the sum corresponds to the square Laplacian while the second corresponds to the quadratic variation. Thus, for $\epsilon = 1$ and $\beta = 0$, the functional reduces to square Laplacian. For $\epsilon = 0$ and $\beta = 2$, the functional reduces to quadratic variation. Finally, if $\epsilon = \frac{1}{2}$ and $\beta = -1$ we obtain a functional which corresponds to the approximation to the integral of square Gaussian curvature derived in Section 6.1.4.

Thus, we have answered our second question. There are other possible functionals, but they are all linear combinations of the two basic functionals, the square Laplacian and the quadratic variation.

6.4 How Do the Functionals Differ?

Given that there are many possible functionals, all linear combinations of the square Laplacian, Θ_4, and the quadratic variation, Θ_7, we must consider how the solutions to the square Laplacian and the quadratic variation differ. In other words, is there any noticeable difference in the surfaces that minimizes these two functionals, subject to fitting through the stereo data?

6.4.1 Calculus of Variations

To answer this question, we shall rely on the Calculus of Variations, which is reviewed in Appendix V (see also, for example, Courant and Hilbert [1953] and Forsyth [1960]). The salient points are outlined below.

The calculus of variations is frequently used to solve problems of mathematical physics, and is applicable to our surface interpolation problem. In particular, we can use the calculus of variations to formulate differential equations associated with problems of minimum energy. Suppose we are given a thin elastic plate, whose equilibrium position is a plane, and whose potential energy under deformation is given by an integral of the quadratic form in the principal curvatures of the plate. We can consider the interpolation problem as one of determining the surface formed by fitting a thin elastic plate over a region $\Re$ (with boundary Γ) and through the known points. The solution to the interpolation problem is then the surface which has the minimum potential energy.

The calculus of variations can be used to characterize this problem by providing a set of differential equations (called the Euler equations) which the solution surface must satisfy. We show in Appendix V (see also Courant and Hilbert, [1953, p.251]) that the Euler equations for the interior of any region $\mathcal{R}$ are given by

$$\nabla^4 f = f_{xxxx} + 2f_{xxyy} + f_{yyyy} = 0.$$

Along the boundary contour Γ of the region, the solution surface must satisfy the equations (called the *natural boundary conditions*):

$$M(f) = -\nabla^2 f + (1 - \mu)(f_{xx}x_s^2 + 2f_{xy}x_s y_s + f_{yy}y_s^2) = 0$$

$$P(f) = \frac{\partial}{\partial n}\nabla^2 f + (1 - \mu)\frac{\partial}{\partial s}\left(f_{xx}x_n x_s + f_{xy}(x_n y_s + x_s y_n) + f_{yy}y_n y_s\right) = 0,$$

where $\partial/\partial n$ is a derivative normal to the boundary contour, $\partial/\partial s$ is a derivative with respect to arclength along the boundary contour and x_s, y_s and x_n, y_n are the direction cosines of the tangent vector and the outward normal respectively. The constant μ denotes the tension factor associated with the elastic material of the plate.

There are two subcases of particular interest. In the first case, suppose that the tension factor is given by $\mu = 1$. The energy equation reduces to

$$\int\int_{\mathcal{R}} (\nabla^2 f)^2 \, dx \, dy$$

which is simply the square Laplacian condition derived previously. The Euler equation is the biharmonic equation $\nabla^4 f = 0$ while the natural boundary conditions are

$$\nabla^2 f = 0$$

$$\frac{\partial}{\partial n}\nabla^2 f = 0,$$

along the boundary contour Γ. In the second case, suppose that the tension factor is given by $\mu = 0$. The energy equation reduces to

$$\int\int_{\mathcal{R}} (f_{xx}^2 + 2f_{xy}^2 + f_{yy}^2) \, dx \, dy$$

which is simply the quadratic variation condition, also derived previously. The Euler equation is identical to that of the square Laplacian, namely the biharmonic equation $\nabla^4 f = 0$. The natural boundary conditions are different, however. They are given by

$$-\nabla^2 f + \left(f_{xx}x_s^2 + 2f_{xy}x_s y_s + f_{yy}y_s^2\right) = 0,$$

$$\frac{\partial}{\partial n}\nabla^2 f + \frac{\partial}{\partial s}\left(f_{xx}x_n x_s + f_{xy}(x_n y_s + x_s y_n) + f_{yy}y_n y_s\right) = 0.$$

In the simple case of a square boundary, oriented with respect to the coordinate axes, the boundary conditions reduce to:

$$f_{yy} = 0$$

$$2f_{xxy} + f_{yyy} = 0$$

along the boundary segments parallel to the x axis, and

$$f_{xx} = 0$$

$$2f_{yyx} + f_{xxx} = 0$$

along the boundary segments parallel to the y axis.

These boundary conditions can be straightforwardly simplified to:

$$f_{yy} = 0$$

$$f_{xxy} = 0$$

along the boundary segments parallel to the x axis, and

$$f_{xx} = 0$$

$$f_{yyx} = 0$$

along the boundary segments parallel to the y axis.

We have thus answered our question. For both the square Laplacian and the quadratic variation, the Euler equations are identical in the interior. The only difference to be noted in the extremal solutions to the two functionals will be observed at the boundaries of the surfaces. When we look at examples of solving these equations in Chapter 8, this difference will become important.

There is a second manner in which the minimal solutions to the functionals will differ, in part related to the difference in boundary conditions of the two solutions. While the form of the minimal surface under either functional is roughly the same, except at the boundaries, this minimal surface will be uniquely determined only to within an element of the null space of the functional. This will be an important factor in determining which functional is best suited to our problem, since we would like the boundary conditions provided by the stereo data to completely determine a unique solution. The null spaces of the two functionals differ greatly, since the null space of the quadratic variation is the space of all linear functions, while the null space of the square Laplacian is the much larger space of all harmonic functions. We shall consider the effect of this difference later.

6.5 The Best Functional

Given that the set of possible functionals forms a vector space spanned by the square Laplacian and the quadratic variation, what criteria can be applied to determine the best functional? Since the Euler equation for both of these basis operators is the biharmonic equation $\nabla^4 f = 0$, the same will be true of any other operator in the vector space. This implies that aside from boundary conditions at the edge of the region being interpolated, the surfaces provided by any operator in this space will be basically the same.

This being the case, the only other characteristic that can distinguish between the possible functionals is the size of their respective null spaces. Let us denote the null space of the square Laplacian by $\mathcal{N}_1$ (the space of all harmonic functions) and the null space of the quadratic variation by $\mathcal{N}_2$ (the space of all linear functions). Note that $\mathcal{N}_2$ is a subspace of $\mathcal{N}_1$. Now the null space for any linear combination of these two operators must contain at least the space spanned by the intersection of the two null spaces $\mathcal{N}_1$ and $\mathcal{N}_2$. Hence, the null space of any other operator must consist at least of the linear functions. Thus, no possible operator can have a null space smaller than that corresponding to quadratic variation.

The importance of the null space is that it helps determine the family of surfaces that are minimal under the functional. The requirement we impose on the best functional is that the member of this family corresponding to the minimal surface be uniquely determined, when combined with the requirement that the surface must pass through the known points provided by the stereo algorithm. Clearly the smaller the size of the null space, the fewer the requirements we must impose on the output of the stereo algorithm in order to insure a unique solution.

We may view this criterion in the following manner. Initially, we start with the space of all possible functions, namely, the space of all second differentiable functions of two real variables, denoted $C^2(\Re^2)$. If we restrict our attention to those surfaces that pass through the boundary conditions imposed by the stereo or structure-from-motion data, we define a convex subset U of this space. If we define a functional on this space, the set of surfaces that are minimal under the functional are given by

$$\{v + w \mid w \in W\}$$

where

$$W = \{v - u \mid u \in U\} \cap \mathcal{N},$$

for some minimal surface $v \in U$. We are guaranteed a unique solution to the interpolation problem if W is empty (or equivalently, consists only of the null surface, defined to be zero everywhere). The key question becomes: can we have two surfaces that fit through the known points, have the same measure of surface consistency (the same value as measured by the functional) and differ by an element of the null space? If not, we are done, as the minimal surface is then guaranteed to be unique. Thus, the structure of the boundary conditions provided by the stereo algorithm (or the structure-from-motion algorithm) may be important in deciding which functional is more suitable. Clearly, the smaller the subspace of minimal surfaces, the more likely we are to have a unique minimal surface fitting the known data, as the set W is more likely to be empty.

Recall that the null space of the square Laplacian

$$\Theta(f) = \left\{ \int \int \left(\nabla^2 f \right)^2 dx dy \right\}^{\frac{1}{2}}$$

is the set of all harmonic functions. We wish to know what form of the boundary conditions will uniquely determine the harmonic function. This problem is known as the Dirichlet problem in classical analysis, and it has long been known that if the boundary conditions consist of a series of closed, bounded Jordan curves, then the harmonic function is uniquely determined. These are, of course, sufficient, but not necessary conditions. It would appear, however, from these conditions that it is unlikely that the boundary conditions provided by the stereo algorithm will be sufficient to uniquely determine the component of the null space. This follows from the observation that the stereo algorithm is capable of providing boundary values at scattered points in the image, corresponding to the zero-crossings of the convolved image, while the Dirichlet problem is uniquely determined if the boundary values form a closed, bounded Jordan curve. Thus, in the case of the square Laplacian, the best we can do is determine a family of most consistent surfaces, which differ by harmonic functions. Referring back to our earlier question, we see that in this case, we could have two (or more) surfaces which fit through the known points, have the same measure of surface consistency, and differ by an element of the null space. The variation in such a family of surfaces is not consistent with our intuitive notion of indistinguishable surfaces, that is, the difference in the shape of two surfaces which have identical minimal values for the square Laplacian measured over the surface can be noticeably large. As a consequence, we consider the square Laplacian to be a poor choice for the functional.

On the other hand, the null space of the quadratic variation

$$\Theta(f) = \left\{ \int \int \left(f_{xx}^2 + 2f_{xy}^2 + f_{yy}^2 \right) dx dy \right\}^{\frac{1}{2}}$$

is the set of all linear functions. The boundary conditions required in this case to uniquely determine the component of the null space are much simpler. In particular, if the stereo algorithm provides at least four non-coplanar points, the element of the null space is uniquely determined to be the null surface (the surface which is zero everywhere). It is clear that in almost all imaging situations, the stereo algorithm will be capable of providing the necessary boundary conditions, and thus the most consistent surface is uniquely determined.

Thus, we have seen that the only possible functionals that can be used to measure the *surface consistency constraint* form a vector space spanned by the square Laplacian operator and the quadratic variation operator. The minimal surface for any such operator satisfies the biharmonic equation in the interior of the region being interpolated, but along the boundaries of the region it may satisfy different differential equations than the minimal solution of any other operator. In general, this implies that the solution surfaces corresponding to different operators will generally differ in shape only near the boundaries. To distinguish between possible operators, we examined the form of their null spaces. We showed that the operator with the smallest null space was the quadratic variation. Further, the stereo data is in general sufficient to uniquely determine the component of the null space corresponding to the minimal surface. That is, the surface that minimizes the quadratic variation, subject to passing through the known points provided by the stereo or structure-from-motion algorithms, is uniquely determined.

6.6 The Computational Problem

By combining the results of the last two chapters, it is now possible to state the computational theory of the problem of interpolating visual surface information.

The Interpolation of Visual Information: Suppose one is given a representation consisting of surface information at the zero-crossings of a Primal Sketch description of a scene (this could be either from the Marr-Poggio stereo algorithm, or from the Ullman structure-from-motion algorithm, or both). Within the context of the visual information available, the best approximation to the original surface in the scene is given by the minimal solution to the quadratic variation in gradient (or surface orientation)

$$\Theta(f) = \left\{ \int \int \left(f_{xx}^2 + 2f_{xy}^2 + f_{yy}^2 \right) dx dy \right\}^{\frac{1}{2}}.$$

Such approximations are guaranteed to be uniquely "best" to within an element of the null space of the functional Θ. In the case of quadratic variation, the null space is the set of all linear functions. Provided the set of known points supplied by the stereo algorithm or by the structure from motion algorithm includes at least four non-coplanar points, the component of the surface due to the null space is uniquely determined to be the null surface. Hence, the surface most consistent with the visual information is uniquely determined.

It is worth noting that although the above statement is phrased in terms of zero-crossings obtained from images convolved with $\nabla^2 G$ filters, the heart of the statement is much broader in scope. The key point is that to interpolate any surface representation which contains explicit information only at sparse points in the representation, we need to find the "most conservative" surface consistent with the input information. This implies that between the known surface points, the surface should vary as little as possible. Thus, whether those known points correspond to zero-crossings, edges, or some other basic descriptor of image changes, the surface interpolation algorithm should construct the surface which minimizes variation in the surface between the known points.

It is interesting to compare the criteria for surface interpolation developed in the last two chapters, as well as the specific theory of surface interpolation stated above with the work of Barrow and Tenenbaum, [1981].

CHAPTER 7

CONSTRAINED OPTIMIZATION

Our goal throughout the second part of this book has been to find the surface that best fits the known data provided by the stereo algorithm or the structure-from-motion algorithm. In Chapter 6, we saw that such a "best" surface exists and is characterized as the surface that minimizes the functional of quadratic variation, measured over the surface. The problem we address in this chapter is how to find that minimal surface. What is meant by "finding the minimal surface"? Our goal is to derive an algorithm that computes explicit surface values (such as depth, relative depth, or even disparity) at all points on a discrete grid, m points on a side. (That is, the scene will be partitioned into an $m \times m$ grid, and to each grid point, we want to associated a surface value.)

In general terms, we are seeking an algorithm to solve an optimization problem, that is, we want to compute the values of a set of parameters that optimize some function. In our case, the parameters correspond to the surface values at the grid points, and the function to be optimized is the measure of a discrete correlate to quadratic variation over the surface. We will restrict our attention to the class of optimization algorithms that satisfy three simple criteria of biological feasibility — parallelism, local-support, and uniformity. These three criteria, together with the form of the input data — scattered contours of known points — preclude many of the possible techniques for solving an optimization problem, but also suggest the use of techniques such as those of mathematical programming.

In this chapter, we will review the basic characteristics of mathematical programming (for a more complete development, see, for example, Luenberger [1973]). In simplest terms, the algorithms of mathematical programming can be viewed as follows. Since we want to compute surface values at all points on an $m \times m$ grid, we can consider each possible surface as a point in an m^2-dimensional vector space, with each dimension representing the value of one point on the grid. This m^2-dimensional vector space can be embedded in an $m^2 + 1$-dimensional vector space, where the final dimension corresponds to the consistency of the surface. Thus, to each point in the original m^2-dimensional vector space (corresponding to some surface) we can associate a value corresponding to the quadratic variation measured over that surface. By associating a measure of quadratic variation with each possible surface, we can construct a *hypersurface* (called the *objective surface*) in the $m^2 + 1$-dimensional space. Our goal is to find a method for locating the "lowest" point on this objective hyper-surface, since that point will correspond to the minimal surface under quadratic variation — the surface that best fits our stereo or structure-from-motion data.

The most straightforward method for locating a minimum point on the hyper-surface is simply to apply an exhaustive search; that is, compare all points on the hypersurface and choose the smallest. Clearly, for a reasonable size grid, the number of surfaces to be compared becomes astronomical, even if only a finite number of values can be assumed by each surface point. To avoid this difficulty, we will restrict our attention to a class of algorithms that satisfy three criteria — parallelism, uniformity, and local-support. In terms of our hypersurface, this amounts to considering iterative algorithms which operate by:

1. considering some point on the hypersurface,
2. examining a local region about that point, and choosing the lowest point on the hypersurface in that region, and
3. moving to this new point and reapplying the process.

Because of the local nature of the process by which the algorithms step along the hypersurface, they are subject to one major drawback — they can only detect local minima. To see this, consider the following example. Imagine a piece of stretched plastic, upon which are placed a number of small, heavy objects (for example, pebbles and stones). Each object will locally depress the surface of the plastic, some more than others. Now consider a small homunculus which can walk along the plastic surface. As he walks along the surface, he will seek to move towards the lowest point he can see. Because of his size, he can only see a small portion of the surface around him, however. Thus, he will eventually move to one of the local low points, caused by some pebble, but will not be able to tell (without having seen the entire surface) whether this is the lowest point over all the surface, or just a local depression.

For local algorithms, there is no way to overcome this problem; they can detect local minima, but not global ones. We can avoid the problem, however. We show that if the hypersurface has a particular form (which the hypersurface formed by quadratic variation does have) then all the local minima are also global minima, and local algorithms will succeed. Thus, in this chapter, we will develop two local algorithms, which we will apply to visual surface interpolation in Chapter 8. One algorithm yields a solution to unconstrained problems (we can move anywhere on the hypersurface) and will be applied in Chapter 8 to surface approximation problems. The other yields a solution to constrained problems (we can only move in certain regions of the hypersurface) and will be applied in Chapter 8 to surface interpolation problems.

7.1 The Role of Algorithmic Criteria

An essential problem for any computational theory about early visual processing is to determine the implicit assumptions used by the visual system to perform the computation. These are valid assumptions about the environment that are explicitly incorporated into the computation. Ullman's rigidity assumption in visual motion perception [Ullman, 1979a], Marr and Hildreth's condition of linear variation and spatial coincidence assumption [Marr and Hildreth, 1979], and Marr and Poggio's assumptions of uniqueness and continuity [Marr and Poggio, 1979] are three examples. Such assumptions may be considered as computational constraints on the problem.

There is a second set of criteria that may be applied to any theory and, more importantly, to any algorithm for a theory. They deal with the requirement of biological feasibility, and are important if one is to describe a model of the human system. They will be termed *algorithmic criteria*. Ullman [1979b] has listed a number of such criteria that should apply to any biologically feasible algorithm. A similar set is briefly sketched here.

Parallelism

The need to process large amounts of input data in short amounts of time implies the use of computations that can be implemented in a parallel manner, using a large number of interconnected processors.

Local Support

If the number of processors involved in the computation is large, it becomes infeasible to connect each one to all of the others. Rather, there should only be local connections between the processors. Here, "local" means not only that the number of connections be small, but also that since the information being processed has a two-dimensional plane as an underlying coordinate system, the connections should also be local in a spatial sense. If the support of a function, defined on a two-dimensional grid, is the set of points on the grid that contribute in a non-trivial manner to the computation of the function, then our requirement is that the processors implementing our computation must have local support.

Uniformity

One final consideration, though not as critical as the first two, concerns the uniformity of the processors. If it is possible, an algorithm that utilizes parallel networks of identical processors will be favored over other algorithms. Such a requirement is not crucial, however.

Although the original motivation for such restrictions on an algorithm arises from consideration of the human visual system and restrictions of biological feasibility, they could apply equally well to other types of image processing systems. As such, they are taken as general criteria for the computations to be investigated, regardless of whether the algorithm serves as a model of the human system. In designing algorithms to solve a particular visual process, the first step is to seek a method that solves the problem. Having done so, one can then consider its applicability in light of the criteria outlined above, and possible modifications to the algorithm in order to satisfy those criteria.

7.2 Mathematical Programming

The surface interpolation problem, as we have developed it, can be viewed as an optimization problem; that is, the solution to the surface interpolation problem is equivalent to the minimal point of an objective hypersurface. There is a large body of literature on methods for finding the solution to optimization problems in general. In considering which one to apply to our problem, we take two factors into account. The first is the form of the input data supplied by stereo (and possibly also structure-from-motion). The key point is that the set of known points will generally consist of a series of zero-crossing contours, along which the depth is known. These contours are not closed, since the horizontal components will have no disparity value, and hence no depth value, assigned to them. Further, they tend to be scattered at random rather than distributed uniformly over the grid. (This removes many methods from further consideration.) The second factor is the architecture of the possible algorithm, outlined by the algorithmic criteria of the previous section. As a consequence of these two factors, many of the possible methods, while perfectly valid solutions mathematically, are not readily applicable to our problem. A comprehensive review of the types of methods may be found in Schumaker [1976] (see also Grimson [1980b, Chapter 7]). In Appendix VI, many of these methods are outlined and discussed from the viewpoint of the two factors presented above.

Given that an algorithm used to solve the visual surface interpolation problem must be local, parallel and uniform, and must be capable of dealing with scattered input data, one of the best methods to use is *mathematical programming*, and in particular, nonlinear programming. Ullman [1979b] has shown that many problems of relaxation and constrained optimization can be solved by local nonlinear programming processes (see also Hummel and Zucker [1980]). Indeed, a method similar to that outlined here was used by Ullman in solving the motion correspondence problem [Ullman, 1979a].

Recall that the problem with which we are faced is to find the surface that minimizes a functional measuring surface consistency. The most likely candidate for this functional is the quadratic variation. The boundary conditions with which the surface must agree are depth values along the zero-crossings, given either by the Marr-Poggio stereo algorithm or the Ullman structure-from-motion algorithm. These boundary conditions can be met in one of two ways. If the surface is required to fit exactly through the boundary points, the problem is one of surface interpolation. If the surface is required only to pass near the known points, while minimizing some error function, the problem is one of surface approximation. In the following sections, both problems will be examined.

The relevant aspects of mathematical programming are briefly outlined (for a more complete development, see for example Luenberger, [1973]). Two cases will be examined: unconstrained optimization, which is applicable to the approximation problem, and constrained optimization, which is applicable to the interpolation problem. Specific algorithms for computing the solution to the optimization problem will be sketched for each case.

7.2.1 The Basis of Mathematical Programming

The basic notion of mathematical programming can be sketched as follows. Suppose we are given some set of parameters whose values we want to determine, which we denote by an n-vector

$$\mathbf{x} = \{x_1, \ldots, x_n\}.$$

(For example, these parameters could be the set of surface values at the points of our $m \times m$ grid.) Let f be any real-valued function on n variables, usually called the objective function. The general problem of unconstrained optimization is to find the values of $x_1, \ldots, x_n$ in Euclidean n-space such that the function $f(\mathbf{x})$ is minimized. (For example, the function $f(\mathbf{x})$ could measure the quadratic variation over the $m \times m$ grid.) Thus, we seek a solution to the problem:

$$\text{minimize} \quad f(\mathbf{x})$$

$$\text{subject to} \quad \mathbf{x} \in E^n,$$

where E^n is an n-dimensional Euclidean space.

One can think of this problem intuitively as follows. The function f defines a "surface" (called a hypersurface) on the n-dimensional space E^n. We are looking for the location in the space (given by the coordinate values for $x_1, \ldots, x_n$) at which the surface is "lowest". We will first determine what conditions on the hypersurface characterize a "lowest point". These conditions will then allow us to determine when a local "lowest" point has been reached, and are simply extensions to n-dimensional space of the well-known derivative conditions for a function of a single variable that hold at a maximum point or a minimum point. In the general case, we can distinguish two kinds of solution points: *local minimum points*, and *global minimum points*. A point $\mathbf{x}'$ is defined as a *local minimum point* if the value of the function f is at least as large for all other points within a neighborhood of $\mathbf{x}'$. If the value of f is strictly smallest at $\mathbf{x}'$ then the point is called a *strict local minimum point*. A point is called a *global minimum point* or a *strict global minimum point* if the same definition holds over the entire space E^n rather than a local neighborhood.

We are, of course, seeking global minimum points as solutions to our problem. If we are using local iterative algorithms, however, we may only be able to guarantee the ability to locate a local minimum. This follows from the intuitive argument that if the surface f contains several widely separated local minima, there will be a set of non-overlapping regions, each centered about a local minimum, with the property that a local algorithm starting at any point in that region will necessarily converge to the associated local minimum. As a consequence we may not be able to locally determine the global minimum, only a local one. Further, in deriving necessary conditions for a minimum point, based on the differential calculus, comparisons of the values of nearby points is all that is possible and we are again forced to consider local minima. In general, global solutions and global conditons can only be found if the problem possesses certain convexity properties that guarantee that any local minimum is a global minimum. In terms of our intuitive argument, this means that the surface f must have a "convex" shape, so that all local minima are also global minima. We shall return to this point later.

While it is easiest to develop the techniques of mathematical programming in the context of unconstrained optimization problems, where we only require that the hypersurface be minimized, there are many situations in which this will not suffice. For example, in the visual surface interpolation problem, we require not only that the quadratic variation be minimized, but also that the surface pass through a set of known points. These latter conditions *constrain* the problem somewhat, by restricting the regions of the hypersurface over which a minimum is sought. After we have developed the unconstrained case, we will consider extensions to constrained optimization. That is, we will consider the problem:

$$\text{minimize} \quad f(\mathbf{x})$$

$$\text{subject to} \quad \mathbf{x} \in \Omega \subset E^n,$$

where we define Ω to be the subspace of *feasible* points.

7.2.2 Unconstrained Optimization

Suppose we are given some set of parameters whose values we want to determine, denoted by

$$\mathbf{x} = \{x_1, \ldots, x_n\},$$

and let f be any real-valued function on n variables, called the objective function. The general problem of unconstrained optimization is to find the values of $x_1, \ldots, x_n$ within some region Ω of Euclidean n-space such that the function $f(\mathbf{x})$

is minimized. That is, we seek a solution to the problem:

$$\text{minimize} \quad f(\mathbf{x})$$

$$\text{subject to} \quad \mathbf{x} \in \Omega \subset E^n.$$

The *feasible* region Ω is defined as the region of E^n over which a solution is sought and initially will be taken to be the entire Euclidean n-space.

To derive necessary conditions satisfied by a local minimum point, we consider movement away from a point on the hypersurface defined by f, in some direction. We will denote this direction by a vector $\mathbf{d}$. Along any given direction, f can be regarded as a function of a single variable, the parameter defining movement in this direction. As a consequence, we can apply the ordinary calculus of a single variable.

We begin by presenting the notion of a feasible direction on the hypersurface defined by f. For any point $\mathbf{x} \in \Omega$ we say that a vector $\mathbf{d}$ is a *feasible direction* if we can move in this direction without leaving the feasible region Ω. That is, there is an α such that for all $\beta, 0 \leq \beta \leq \alpha$, the point $\mathbf{x} + \beta\mathbf{d}$ lies in Ω. Using this notion of a feasible direction, we will apply the calculus in a straightforward manner to make a first-order approximation to the function f, which will yield a set of first-order conditions to be satisfied by local minimum points.

Some definitions will aid the discussion that follows. If f is a function with continuous first partial derivatives, the *gradient* of f is the vector

$$\nabla f(\mathbf{x}) = \left[\frac{\partial f(\mathbf{x})}{\partial x_1}, \ldots, \frac{\partial f(\mathbf{x})}{\partial x_n} \right].$$

If f has continuous second partial derivatives, the *Hessian* of f at $\mathbf{x}$ is the $n \times n$ matrix denoted $\nabla^2 f(\mathbf{x})$ or $\mathbf{F}(\mathbf{x})$ and defined as

$$\mathbf{F}(\mathbf{x}) = \left[\frac{\partial^2 f(\mathbf{x})}{\partial x_i \partial x_j} \right].$$

For a vector-valued function, $\mathbf{f} = (f_1, \ldots, f_k)$ the first derivative is defined as the $k \times n$ matrix

$$\nabla \mathbf{f}(\mathbf{x}) = \left[\frac{\partial f_i(\mathbf{x})}{\partial x_j} \right].$$

If $\mathbf{f}$ has continuous second partial derivatives, it is possible to define the k Hessians $\mathbf{F}_1(\mathbf{x}), \ldots, \mathbf{F}_k(\mathbf{x})$ corresponding to the k component functions. Also, given any $\lambda = [\lambda_1, \ldots, \lambda_k]$ the real-valued function $\lambda\mathbf{f}$ has gradient equal to $\lambda \nabla \mathbf{f}(\mathbf{x})$ and Hessian, denoted $\lambda\mathbf{F}(\mathbf{x})$, equal to

$$\lambda\mathbf{F}(\mathbf{x}) = \sum_{i=1}^{k} \lambda_i \mathbf{F}_i(\mathbf{x}).$$

Having defined some useful notation, we can return to the determination of a set of conditions on a local minimum. Applying the ordinary calculus of a function of a single variable, we get the following conditions.

First-order Necessary Conditions: Let Ω be a subset of E^n and let $f \in C^1$ be a function on Ω. If x^* is a relative minimum point of f over Ω, then for any $d \in E^n$ that is a feasible direction at x^*, it must hold that $\nabla f(x^*)d \geq 0$. ∎

If the point x lies in the interior of Ω, then there are feasible vectors emanating in every direction from the point, and hence $\nabla f(x)d \geq 0$ for all $d \in E^n$. This implies that $\nabla f(x) = 0$, as might be expected from the calculus of a function of a single variable.

Second order conditions on the local minimum points can be derived by considering a second-order approximation to f.

Second-order Necessary Conditions: Let Ω be a subset of E^n and let $f \in C^2$ be a function on Ω. If x^* is a relative minimum point of f over Ω, then for any $d \in E^n$ that is a feasible direction at x^* it must hold that

1. $\nabla f(x^*)d \geq 0$
2. *if $\nabla f(x^*)d = 0$, then $d^T \nabla^2 f(x^*)d \geq 0$.* ∎

These conditions hold in general for any objective function f. Based on these conditions, one can derive algorithms for finding a relative minimum point, simply by moving along feasible directions until it is no longer possible to reduce the objective function. As we have already seen, however, such methods will in general only guarantee a relative minimum point. We suggested earlier that the only way to overcome this problem is to avoid it. We need to consider what types of hypersurfaces will guarantee that local minima are also global minima, so that local algorithms will be guaranteed to find global minimum points. If the objective function is restricted to convex functions defined on convex sets, then the search for a global minimum point is possible. In particular, the following three classical results may be obtained [see, for example, Luenberger, 1973].

Theorem 3. Let f be a convex function defined on the convex set Ω. Then the set Γ where f achieves its minimum is convex, and any relative minimum of f is a global minimum. ∎

This theorem basically says that for convex functions, the minimum points are located together and all local minima are also global minima. This is important since local algorithms based on it are guaranteed to find a global minimum point.

Theorem 4. Let $f \in C^1$ be convex on the convex set Ω. If there is a point $x^* \in \Omega$ such that, for all $y \in \Omega$, $\nabla f(x^*)(y - x^*) \geq 0$, then x^* is a global minimum point of f over Ω. ∎

This theorem says that if the function f is continuously differentiable as well as convex, then satisfaction of the first order necessary conditions are both necessary and sufficient for a point to be a global minimizing point. The same is not true, however, when considering the maximization of a convex function, as indicated by the following theorem.

Theorem 5. Let f be a convex function defined on the bounded, closed convex set Ω. If f has a maximum over Ω it is achieved at an extreme point of Ω. ∎

Thus, if our hypersurface is convex, we know that all local minima are also global minima. In the case of quadratic variation, the hypersurface is in fact convex, so we need not worry about the local nature of the algorithms. Further, we know that we need only construct a local algorithm which moves "downhill" until it reaches a point at which

$$\nabla f(x)d \geq 0$$

for all feasible directions **d**. We now turn to the problem of finding an algorithm for computing this solution point.

7.2.3 Conjugate Gradient Method

We have seen that a local minimum lacks a feasible direction in which one can move to further reduce the objective function. One of the most common iterative methods for locating such a point is to use a descent method, wherein one moves "downhill" on the objective surface f, until it is no longer possible to do so. The basic structure for descent algorithms is to choose an initial point; determine a direction in which to move; and then move along that direction to a local minimum of the objective function on that line. At the new point the process is repeated. Most descent algorithms differ only in the manner in which one chooses the next direction of movement.

One of the simplest methods to use is *steepest descent*. For any given point x on the objective surface f, we can obtain the gradient of the surface at that point, $g(x) = \nabla f(x)$. The gradient is a vector that points in the direction of steepest descent from the point x. In the steepest descent method, we use the gradient to define the direction of motion at each stage, and then move along that direction until we reach the point which minimizes the objective function along that direction.

The steepest descent method will converge and does meet our general requirements of involving local parallel computations. Unfortunately, its convergence rate is generally somewhat slow. We can accelerate this slow convergence while still avoiding computationally expensive and global algorithms such as Newton's method (which involves the evaluation and inversion of the Hessian at each stage, in order to compute the direction of movement). To do this, we consider conjugate direction methods, and in particular, the method of conjugate gradients.

The basic notion behind the conjugate gradient method is to optimize the choice of the feasible direction in which to move at any point in the algorithm. In order to reduce the objective function, a simple steepest descent method would choose the direction in which the gradient of the objective function has the largest decrease as the next direction in which to move. While this is locally sound, (and can, in fact, lead eventually to a global minimum, provided the structure of the objective function is right), it may not be globally optimal in terms of the number of steps needed to reach the minimum. In order to improve the method, an extension to the notion of orthogonality is considered.

To discuss the conjugate gradient method, we shall restrict our attention to quadratic problems, that is, hypersurfaces defined by functions involving only linear and quadratic terms. The problem is defined by:

$$\text{minimize} \quad \frac{1}{2}\mathbf{x}^T Q\mathbf{x} - \mathbf{b}^T\mathbf{x}$$

$$\text{subject to} \quad \mathbf{x} \in \Omega \subset E^n$$

where Q is an $n \times n$ symmetric positive definite matrix. Although the techniques developed for this case can be extended to general objective functions, we will see in Chapter 8 that the quadratic case is sufficient for our problem of visual surface interpolation, since quadratic variation, square Laplacian and any linear combination of these two operators are all quadratic operators.

The basic notion behind conjugate direction methods is to optimize the direction in which each new step is taken. The first step taken by the algorithm will serve to optimize the objective function along the line specified by the current direction vector. The second step taken by the algorithm will optimize the objective function along a new line, specified by the new direction vector. It would be wasteful to undo some of the work done in optimizing the objective function along the first line, so we would like to choose the new direction vector so that the objective function is not only optimized along the line of the vector, but also over the subspace spanned by the first two direction vectors. In general, as we continue the algorithm, we would like to choose the new direction vector so that when we optimize the objective function along this line, we are also certain that we have not undone any work — that the new minimum point also optimizes the objective function over the subspace spanned by all previous direction vectors. The notion of conjugate directions accomplishes this task. In the remainder of this section, we will define the notion of conjugate directions formally, and show that an algorithm that iteratively minimizes the objective function along a set of conjugate directions is guaranteed to also iteratively optimize the objective function over an expanding set of subspaces of the Euclidean space E^n. We will then show one method for choosing a set of conjugate directions, and combine this to derive the *conjugate gradient algorithm.*

Definition: Given a symmetric matrix Q, two vectors $\mathbf{d}_1$ and $\mathbf{d}_2$ are said to be Q-orthogonal, or conjugate, with respect to Q if $\mathbf{d}_1^T Q\mathbf{d}_2 = 0$. ∎

Note that if Q is the identity matrix I, then conjugacy is identical to the normal notion of orthogonality. The key factor in allowing an optimization of the choice of feasible directions to be used in the algorithm is the following fact.

Proposition: If Q is positive definite and the set of nonzero vectors $d_0, d_1, \ldots, d_k$ are Q-orthogonal, then these vectors are linearly independent. ∎

The importance of a set of conjugate directions can be seen by the following argument. Consider the quadratic problem

$$\text{minimize } \tfrac{1}{2} x^T Q x - b^T x$$

where Q is positive definite. It can easily be shown that the unique solution to this problem is also the unique solution to the linear equation

$$Qx = b$$

and hence that the quadratic minimization problem is equivalent to a linear equation problem.

Given the positive definite matrix Q, consider a set of n non-zero Q-orthogonal vectors, $d_0, d_1, \ldots, d_{n-1}$. Since they are linearly independent (by the above proposition), the solution to the optimization problem can be expanded in terms of them as

$$x' = a_0 d_0 + \cdots + a_{n-1} d_{n-1}$$

for some set of scalars a_i. As a consequence, if we could determine the scalar constants and a set of Q-orthogonal vectors, we could derive an algorithm which would be guaranteed to converge to the solution in at most n steps. The orthogonality of the vectors implies that multiplying by Q and taking the scalar product with d_i causes all the terms, except the ith to vanish, yielding

$$a_i = \frac{d_i^T Q x'}{d_i^T Q d_i} = \frac{d_i^T b}{d_i^T Q d_i}.$$

Thus, the scalar coefficients a_i and hence the solution itself can be found by evaluation of simple scalar products. Note that this would be true even if the d_i's were orthogonal in the normal sense. The second key observation is that by using Q-orthogonality, the above expression for the a_i's can be expressed in terms of the known vector b rather than the unknown solution vector x',

$$x' = \sum_{i=0}^{n-1} \frac{d_i^T b}{d_i^T Q d_i} d_i.$$

The expansion for the solution x' can be considered as the result of an iterative process of n steps, where at the ith step, the term $a_i d_i$ is added. In this way, the following result can be proven [see, for example, Luenberger, 1973].

Conjugate Direction Theorem: Let $\{d_i\}_{i=0}^{n-1}$ *be a set of non-zero* Q-*orthogonal vectors. For any* $x_0 \in E^n$ *the sequence* $\{x_k\}$ *generated according to*

$$x_{k+1} = x_k + \alpha_k d_k, \qquad k \leq 0$$

with

$$\alpha_k = -\frac{g_k^T d_k}{d_k^T Q d_k}$$

and

$$g_k = Q x_k - b,$$

converges to the unique solution, x', *of* $Qx = b$ *after* n *steps.* ∎

The final point to consider, is how to generate the sequence of Q-orthogonal direction vectors. The conjugate gradient method provides one way. It is based on the notion of selecting the successive direction vectors as a conjugate version of the successive gradients obtained as the method proceeds. Hence, at each step, the next direction vector is determined, based on the current state of the objective function and its gradient vector. The algorithm, which is guaranteed to converge in at most n steps, is outlined below.

The Conjugate Gradient Algorithm

Starting at any point $x_0 \in E^n$ define $d_0 = -g_0 = b - Qx_0$ and

$$x_{k+1} = x_k + \alpha_k d_k$$
$$\alpha_k = -\frac{g_k^T d_k}{d_k^T Q d_k}$$
$$d_{k+1} = -g_{k+1} + \beta_k d_k$$
$$\beta_k = \frac{g_{k+1}^T Q d_k}{d_k^T Q d_k}$$

where $g_k = Q x_k - b$. ∎

We will apply this algorithm, for the case of unconstrained optimization, to the problem of visual surface interpolation in Chapter 8. Because the algorithm is solving an unconstrained optimization problem, it will be applicable to the surface approximation problem, where the surface is required to pass near, but not necessarily through, the known points.

7.2.4 Constrained Optimization

The general nonlinear programming problem has the following form. Let x be an n-vector,

$$x = \{x_1, x_2, \ldots, x_n\},$$

let g(x) be a p-vector,

$$g(x) = \{g_1(x), \ldots, g_p(x)\},$$

and let h(x) be an m-vector,

$$h(x) = \{h_1(x), \ldots, h_m(x)\}.$$

Let $f(x)$ be any function. The problem is then:

$$\text{minimize} \quad f(x)$$

$$\text{subject to} \quad h(x) = 0, \quad g(x) \le 0.$$

The problem of finding the vector x' that maximizes $f(x)$ subject to these constraints h, g is known as a *problem of constrained optimization*. The constraints $g_1(x) \le 0, \ldots, g_p(x) \le 0$ each restrict the solution point to lie on one side of a hypersurface in our n-dimensional space. The constraints $h_1(x) = 0, \ldots, h_m(m) = 0$ each restrict the solution point to lie on a hypersurface in the n-dimensional space. Thus, the constrained optimization problem differs from the unconstrained one in that only certain sections of the n-space, and hence only certain portions of the objective hypersurface f, will be considered in the search for a minimum point.

As before, there is a notion of feasibility associated with possible points on an objective hypersurface. A point x that satisfies all the constraints is said to be *feasible*. In our particular problem, all constraints are equality constraints of the form

$$s(x, y) - c_{(x,y)} = 0$$

where $s(x, y)$ is the value of the surface at the point (x, y), which has an associated known point, and $c_{(x,y)}$ is a constant representing the value of the known point. We will thus restrict our attention to constrained problems in which only equality constraints are involved:

$$\text{minimize} \quad f(x)$$

$$\text{subject to} \quad h(x) = 0.$$

Let x' be a point satisfying the constraints

$$h(x') = 0.$$

If the gradient vectors $\nabla h_i(x')$ are linearly independent, then x' is said to be a *regular point* of the constraints. We will develop conditions which depend on finding points with such properties, and then will develop algorithms for finding such points. Perhaps the most important result concerning constrained optimization problems is the first-order necessary conditions on a solution point, given by the Kuhn-Tucker theorem.

7.2.4.1 Kuhn-Tucker Conditions

In the restricted case of equality constraints, the first-order necessary conditions for a constrained optimum are given by the following theorem. (For a proof, and further development see Kuhn and Tucker, [1951]; Arrow, Hurwicz and Uzawa, [1958]; or Luenberger, [1973].)

Theorem 6 (Kuhn-Tucker Conditions): *Let* x' *be a local extremum point of* f *subject to the constraints* $h(x) = 0$. *Assume further that* x' *is a regular point of these constraints. Then there is a* $\lambda \in E^m$ *such that*

$$\nabla f(x') + \lambda \nabla h(x') = 0.$$

∎

These conditions state that a local extremal point of a constrained problem is also characterized by a simple condition on the gradient of the objective hypersurface, which in this case must be expanded to include a condition on the hypersurfaces formed by the constraint equations. The first order necessary conditions given by the theorem, together with the constraints give a total of $n + m$ nonlinear equations in the $n + m$ variables included in x', λ. As a consequence, the necessary conditions are a complete set since, at least locally, they determine a unique solution.

Second order conditions can also be developed for this problem. In order to state these conditions, we develop the notion of the tangent plane. As stated above, the set of equality constraints $h(x) = 0$ defines a hypersurface in E^n. If the constraint functions $h_1, \ldots, h_m$ belong to C^1, the hypersurface is said to be *smooth*. To any point on a smooth surface, one can associate a *tangent plane* at that point. This tangent plane is defined by the following technique. A *curve* on a surface S is simply a continuously parameterized family of points $x(t) \in S$, $a \leq t \leq b$. The curve is differentiable if the parametric derivative $(d/dt)x(t)$ exists. The derivative of a curve at a point is, of course, a vector in E^n. Consider all differentiable curves on the hypersurface S passing through a point. For each such curve, there is a derivative vector. The *tangent plane* at a point is defined as the collection of all of these derivatives, and forms a subspace of E^n.

The key result concerning the tangent plane is:

Lemma: At a regular point x' *of the hypersurface* S *defined by* $h(x') = 0$ *the tangent plane is equal to*

$$M = \{y: \nabla h(x')y = 0\}.$$

∎

For a proof of this statement, see Luenberger [1973, p.223].

The second-order conditions can now be stated. Proofs can again be found in Luenberger.

Second-Order Necessary Conditions: Suppose that x' *is a local minimum of* f *subject to* $h(x) = 0$ *and that* x' *is a regular point of these constraints. Then there is a* $\lambda \in E^m$ *such that*

$$\nabla f(x') + \lambda \nabla h(x') = 0.$$

If we denote by M *the tangent plane* $M = \{y: \nabla h(x')y = 0\}$, *then the matrix*

$$L(x') = F(x') + \lambda H(x')$$

is positive semidefinite on M, *that is,* $y^T L(x')y \geq 0$ *for all* $y \in M$. ∎

Second-Order Sufficient Conditions: Suppose there is a point x' *satisfying* $h(x') = 0$, *and a* $\lambda \in E^m$ *such that*

$$\nabla f(x') + \lambda \nabla h(x') = 0.$$

Suppose also that the matrix $L(x') = F(x') + \lambda H(x')$ *is positive definite on* $M = \{y: \nabla h(x')y = 0\}$, *that is, for* $y \in M$, $y \neq 0$ *there holds* $y^T L(x')y > 0$. *Then* x' *is a strict local minimum of* f *subject to* $h(x) = 0$.

The components of the vector λ are usually called *Lagrangian multipliers*. It is convenient to introduce the *Lagrangian* associated with the constrained problem, defined as

$$l(x, \lambda) = f(x) + \lambda h(x).$$

The necessary conditions can then be expressed in the form

$$\nabla_x l(x, \lambda) = 0$$

$$\nabla_\lambda l(x, \lambda) = 0$$

the last one of these being simply a restatement of the constraints.

These results can easily be extended to the case of inequality constraints by considering only the active inequality constraints along with the equality constraints. For details, the reader is referred to Luenberger [1973].

The main point about the Kuhn-Tucker conditions is that they relate the solution of a constrained optimization problem to the position of a saddle-point of the associated Lagrangian. In other words, the constraints can be dealt with by considering a hypersurface in a larger $n + m$-dimensional space, and search this hypersurface for a saddle-point, rather than a minimum point. A consequence of this fact is that it should be possible to design local algorithms similar to those used in the unconstrained case to compute the optimal solution by searching for these saddle-points.

7.2.5 Gradient Projection Method

As in the case of unconstrained optimization, there are many methods available for computing the solution to the optimization problem. For the case of constrained optimization, the gradient projection method will be outlined. Because of the structure of the visual surface interpolation problem, it is possible to consider the somewhat simpler problem of linear constraints, rather than the general problem of nonlinear constraints.

The problem becomes:

$$\text{minimize} \quad f(\mathbf{x})$$

$$\text{subject to} \quad \mathbf{a}_i^T(\mathbf{x}) \leq b_i, \qquad i \in I_1$$

$$\mathbf{a}_i^T \mathbf{x} = b_i, \qquad i \in I_2.$$

It will be assumed that an initial feasible point has been found. (This corresponds to setting up an initial surface which at least satisfies the known depth points.) The descent process will proceed to find a new feasible direction, and then move in that direction. At a given feasible point $\mathbf{x}$ there will be a certain number p of active constraints satisfying $\mathbf{a}_i^T \mathbf{x} = b_i$ and some inactive constraints $\mathbf{a}_i^T \mathbf{x} < b_i$. The set of indices corresponding to the active constraints will be denoted by $I(\mathbf{x})$.

At any point, the feasible direction sought is one such that the projection of the gradient of the objective function onto this direction is negative, so that the movement in this direction will cause a decrease in the function f. Initially, the directions will be chosen, if possible, so as to keep all the active constraints active. This is equivalent to requiring that the direction vector $\mathbf{d}$ lie in the tangent subspace M defined by the active constraints. The particular direction vector that will be used is the projection of the negative gradient onto this subspace.

To compute this projection, let A_p be defined as the matrix composed of the rows of active constraints. If the constraints are assumed to be regular, so that the constraints are linearly independent, then A_p will be a $p \times n$ matrix of rank p. The tangent subspace M in which the vector $\mathbf{d}$ must lie is the subspace of vectors orthogonal to A_p, that is, satisfying $A_p \mathbf{d} = 0$. Thus, the subspace spanned by the (linearly independent) rows of A_p is complementary to the tangent subspace M. (Note that this subspace consists of all vectors of the form $A_p^T \mathbf{v}$ for $\mathbf{v} \in E^p$.) Any vector can be decomposed into the sum of two vectors from these two complementary subspaces. In particular, the negative gradient vector can be written as

$$-\mathbf{g}_k = \mathbf{d}_k + A_p^T \mathbf{v}_k$$

where $\mathbf{d}_k \in M$ and $\mathbf{v}_k \in E^p$. Since it is required that $A_p \mathbf{d}_k = 0$, one can solve for $\mathbf{v}_k$,

$$\mathbf{v}_k = -\left(A_p A_p^T\right)^{-1} A_p \mathbf{g}_k.$$

As a consequence, the direction vector is given by

$$\mathbf{d}_k = -\left[I - A_p^T\left(A_p A_p^T\right)^{-1} A_p\right]\mathbf{g}_k = -P_k \mathbf{g}_k$$

where the matrix

$$P_k = \left[I - A_p^T \left(A_p A_p^T \right)^{-1} A_p \right]$$

is called the projection matrix corresponding to the subspace M. In essence, it transforms any vector into the projection of that vector onto M.

It is easy to show that if $d_k \neq 0$ then it is a direction of descent.

Gradient Projection Algorithm

The entire algorithm may be summarized as follows.

1. Find the subspace of active constraints M, and form the matrix A_p.

2. Calculate the projection matrix $P_k = \left[I - A_p^T \left(A_p A_p^T \right)^{-1} A_p \right]$ and the direction vector $d = -P_k \nabla f(x)^T$.

3. If $d \neq 0$, find the scalar c_1 that maximizes

$$\{\alpha: x + \alpha d \text{ is feasible}\}$$

and the scalar c_2 that minimizes

$$\{f(x + \alpha d): 0 \leq \alpha \leq c_1\}$$

as a function of α. Set x to $x + c_2 d$ and return to (1).

4. If $d = 0$, find $\beta = -\left(A_p A_p^T \right)^{-1} A_p \nabla f(x)^T$. If $\beta_j \geq 0$, for all j corresponding to active inequalities, stop, as x satisfies the Kuhn-Tucker conditions. Otherwise, delete the row from A_p corresponding to the inequality with the most negative component of β and return to (2). ∎

We will apply this algorithm, for the case of constrained optimization, to the problem of visual surface interpolation in Chapter 8. Because the algorithm is solving a constrained optimization problem, it will be applicable to the surface interpolation problem, where the surface is required to pass through the known points.

7.3 Summary

In this chapter, we have investigated the problem of deriving an algorithm for solving the surface interpolation problem. We argued that, if possible, we want a local-support, parallel, uniform algorithm. We then outlined the methods of non-linear programming and sketched two algorithms, the conjugate gradient algorithm and the gradient projection algorithm. The conjugate gradient algorithm is appropriate for the case of approximating the surface, by requiring that the surface minimize an objective function (in our case, the quadratic variation) and pass near the known points. The gradient projection algorithm is appropriate for the case of interpolating the surface, by requiring that the surface minimize an objective function (the quadratic variation) and pass exactly through the known points. Both of these algorithms meet our algorithmic criteria, and are well suited to the form of the input data provided by stereo or structure-from-motion. In the next chapter, we will apply these algorithms to the visual surface interpolation problem.

CHAPTER 8

THE INTERPOLATION ALGORITHM

The algorithms of the previous chapter can now be applied to the problem at hand, the interpolation (or approximation) of visual surfaces from the stereo data. Recall that the interpolation problem was stated as:

The Interpolation of Visual Information: Suppose one is given a representation consisting of surface information at the zero-crossings of a Primal Sketch description of a scene (this could be either from the Marr-Poggio stereo algorithm, or from the Ullman structure-from-motion algorithm, or both). Within the context of the visual information available, the best approximation to the original surface in the scene is given by the minimal solution to the quadratic variation in gradient

$$\Theta(s) = \left\{ \int \int \left(s_{xx}^2 + 2s_{xy}^2 + s_{yy}^2 \right) dx dy \right\}^{\frac{1}{2}},$$

(where s denotes a surface). Such approximations are guaranteed to be uniquely "best" to within an element of the null space of the functional Θ. In the case of quadratic variation, the null space is the set of all linear functions. Provided the set of known points supplied by the stereo algorithm or by the structure-from-motion algorithm includes at least four non-coplanar points, the component of the surface due to the null space is uniquely determined to be the null surface. Hence, the surface most consistent with the visual information is uniquely determined.

We shall consider solving this optimization problem both in the case of interpolation (the surface passes exactly through the data) and in the case of approximation (the surface passes near the data). Although the algorithms could be either applied to the square Laplacian or to the quadratic variation, we shall examine only the case of the quadratic variation.

8.1 Conversion to the Image Domain

The problem, as stated, lies clearly within the domain of continuous functions. Yet this is not appropriate to the case at hand. In order to establish an algorithm for transforming the visual information into a representation of the surface shape, a number of conversions must take place.

The first point to note is that the functional $\Theta(s)$ consists of a square root. (Note that we will use s to denote the surface which we are fitting to the known points, to distinguish it from the notation of s used in the previous chapter to denote the objective function.) However, clearly any function which minimizes the functional $\Theta(s)$ also minimizes the functional $\Theta^2(s)$, and vice versa, provided that the functional is always positive in value. Hence, without loss of generality, one may consider the minimization of

$$\Theta(s) = \int \int \left(s_{xx}^2 + 2s_{xy}^2 + s_{yy}^2 \right) dx dy.$$

Throughout this section, this will be the functional to be minimized.

In order to determine the structure of the algorithm, one must address the issue of the form of the output representation, since that will have a major effect on the actual algorithm. In this case, it is desired that the surface information be specified only at particular places within the representation of the scene. This will be accomplished by requiring that the interpolation algorithm compute explicit depth values at all locations within a Cartesian grid of uniform spacing. Although both the spatial resolution of the grid and the resolution of the depth information stored within that grid should be determined, it is considered that such parameters are not critical to the development of the algorithm. Hence, these parameters will be assigned arbitrary values.

The continuous functional must now be converted to a form applicable to a discrete grid. Without loss of generality, assume that the grid is of size $m \times m$. Each point on the grid may be represented by its coordinate location, so that the point (i, j) corresponds to the grid point lying on the ith row and the jth column. At each point (i, j) on the grid, a surface value may be represented by $s_{(i,j)}$. Each such surface value may be considered as an independent variable, subject to the constraints of the problem, of course. Using either row major order or column major order, these variables $s_{(i,j)}$ may be considered as a vector of variables, denoted $s = \{s_{(0,0)}, s_{(0,1)}, \ldots, s_{((m-1),(m-1))}\}$. (For clarity, a straightforward transformation from the doubly-indexed grid coordinates into a singly-indexed vector coordinate can be established. For example, the grid point (i, j) can be mapped to the vector point $k = mi + j$, and the vector point k can be mapped to the grid point $(i, j) = (\lfloor k/m \rfloor, k - m\lfloor k/m \rfloor)$.) It is this vector which will be modified using the non-linear programming algorithms, and the final value of which will form the solution to the optimization problem and thus correspond to the desired interpolated surface.

Having converted the surface function to a discrete grid format, it is now necessary to convert the objective function of the optimization problem to a discrete format. This means that the differential operators must be converted to difference operators. There are many possible discrete approximations to the differential operators. We choose to use the following approximations [Abramowitz and Stegun, 1965, p. 884].

The second partial derivative in the x direction may be approximated by

$$\frac{\partial^2 s_{(i,j)}}{\partial x^2} = \frac{1}{h^2}\left[s_{(i+1,j)} - 2s_{(i,j)} + s_{(i-1,j)}\right] + O(h^2)$$

where h is the grid spacing, and $O(h^2)$ indicates that the approximation is valid to terms of order h^2. Similarly, the second partial derivative in the y direction may be approximated by

$$\frac{\partial^2 s_{(i,j)}}{\partial y^2} = \frac{1}{h^2}\left[s_{(i,j+1)} - 2s_{(i,j)} + s_{(i,j-1)}\right] + O(h^2).$$

The cross second partial derivative can be approximated by

$$\frac{\partial^2 s_{(i,j)}}{\partial x \partial y} = \frac{1}{4h^2}\left[s_{(i+1,j+1)} - s_{(i+1,j-1)} - s_{(i+1,j-1)} + s_{(i-1,j-1)}\right] + O(h^2).$$

Note that such approximations have frequently been used in the image processing literature, (for example, see the reviews of Davis [1975], Rosenfeld and Kak [1976], Pratt [1978]). Little is knwon of the affect of these approximations on the behavior of the result.

Having converted the surface function and the differential operators, one must convert the double integral to a discrete equivalent. This can easily be done, by using a double summation over the finite difference operators applied to the discrete grid. One minor point is noted. While it is straightforward to form the discrete equivalent to the double integrals $\int\int s_{xx}^2 \, dx dy$ and $\int\int s_{yy}^2 \, dx dy$, the cross term $2\int\int s_{xy}^2 \, dx dy$ is handled differently. In particular, consider a second grid, superimposed on the first, which has twice the spatial resolution of the first (that is, all integer points are represented as are all points $(\frac{i}{2}, \frac{j}{2})$). For the cross term, we shall apply the finite difference operator to all half integral points on this finer grid. The combination of these operators yields the discrete objective function:

$$\text{minimize} \quad \sum_{i=1}^{m-2}\sum_{j=0}^{m-1}\left(s_{(i-1,j)} - 2s_{(i,j)} + s_{(i+1,j)}\right)^2$$

$$+ \sum_{i=0}^{m-1}\sum_{j=1}^{m-2}\left(s_{(i,j-1)} - 2s_{(i,j)} + s_{(i,j+1)}\right)^2$$

$$+2\sum_{i=0}^{m-2}\sum_{j=0}^{m-2}\left(s_{(i,j)} - s_{(i+1,j)} - s_{(i,j+1)} + s_{(i+1,j+1)}\right)^2.$$

Finally, the characterization of the constraints must be considered. The case of interpolation will be considered first, where the interpolated surface is required to pass through the known points. Let $\mathcal{G} = \{(i,j) \mid$ there is a known depth value at the grid point $(i,j)\}$ be the set of grid points for which a depth value is known. Then the constraints on the optimization problem have the form $s_{(i,j)} - c_{(i,j)} = 0$ for all points (i,j) in the set $\mathcal{G}$, and where the $c_{(i,j)}$'s are a set of constants reflecting the stereo data. Note that the set of constraints are all equality constraints.

8.2 The Gradient Projection Interpolation Algorithm

It is now possible to consider applying the gradient projection method to this problem:

$$\text{minimize} \quad \sum_{i=1}^{m-2} \sum_{j=0}^{m-1} \left(s_{(i-1,j)} - 2s_{(i,j)} + s_{(i+1,j)} \right)^2$$

$$+ \sum_{i=0}^{m-1} \sum_{j=1}^{m-2} \left(s_{(i,j-1)} - 2s_{(i,j)} + s_{(i,j+1)} \right)^2$$

$$+2 \sum_{i=0}^{m-2} \sum_{j=0}^{m-2} \left(s_{(i,j)} - s_{(i+1,j)} - s_{(i,j+1)} + s_{(i+1,j+1)} \right)^2.$$

$$\text{subject to} \quad s_{(i,j)} - c_{(i,j)} = 0, \ \forall (i,j) \in \mathcal{G}.$$

To apply the method of gradient projection, it is necessary to determine the set of active constraints, and the projection matrix onto the subspace spanned by the active constraints. Clearly, since all the constraints are equality constraints, they are all active at every iteration. Thus, the matrix A^p (where $p = |\mathcal{G}|$) has rows consisting of a 1 in the position corresponding to the grid point (i,j) for $(i,j) \in \mathcal{G}$ and 0's elsewhere. One can easily show that $A_p A_p^T = I$ and that $A_p^T A_p = \delta_{\mathcal{G}}$ where $\delta_{\mathcal{G}}$ is a matrix consisting on 0's except for those rows corresponding to a point in $\mathcal{G}$, such rows containing a 1 for the diagonal element. Thus, the projection matrix $P = I - \delta_{\mathcal{G}}$ consists of all 0's except for the diagonal elements in those rows corresponding to a grid point not in $\mathcal{G}$, such elements being 1. The effect of the projection matrix P is to ignore any components of the direction vector $\mathbf{d}$ corresponding to a known point, while preserving all other components, unaltered.

Recall that the direction vector $\mathbf{d}$ is determined by the projection of the negative gradient of the objective function. By expanding the double summation and performing the differentiation, the components of the gradient of the objective function are given, in this case, by the following:

For all elements in the center of the grid, apply the following stencil to the grid representation of the surface function **s**:

$$\begin{bmatrix} & & 2 & & \\ & 4 & -16 & 4 & \\ 2 & -16 & 40 & -16 & 2 \\ & 4 & -16 & 4 & \\ & & 2 & & \end{bmatrix}.$$

By this, we mean that given a two-dimensional grid representation of the current surface approximation, **s**, the value of the component of the gradient of the objective surface at some point (i, j) on the grid is obtained by applying the above stencil centered over that point (i, j), multiplying the value of each of the stencil points with the value of the surface at that point and summing these products. The value of the components of the gradient can be computed in this manner by applying the stencil to all points in the center of the grid.

Along the outer edges of the grid, the above stencil does not apply. Instead, a careful expansion of the gradient of the objective function shows that the following stencils should be used.

For elements in the corners of the grid, apply the following stencil (or its appropriate rotations and reflections) to the grid representation of the surface function **s**:

$$\begin{bmatrix} 2 & & \\ -8 & 4 & \\ 8 & -8 & 2 \end{bmatrix}.$$

For elements along an outside row of the grid, one point removed from the corner, apply the following stencil (or its appropriate rotations and reflections) to the grid representation of the surface function **s**:

$$\begin{bmatrix} & 2 & & \\ 4 & -12 & 4 & \\ -8 & 20 & -12 & 2 \end{bmatrix}.$$

For elements along an outside row of the grid, more than one point removed from any corner, apply the following stencil (or its appropriate rotations and reflections) to the grid representation of the surface function **s**:

$$\begin{bmatrix} & 2 & & \\ 4 & -12 & 4 & \\ 2 & -12 & 22 & -12 & 2 \end{bmatrix}.$$

For elements along a row second from the outside of the grid, located one element from each of two outside rows, apply the following stencil (or its appropriate rotations and reflections) to the grid representation of the surface function **s**:

$$\begin{bmatrix} & & 2 & & \\ & 4 & -16 & 4 & \\ -12 & 36 & -16 & 2 \\ & 4 & -12 & 4 & \end{bmatrix}.$$

For all other elements along a row second from the outside of the grid, apply the following stencil (or its appropriate rotations and reflections) to the grid representation of the surface function **s**:

$$\begin{bmatrix} & & 2 & & \\ & 4 & -16 & 4 & \\ 2 & -16 & 38 & -16 & 2 \\ & 4 & -12 & 4 & \end{bmatrix}.$$

Thus, the direction vector has zero valued components at all points corresponding to known depth values, and non-zero valued components elsewhere, with value given by the result of convolving the above stencils with the current surface approximation. It is interesting to note that the stencil used in the interior of the grid is a finite difference approximation to the biharmonic equation $\nabla^4 s = 0$ [Abramowitz and Stegun, 1965, p.885]. This should not be surprising, since the Euler equation, derived from the calculus of variations in Chapter 8, was precisely this equation. Thus, we see that the quadratic programming algorithms implicitly solve the Euler equation.

We have determined the form of the direction vector, which specifies the direction in which to move in order to reduce the objective function and refine the surface approximation. To determine the amount to move in this direction, it is necessary to determine the minimum value of the objective function along this direction, that is, to determine the value of α such that

$$\sum_{i=1}^{m-2} \sum_{j=0}^{m-1} \left(s_{(i-1,j)} - 2s_{(i,j)} + s_{(i+1,j)} \right.$$

$$\left. + a d_{(i-1,j)} - 2a d_{(i,j)} + a d_{(i+1,j)} \right)^2$$

$$+ \sum_{i=0}^{m-1} \sum_{j=1}^{m-2} \left(s_{(i,j-1)} - 2s_{(i,j)} + s_{(i,j+1)} \right.$$

$$\left. + a d_{(i,j-1)} - 2a d_{(i,j)} + a d_{(i,j+1)} \right)^2$$

$$+ 2 \sum_{i=0}^{m-2} \sum_{j=0}^{m-2} \left(s_{(i,j)} - s_{(i+1,j)} - s_{(i,j+1)} + s_{(i+1,j+1)} \right.$$

$$\left. + a d_{(i,j)} - a d_{(i+1,j)} - a d_{(i,j+1)} + a d_{(i+1,j+1)} \right)^2$$

is minimized. A straightforward application of calculus determines that this value for α is given by the ratio of $\alpha = \frac{\alpha_1}{\alpha_2}$ where

$$\alpha_1 = \sum_{i=1}^{m-2} \sum_{j=0}^{m-1} \left(s_{(i-1,j)} - 2s_{(i,j)} + s_{(i+1,j)} \right)$$

$$\left(d_{(i-1,j)} - 2d_{(i,j)} + d_{(i+1,j)} \right)$$

$$+ \sum_{i=0}^{m-1} \sum_{j=1}^{m-2} \left(s_{(i,j-1)} - 2s_{(i,j)} + s_{(i,j+1)} \right)$$

$$\left(d_{(i,j-1)} - 2d_{(i,j)} + d_{(i,j+1)} \right)$$

$$+ 2 \sum_{i=0}^{m-2} \sum_{j=0}^{m-2} \left(s_{(i,j)} - s_{(i+1,j)} - s_{(i,j+1)} + s_{(i+1,j+1)} \right)$$

$$\left(d_{(i,j)} - d_{(i+1,j)} - d_{(i,j+1)} + d_{(i+1,j+1)} \right)$$

and

$$a_2 = \sum_{i=1}^{m-2} \sum_{j=0}^{m-1} \left(d_{(i-1,j)} - 2d_{(i,j)} + d_{(i+1,j)} \right)^2$$

$$+ \sum_{i=0}^{m-1} \sum_{j=1}^{m-2} \left(d_{(i,j-1)} - 2d_{(i,j)} + d_{(i,j+1)} \right)^2$$

$$+ 2 \sum_{i=0}^{m-2} \sum_{j=0}^{m-2} \left(d_{(i,j)} - d_{(i+1,j)} - d_{(i,j+1)} + d_{(i+1,j+1)} \right)^2.$$

Thus, the algorithm is completely determined. The steps consist of:

0.   Determine a feasible initial surface approximation (any surface approximation which contains the known stereo depth values $c_{(i,j)}$ at the known points $(i, j) \in \mathcal{S}$ will suffice).

1.   Compute the gradient of the objective function by convolving the grid representation of the current surface approximation with the stencils listed above. Compute the direction vector by taking the negative of the gradient, setting any components corresponding to known depth points to zero.

2.   Compute the scalar a which specifies the amount to move along the direction vector on the hypersurface defined by the objective function, by the formula given above.

3.   Refine the surface approximation by incrementing the current surface approximation with the scaled direction vector.

4.   Return to step (1) and continue until the magnitudes of all components of the direction vector are smaller than some constant ϵ.

8.3 Examples of Interpolation

We can demonstrate the effectiveness of the surface interpolation algorithm by considering the performance of the gradient projection algorithm on several examples. Although the previous discussion dealt specifically with applying the gradient projection algorithm to the quadratic variation, a similar analysis can be performed for other functionals such as the square Laplacian. (Recall that any feasible functional was a linear combination of these two functionals.)

To demonstrate both the effectiveness of the interpolation algorithm and the difference between the quadratic variation and the square Laplacian, we consider three synthetic examples in Figures 8.1-8.3. In Figure 8.1, the interpolation algorithm is given as boundary conditions a set of closed contours from a cylinder, oriented parallel to the x-axis. It can be seen that the surfaces obtained by minimizing the square Laplacian and the quadratic variation differ markedly along the edge of the region. This is to be expected for two reasons. In Section 6.4,

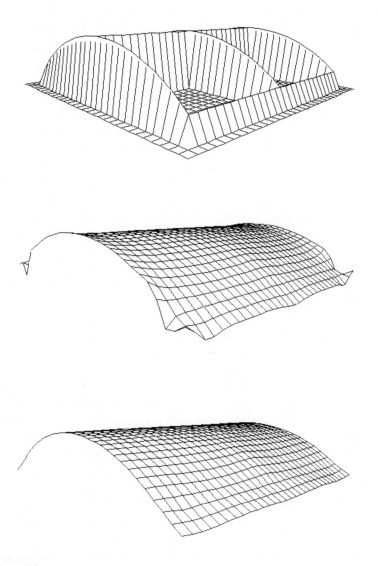

Figure 8.1
Synthetic Example. The top figure shows a synthetic set of boundary conditions, consistent with a cylinder aligned with the axes of the grid. The middle figure shows the surface obtained by applying the gradient projection algorithm to the square Laplacian functional. The bottom figure shows the surface obtained by applying the algorithm to the quadratic variation.

we derived the Euler equations for the interpolation problem, a set of differential equations which must be satisfied by the minimal surface. The Euler equations for the interior of a region were identical for both the square Laplacian and the quadratic variation, namely the biharmonic equation. Along the edges of the region, however, the natural boundary conditions imposed different equations on the solution surface. This fact is reflected in Figure 8.1. The second reason for the different surfaces arises from the form of the stencils obtained in Section 8.2. The stencils to be applied at the edges of a region in the case of quadratic variation are numerically more stable than those to be applied in the case of the square Laplacian. (This may, in fact, simply be a reflection of the difference in Euler equations.) In either case, it can be seen from Figure 8.1 that while minimizing the quadratic variation results in a reasonable approximation to a cylinder, minimizing the square Laplacian yields less acceptable results.

In Figure 8.2, we illustrate a second synthetic example. In this case, the boundary conditions are points lying on a hyperbolic paraboloid, choosen at random so that the known points do not form closed contours. As in the previous case, it can be seen that while the surfaces obtained by minimizing the two functionals are very similar in the interior of the region, the surfaces differ drastically along the edges of the region. Again, minimizing the quadratic variation yields a reasonable approximation to a hyperbolic paraboloid.

In Figure 8.3, we illustrate a third synthetic example. In this case, the boundary conditions are again taken from a cylinder, here oriented at 45 degrees to the x-axis. As in the previous cylinder example, the major difference between the two surfaces occurs along the borders of the region and the minimization of quadratic variation yields a good approximation to the cylinder.

The algorithm can also be applied to the output of the stereo algorithm, as indicated in Figures 8.4 – 8.7. It should be noted that in these examples the interpolation algorithm was applied directly to the disparity values obtained by the stereo algorithm, without converting them to depth information. As a consequence, the displayed surfaces in the figures will not exactly reflect the shape of the surface, since an additional nonlinear transformation from disparity to depth is still required. For the purposes of illustrating the interpolation algorithm, however, the use of interpolated disparity values suffices, since the interpolation algorithm will preserve the general shape of the surfaces (that is, the sign of the surface curvature) as well as the relative differences in depth between different surfaces.

Figure 8.4 shows the surface obtained for the wedding cake random dot stereogram of Chapter 4. The four planar surfaces are clearly visible, although the effect of a small number of incorrect disparity values at the junctions of adjacent planes can be seen. Figure 8.5 shows the surface obtained for the spiral staircase random dot stereogram of Chapter 4. Again, while the general shape of the spiral staircase is clearly apparent, the effect of a small number of incorrect disparity

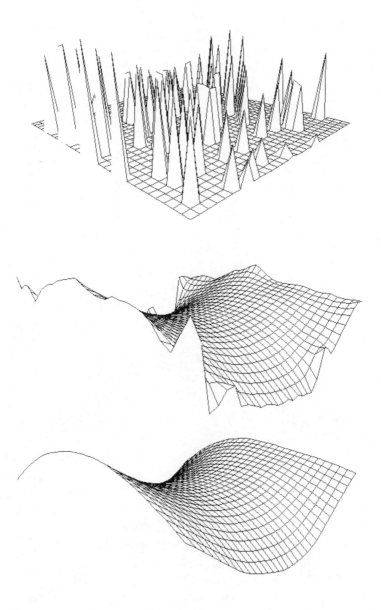

Figure 8.2
Synthetic Example. The top figure shows a synthetic set of boundary conditions, consistent with a hyperbolic paraboloid. The points are chosen at random with a density of 10 percent. The middle figure shows the surface obtained by applying the gradient projection algorithm to the square Laplacian functional. The bottom figure shows the surface obtained by applying the algorithm to the quadratic variation.

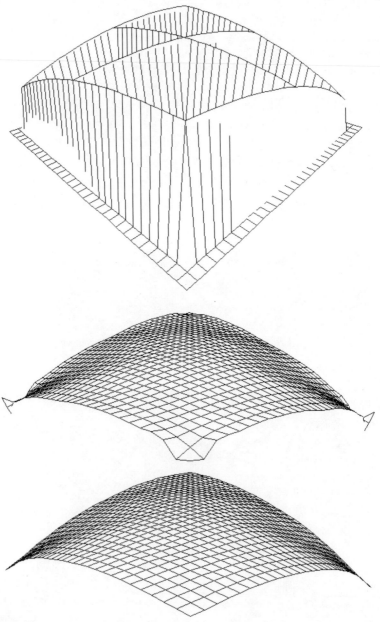

Figure 8.3
Synthetic Example. The top figure shows a synthetic set of boundary conditions, consistent with a cylinder not aligned with the axes of the grid. The middle figure shows the surface obtained by applying the gradient projection algorithm to the square Laplacian functional. The bottom figure shows the surface obtained by applying the algorithm to the quadratic variation.

values can be seen. Figure 8.6 shows the surface obtained for the natural image of the coffee jar of Chapter 3. As in the previous cases, the general shape of the surfaces are clearly evident. Not only is the jar sharply separated in disparity from the background plane (which is slightly slanted), but the overall shape of the jar can be distinguished. Figure 8.7 shows the surface obtained for the natural image of the Moore sculpture of Chapter 4. As in the case of Figure 8.6, the general shape of the surface can be distinguished. Note that because no disparity values can be obtained for the hole in the center of the sculpture, the interpolation algorithm interpolates across the hole as if it were a uniform surface.

8.4 The Conjugate Gradient Approximation Algorithm

Previous sections have addressed the case of interpolating a surface through the known stereo depth values. In this section, the case of approximating a surface relative to the known stereo depth values is considered. There are several reasons for considering an approximation of the known depth values, rather than an exact fit through them. The first reason is that the accuracy of the stereo data may not be sufficient for the purpose of surface approximation. In particular, the algorithm outlined for performing the stereo computation yields disparity matches with an accuracy of one picture element. One must consider if such accuracy is sufficient. As well, one must consider the accuracy with which the zero-crossing positions reflect the location of a point of interest on an object in the scene. Since the operators which extract the zero-crossings have a non-infinitesimal spatial extent, it is possible that the zero-crossing positions undergo slight fluctuations in position, such fluctuations causing a small error in the disparity matches assigned by the algorithm. The second reason is that the stereo algorithm does occasionally make an incorrect match (we saw in Chapter 5 that the number of such points was small, but that such points can occur). If an exact surface interpolation is required, such points will incorrectly cause a change in the shape of the surface, and the effect of such points can spread over a noticeable region of the surface reconstruction. By requiring a surface approximation, the effect of such "bad" disparity points can be minimized.

The basic notion is to combine a measure of "nearness of fit to the known points" with a measure of the consistency of the surface with the zero-crossing information. This can be accomplished by considering a penalty method unconstrained optimization problem. Here, the objective function to minimize is

$$\Theta(s) = \int\int\left(s_{xx}^2 + s_{yy}^2 + 2s_{xy}^2\right)dxdy + \beta\sum_{\mathscr{S}}(s(x, y) - c(x, y))^2$$

where the summation takes place over the set $\mathscr{S}$ of all points in the representation for which there is a known stereo depth value $c(x, y)$. The effect of this objective

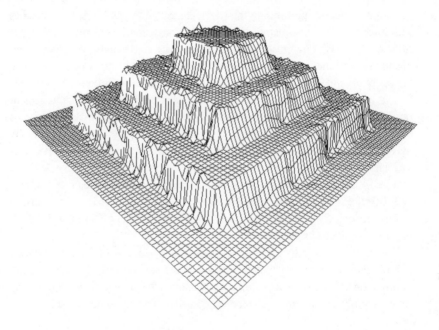

Figure 8.4
The Wedding Cake. The top figure shows the random dot stereogram of a wedding cake. The bottom figure shows the surface obtained by processing the stereo pair with the Grimson implementation of the Marr-Poggio stereo algorithm, and interpolating the result using the quadratic variation.

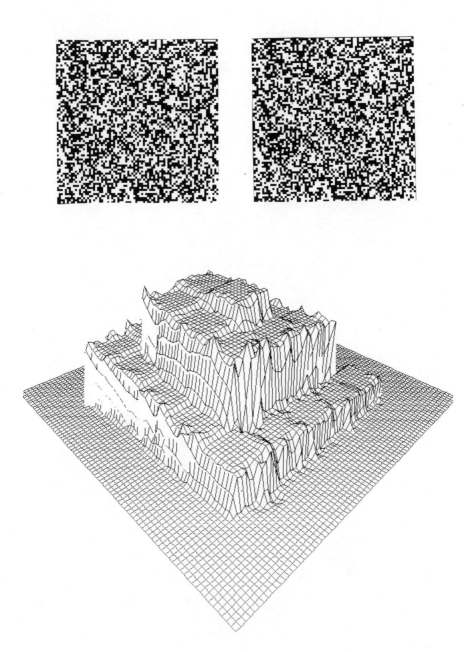

Figure 8.5
The Spiral Staircase. The top figure shows the random dot stereogram of a spiral staircase. The bottom figure shows the surface obtained by processing the stereo pair with the Grimson implementation of the Marr-Poggio stereo algorithm, and interpolating the result using the quadratic variation.

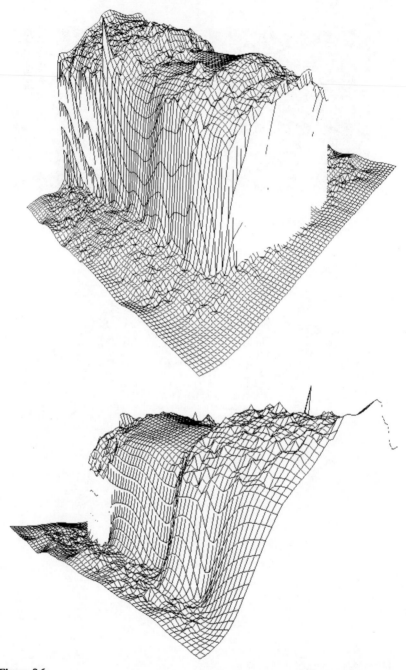

Figure 8.6
The Coffee Jar. The figures show two views of the surface obtained by processing the stereo pair of Figure 3.7 with the Grimson implementation of the Marr-Poggio stereo algorithm, and interpolating the result using the quadratic variation.

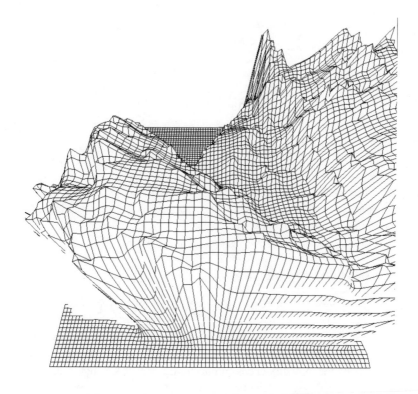

Figure 8.7
The Moore Sculpture. The figure shows a view of the surface obtained by processing
the stereo pair of Figure 4.13 with the Grimson implementation of the Marr-Poggio
stereo algorithm, and interpolating the result using the quadratic variation.

function is to minimize a least-squares fit through the known points, scaled relative to the original minimization problem. The constant β is a scale parameter to be determined by the degree of desired fit. Note that the constraints have, in this case, been incorporated directly into the objective function. Hence, the objective function may be optimized as if it were an unconstrained function.

The translation of this problem into the image domain yields the following discrete version of the objective function:

$$\text{minimize} \quad \sum_{i=1}^{m-2}\sum_{j=0}^{m-1}\left(s_{(i-1,j)} - 2s_{(i,j)} + s_{(i+1,j)}\right)^2$$

$$+ \sum_{i=0}^{m-1}\sum_{j=1}^{m-2}\left(s_{(i,j-1)} - 2s_{(i,j)} + s_{(i,j+1)}\right)^2$$

$$+2 \sum_{i=0}^{m-2}\sum_{j=0}^{m-2}\left(s_{(i,j)} - s_{(i+1,j)} - s_{(i,j+1)} + s_{(i+1,j+1)}\right)^2$$

$$+\beta \sum_{\mathcal{I}}\left(s_{(i,j)} - c_{(i,j)}\right)^2.$$

It is now possible to consider applying the conjugate gradient method to this problem. Recall that this method, when applied to the quadratic case, is considered the minimization of

$$\frac{1}{2}s^T Q s - b^T s.$$

In this case, the vector b is given by

$$b = -2\beta c$$

where c is a vector whose components are the known depth values $c_{(i,j)}$ if the corresponding grid point has such a known value, and 0 otherwise. The matrix Q is given by the discrete stencils outlined in the previous section, with an added diagonal factor of $\delta_{\mathcal{I}}$. One can then straightforwardly apply the conjugate gradient algorithm, with these forms for b and Q.

8.5 Examples of Approximation

The conjugate gradient algorithm, applied to the surface approximation problem, is demonstrated by considering a series of examples, illustrated in Figures 8.8–8.12. These should be compared to Figures 8.4–8.7. As in the case of surface interpolation, the surface approximation algorithm has been applied to disparity values rather than depth information. Again, the general shape of the surface and the relative difference in positions of the surfaces have been preserved by the algorithm, although the exact surface shape has not been reconstructed.

The objective function of the conjugate gradient algorithm in this case contains two factors, the quadratic variation of the surface and a least-squares term embodying a type of "smoothness" requirement. The scalar constant β determines the relative strengths of these two factors. If we let β be very small, then the smoothness requirement essentially vanishes and we return to the case of surface interpolation, discussed in Section 8.2. The conjugate gradient algorithm then becomes identical to the gradient projection algorithm. If we let β become very large, then the quadratic variation factor essentially vanishes and the algorithm reduces to a least-squares fitting of a plane to the known points. Clearly, we require a value of β intermediate to these extreme cases. The figures illustrate this tradeoff between the two factors, as β varies. To determine the optimal value for β, we require an estimate for the density of incorrect disparity values obtained by the stereo algorithm, so that a value for β may be chosen which smooths out the effect of these incorrect values, while not affecting the shape of the surface determined by minimizing the quadratic variation.

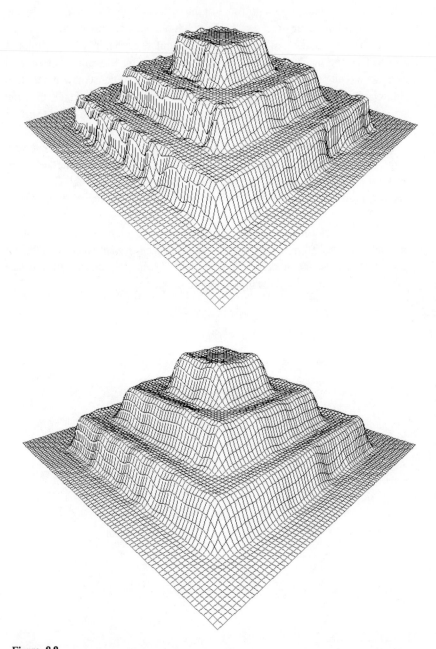

Figure 8.8
The Wedding Cake. The figures show surfaces obtained by approximating the surface using quadratic variation. The scalar constant relating the least squares term to the quadratic term is $\beta = 1$ in the top figure and $\beta = 0.1$ in the bottom figure.

Figure 8.9
The Spiral Staircase. The figures show surfaces obtained by approximating the surface using quadratic variation. The scalar constant relating the least squares term to the quadratic term is $\beta = 1$ in the top figure and $\beta = 0.1$ in the bottom figure.

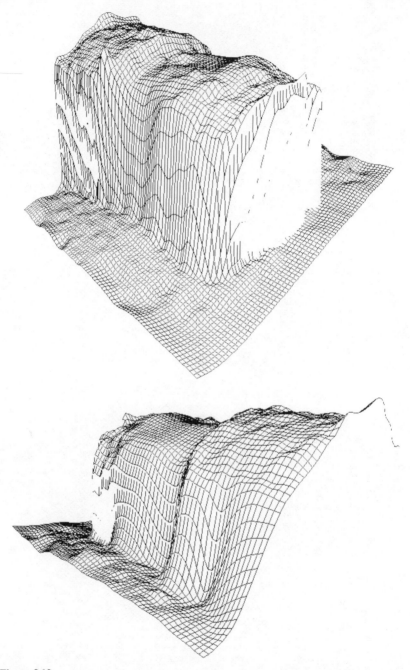

Figure 8.10
The Coffee Jar. The figures show two views of a surface obtained by approximating the surface using quadratic variation. The scalar constant relating the least squares term to the quadratic term is $\beta = 1$.

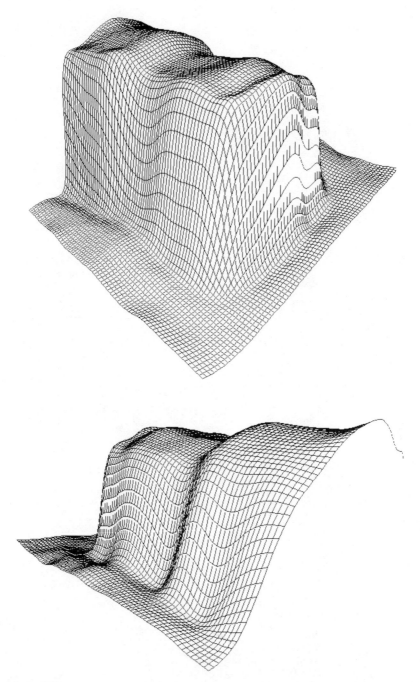

Figure 8.11
The Coffee Jar. The figures show two views of a surface obtained by approximating
the surface using quadratic variation. The scalar constant relating the least squares
term to the quadratic term is $\beta = 0.01$.

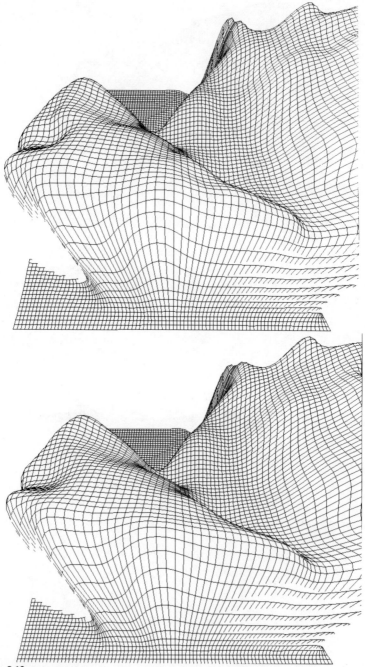

Figure 8.12
The Moore Sculpture. The figures show two approximations of the surface obtained by using quadratic variation. The scalar constant relating the least squares term to the quadratic term is $\beta = 0.5$ in the top figure and $\beta = 0.05$ in the bottom figure.

8.6 Summary

In this chapter, we have completed the final stage in our process of transforming stereo images into representations of surface shape. We transformed the visual interpolation problem derived in Chapter 6 into a form applicable to a discrete grid representation of the image. To solve the resulting problem, we applied the conjugate gradient algorithm and the gradient projection algorithm sketched in Chapter 7. The result was a pair of algorithms which take as input, a representation of the zero-crossings of an image, together with depth information computed by the stereo algorithm along those zero-crossing contours. The algorithms produce as output, a grid reconstruction of the surface most consistent with the stereo data and the zero-crossings of the convolved image.

Thus, we have completed our original goal — we have derived a computational method for obtaining complete representations of surface shape from a pair of stereo images. In the final chapter, we will consider the scope of the process and possible refinements which could improve its performance.

CHAPTER 9

ANALYSIS AND REFINEMENTS

In the previous chapter, we completed the final step in the design of a computational process for constructing, from a pair of stereo images, a complete surface specification, and demonstrated the effectiveness of the algorithm on a set of images. In this final chapter, we consider the scope and performance of the process and discuss possible refinements to it.

9.1 Achieving the Original Goal

We are remarkably adept at interacting with the three-dimensional world about us, even though our visual system obtains only two-dimensional projections of that world. This implies that the human visual system is able to reconstruct a useful representation of that three-dimensional world from its projections onto the retinas. This book was devoted to a computational study of that reconstruction, with emphasis on the method of stereopsis.

We have seen that the process basically consists of three stages (recall Figure 1.2). The first step is to transform the images into the Primal Sketch, a representation of those locations in the images corresponding to positions in the scene at which some physical property of a surface is changing — the zero-crossings of the convolved image. The second step is to match the Primal Sketch representations for the left and right image to obtain depth information at the zero-crossings. This resulted in a sparse representation of surface shape. To obtain a more complete representation, the third step is to interpolate between the known points along the zero-crossing contours to obtain the surface which is most consistent with the zero-crossing information. This most consistent surface constitutes the desired three-dimensional reconstruction.

We also saw that the computational theory developed and the algorithms designed to embody that theory are consistent with evidence, both psychophysical and neurophysiological, about the human visual system. Although much remains to be done in order to demonstrate convincingly that the computational process we have derived is in fact used by the human system, we believe that a solid framework has been developed for understanding some of the processing used by the human early visual system to reconstruct three-dimensional representations of the visual world. The story is not complete, however, and in this chapter we consider some refinements and extensions that may be involved in the reconstruction process.

9.2 Richer Descriptions

The stereo algorithm discussed in Chapters 2–4 transforms a very primitive representation of the image irradiances into a representation of surface depth. This primitive input representation was constructed by applying a series of Laplacian of Gaussian operators ($\nabla^2 G$) to the images, and locating the zero-crossings of the resulting convolved image. These zero-crossings were further characterized by their rough orientation and contrast sign. Based on this description of the image, we demonstrated that the stereo algorithm was able to determine surface shape on a range of random dot patterns and natural images. While this suggests that the stereo algorithm is capable of using such a primitive initial description reliably to effect depth reconstruction, we should also consider the possible role of richer input representations.

There are several possible methods in which the input representation may be enhanced. Mayhew and Frisby [1981] suggest that additional information in the form of the peaks of the convolved image, as well as the zero-crossings, may provide additional useful information for the stereo algorithm. Clearly, if we can add more locations, which can be matched between the two images, to the input to the stereo algorithm without affecting the false targets problem, we should see an improvement in the performance of that algorithm.

A second manner in which the input representation may be enhanced is to use Primal Sketch-like descriptors of edges [Marr, 1976b] in place of the labelled zero-crossings [Arnold, 1978; Arnold and Binford, 1980; Mayhew and Frisby, 1981]. The suggestion is to obtain a representation of edge fragments from the zero-crossings, and to match these edge segments instead. Of course, there is a strong relationship between zero-crossings and edges [Marr and Hildreth, 1980; Hildreth, 1980], but two differences can be distinguished. The first is that while most zero-crossings will closely coincide with edges in the image, the closed nature of the zero-crossing contours requires that some of the zero-crossings do not have a strong relationship to an edge in the image. One possibility is to remove these latter zero-crossings (perhaps on the basis of contrast strength or spatial-coincidence [Marr and Hildreth, 1980; Hildreth, 1980]). It is interesting to note that the stereo algorithm is capable of dealing with such zero-crossings. This follows from the observation that they are unlikely to be correlated between the two images, and the algorithm treats them in the same manner as occluded zero-crossings, no match being assigned to them. However, the performance of the algorithm could be improved by removing such "spurious" zero-crossings before the correspondence process is applied. A second difference between the zero-crossing description and an edge description is that some edges may not be explicitly represented by the zero-crossings (that is, due to the closed nature of the zero-crossing contours, there may be small gaps in the zero-crossing description). While the stereo algorithm is again capable of solving the correspondence problem in the presence of these gaps, its performance would probably be enhanced by using an input representation in which all edges were explicitly represented.

There may be other ways to incorporate the information contained in edge assertions without directly matching such descriptors. For example, Marr and Poggio [1980] suggest the use of edge assertions in the Primal Sketch to drive eye movements, thereby facilitating fusion by aligning the two images. The matching, however, could still be performed at the level of the zero-crossings.

9.3 Other Sources of Information

In this book, we have considered only the processes of stereopsis and surface interpolation. While a three-dimensional reconstruction is possible on the basis of these two processes, it is clear that other visual modules are also involved in obtaining surface information. We have argued that to a first approximation, stereopsis can be considered an independent module of the early visual system, but at some point we must consider the interactions between the stereo system and other early visual systems. For example, what is the interaction between the interpolated surface representation and the stereo matcher? How do modules such as structure-from-motion or texture perception interact with stereo? Can focussing information be used to drive the stereo matching process?

The interpolation algorithm derived in Chapters 6–8 was used specifically for transforming stereo data into a complete surface representation. Thus, the resulting surfaces are those that are most consistent with the stereo information. If we add more initial information about the surface shape, does the performance of the interpolation algorithm improve? We have indicated that the same process could be used to transform the output of Ullman's structure-from-motion algorithm into a complete representation. How should other sources of surface information be incorporated into the interpolation process? For example, how does the computation of shape from shading interact with the interpolation process, and vice versa?

All of these questions need to be investigated, both from the computational viewpoint, and within the context of the human visual system, if we are to gain a more complete model of the early visual system. In the rest of this chapter, we consider some specific refinements in more detail.

9.4 Discontinuities

One of the implicit assumptions of the interpolation algorithm is that the pieces of surface are in fact pieces of a single surface. Of course, this will frequently not be the case. In this section, we consider what modificiations are necessary in order to account for the existence of several surfaces within a scene. In particular, we address the issue of explicitly computing discontinuities in the surface representation, and the effects of explicit discontinuities on the form of the reconstructed surface.

One of the problems associated with the failure to make surface discontinuities explicit is that information about the shape of one surface affects the shape of an adjacent surface. This is illustrated in Figure 9.1. A set of known depth points is given in Figure 9.1(*a*). Intuitively, the most likely surface to fit through these points would be a pair of planes with a discontinuity in depth between them, shown in Figure 9.1(*b*). However, the requirement that a smooth surface fit through these points results in a warping and rippling of the surface that is undesirable, as shown in Figure 9.1(*c*). Thus, the lack of explicit discontinuities can affect the shapes of the interpolated surfaces in an unacceptable manner.

In order to make discontinuities explicit, there are several questions to ask about the process. How are the discontinuities detected? Where are they placed in the representation? When does the detection of discontinuities take place in the overall interpolation process? In the next few sections, we will discuss two possible methods for detecting the discontinuities, and their role in the overall interpolation.

9.4.1 Occlusions in the Stereo Algorithm

Consider the geometry indicated in Figure 9.2. There are regions of the left image which will not have a corresponding region in the right image, and vice versa. Consequently, any zero-crossings in this portion of one image will have no counterpart in the other image, and the stereo program should not assign any match to such zero-crossings. Hence, one possible mechanism for detecting occlusions would be to search for portions of the image which contain unmatched zero-crossings. Then, the interpolation can be restricted to take place only over those sections of the image which are bounded by zero-crossings with known disparity values.

This method would detect the discontinuities before the interpolation, since it uses stereo information directly to locate the occlusions. A problem with the method is that it will not detect all discontinuities, only those in the horizontal direction. Discontinuities that occur in the vertical direction do not cause occlusions. Hence, any method for detecting discontinuities which relies only on the unmatched zero-crossings will be incomplete.

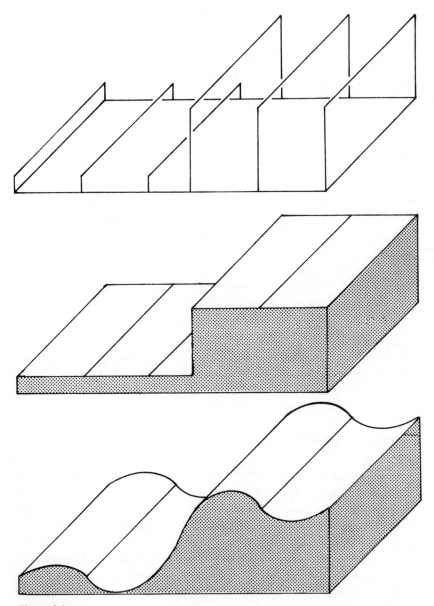

Figure 9.1
Discontinuities in the Surfaces. Figure (a) shows a set of known data points. Intuitively, the correct reconstructed surface would be a pair of planes, with a discontinuity between them, as shown in figure (b). If the interpolation algorithm attempts to reconstruct a surface through the boundary points, without a discontinuity, the result is as shown in figure (c). The sharp change in depth results in a rippling of the surface.

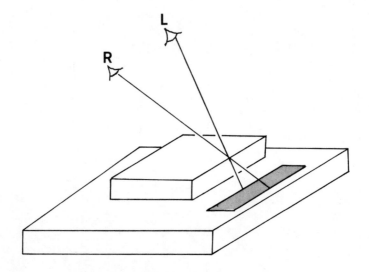

Figure 9.2
Occlusions. The upper surface occludes portions of the lower surface in each eye. These portions are different for the two eyes. The cross-hatched area of the lower surface indicates the region of the surface visible to the left eye, but not to the right.

9.4.2 The Primal Sketch Revisited

An integral part of most computational theories, proposed as models of aspects of the human visual system, is the use of computational constraints based on assumptions about the physical world [Marr, 1976, 1980; Marr and Poggio, 1979; Marr and Hildreth, 1980; Ullman, 1979]. In some of the computational theories, the constraints are explicitly checked for validity within the algorithm (e.g. Ullman's rigidity constraint in recovering structure from motion). In others, the constraints are simply assumed to be true, and are not explicitly checked (e.g. Marr and Poggio's uniqueness constraint in stereopsis). Can any aspect of the surface consistency constraint be explicitly checked and used by the algorithm?

The basic notion of the surface consistency constraint is that the surface cannot undergo a radical change in shape without having an accompanying zero-crossing in the convolved image. Implicit in this constraint is the assumption that the portion of the image being examined in fact corresponds to a single object. Thus, one could propose that if the shape of the interpolated surface forces a zero-crossing in a location for which none exists in the Primal Sketch, then such a zero-crossing indicates a location at which the assumption of a single object is violated. Such zero-crossings could then be taken as indicative of a surface discontinuity.

Perhaps the simplest method of detecting such discontinuities is again to use ideas inherent in the Primal Sketch. Recall that the Primal Sketch created descriptions of points in the image associated with inflections in intensity, for a range of resolutions. Since the image intensities may be considered as a type of three-dimensional surface, the Primal Sketch operators essentially detect discontinuities in the image intensities for a range of resolutions. Thus, one could apply the same type of analysis to the detection of surface discontinuities, where now the surface on which the operators apply is the reconstructed depth surface, rather than the intensity surface.

It is worth noting that not only should the operators be of the form used in the extraction of the Primal Sketch, but that it may also be useful to use a range of operators, as in the Primal Sketch. One reason for using multiple zero-crossing detectors was that surface changes, and hence intensity changes, could take place over a wide range of scales. This is still true in the case of surface descriptions, such as have been constructed for the coffee jar or the wedding cake. Thus, surface discontinuities corresponding to occluding edges will frequently tend to correspond to large surface changes, while internal surface discontinuities, due to a warping of the surface, will tend to correspond to small surface changes. By using a range of $\nabla^2 G$ operators, one can extract both occluding contour discontinuities, as well as ripples or warpings of the surface itself.

Note that this method requires that the surface interpolation already take place, before it can be applied. Since one of the general requirements on an algorithm is that it be rapid, we must consider the consequence of detecting discontinuities after the interpolation of the surfaces. There are two main reasons for the explicit detection of discontinuities. One is that such an explicit representation of this information will allow higher level processes, such as recognition, or extraction of axes for three-dimensional shape analysis, to operate more easily, since the process serves to make implicit information explicit. However, a second reason is to create more accurate surface representations, by removing the type of effect illustrated in Figure 9.1(c). If the process used to isolate discontinuities takes place after interpolation, and if the interpolation process requires the discontinuities to improve the interpolated surface approximation, one must propose an interpolater which passes over the surface information twice; first to produce an initial description, and second to refine the description after the detection of discontinuities. One must then question whether such a two pass process will affect our constraint of rapid algorithms. Fortunately, the answer is no, since the surface approximation obtained without explicitly accounting for the discontinuities is very close to the limiting surface except in the areas of the discontinuities (that is, any effects of the discontinuities are quickly damped out as one moves across the surface). Thus, the initial starting position for the second pass of the interpolation algorithm is very close to the limiting surface, and only a few iterations will be needed to refine the surface approximation.

9.4.3 Interpolation Over Occluded Regions

Even though occluded regions of the image can only be viewed from one eye, the human system still associates a depth value with these regions. This has an interesting implication for the interpolation algorithm. For most occluded regions, the only depth information available is at the edges of the occluded region. Psychophysical experiments have shown that the occluded region is always perceived at the depth of the lower surface. Thus, in Figure 9.2, the occluded region would be perceived at the level of the lower surface. Note that this is consistent with the physics of the situation, since if the occluded region were perceived at the level of the upper surface, then it should in fact be visible to the right eye, and this is not the case.

This observation suggests that when an occlusion is detected, it is explicitly located along the occluding boundary corresponding to the edge of the nearer object. This allows the occluded region itself to be associated with the lower surface, and the interpolation algorithm will fill in surface values for the occluded region from this lower surface.

This raises an interesting psychophysical prediction. The psychophysical literature has examined the case of planar surfaces and their occlusions, as in Figure 9.2. If the interpolation method developed here is given an explicit discontinuity along one edge of the occluded region, it will correctly fill in the region as an extension of the lower plane. Of interest is the case in which the occluded region is not planar. For example, consider a cylindrical object, such as that of Figure 5.2. If the interpolation algorithm is given this type of input, it will fill in the occluded portions of the surfaces as a smooth continuation of the curved cylinder. If the interpolation algorithm correctly models interpolation by the human visual system, then this predicts that the surface perception for human observers in this situation should also be that of a smooth cylinder. This has not yet been rigourously tested psychophysically.

9.5 Noise Removal

Although in general the Marr-Poggio stereo algorithm is very good at matching zero-crossings correctly (especially for random dot patterns), incorrect disparity values may sometimes be assigned to regions of the image. These incorrect values can be considered as noise superimposed on the correct surface. Since the surface interpolator explicitly attempts to fit a surface through all the disparity points, such noise points can affect the shape of the surface approximation. Indeed, the effect of these noise points can spread over a noticeable portion of the surface, before the nearby disparity values can damp out its effect. Thus, it would be preferable to remove these noise points, or at least neutralize their effect on the approximated surface shape. One possibility is that if a two pass interpolator is used, as suggested in the previous section, the detection of surface discontinuities will isolate such noise points from the rest of the surface, and the second pass of the interpolator will adjust the surface approximation to remove the influence of the noise points on the first pass approximation. Certainly this will be true for noise points with disparity values far removed from the correct values. For noise points whose disparity values are only slightly different from the correct surface disparities, the difference does not really matter. However, the final result would be that the noise points, while being isolated from the rest of the correct surface, would still remain in the final surface description. It would be preferable to completely remove such points.

Is it possible to identify and remove noise points from the disparity map? If the noise points are isolated spatially, then it is possible to identify them as undesirable. This follows from the form of the primal sketch operators. The case to consider is that in which one must distinguish between a set of noise points in a disparity map and a small object separated in depth from the rest of the scene. For the small object, the size of the zero-crossing contour is limited by the size of the available operator, and hence there is a minimum size of zero-crossing contour which the operator will yield about the object. If the number of zero-crossing points which differ significantly from their neighbors is less than this minimum, one may conclude that the points are noise, and thus remove them. This will result in an improved surface approximation.

9.6 Acuity

It can be seen from the example of the interpolated coffee jar in Figures 8.6 and 8.7, that the interpolated surface contains a bumpy quality which clearly is not consistent with the original object. How can this be explained? The effect occurs because the disparity values are specified only to within a pixel. This yields a fairly coarse disparity map which results in the bumps observed in the interpolated coffee jar of Figures 8.9 and 8.10. Hence, one method of removing the bumps would be to improve the accuracy of the disparities obtained by the algorithm. Note that some improvement in disparity accuracy is necessary if the algorithm is to be consistent with the human system. If we roughly equate pixels with receptors, then a pixel corresponds to roughly 27 seconds of arc. The implementation of the stereo algorithm computed disparity to within a pixel, while humans are capable of stereo acuity to a resolution of $2 - 10$ seconds [Howard, 1919; Woodburne, 1934; Berry, 1948; Tyler, 1977].

In order to account for finer disparity values, it is necessary to localize the zero-crossing to a better accuracy than has been done so far. Since the convolution values are only specified at each pixel, one method for more accurately specifying the zero-crossing positions is to interpolate between the known convolution values [Crick, Marr and Poggio 1980, Marr, Poggio and Hildreth 1979, Hildreth 1980]. Perhaps the simplest method is to rely on the observation of Hildreth that for most cases, even a simple linear interpolation will give extremely accurate localization of the zero-crossings. The addition of finer resolution depth information may improve the performance of the algorithm.

This example also raises a question of scale. Depending on the application of the surface specification, different amounts of resolution may be required. For example, if the ultimate goal of the surface specification is to obtain a rough idea of the position and shape of the surfaces in a scene, the spatial resolution at which surface information must be made explicit may not be critical. In this case, the known data from the stereo algorithm may be sampled at a coarser resolution, before the interpolation takes place. This should result in a smoother surface approximation. Further, although the reconstructed surface is less exact in terms of fine variation of the surface shape, the overall shape of the bottle is still preserved in this interpolation.

9.7 Retinal Mappings

The operators used to create the symbolic image descriptions matched by the Marr-Poggio stereo matcher were derived in part from evidence about the human visual system [Wilson and Bergen, 1979]. One aspect of this evidence is that the size of each operator scales with eccentricity, being larger in the periphery than in the fovea. However, in the development of the stereo implementation, the operations were assumed to be uniform for each size mask. Modification of the implementation, to be more consistent with the human evidence, is now considered.

There are two possible modifications that could be made. First, the size of the convolution operators, as well as the size of the matching neighborhoods, should explicitly increase with eccentricity. For a parallel implementation, such as in the human brain, there is no great difficulty in imposing this variance in size on the individual processors. However, for a serial computer implementation, such a variation in operator size introduces several practical difficulties.

There is an alternative implementation [Schwartz, 1977] which avoids these difficulties. Suppose that the retinal images are transformed, mapping them to a representation with coordinate axes given by orientation relative to the fovea, θ, along one axis, and log(radius) along the other axis. Such a mapping has the feature that in the new representation, the application of an operator of varying size over the entire transformed image is equivalent to the application of a varying size operator over the entire original image. Since the variation in operator size with eccentricity affects both the extraction of the convolutions, and the size of the matching neighborhood, it is necessary to perform the stereo matching in this transformed representation, before mapping back to a normal coordinate system. However, note that in this transformed representation, direction is only preserved locally. In the original implementation, given the location of a zero-crossing in one image, the location of the matching zero-crossing was performed by searching a horizontal neighborhood about the corresponding location in the other image. In the transformed image, one cannot simply apply the same matching algorithm since the horizontal direction in the original image does not correspond to the horizontal direction in the transformed image. Rather, for each value of θ, the orientation of the matching neighborhood must be changed from horizontal to something else, depending on the exact value of θ. The matching algorithm can be modified to account for this.

Once the matching has been performed in this transformed representation, the resulting disparity values can be transformed back to the original retinal coordinate system. This method has not yet been tested.

9.8 Multiple Representations

One final point concerns the question of the resolution of the depth representation. In the previous sections, we have outlined a method which creates a single disparity map, interpolates it, and then finds discontinuities and inflections in depth using a range of $\nabla^2 G$ operators. Rather than combining the depth information from the multiple stereo channels into a single representation, only to later create multiple descriptions of the inflections in depth, at varying resolutions, one could consider maintaining separate levels of description. In this manner, one would interpolate the disparity information obtained at each scale, using the output of each stereo channel. Then the inflections in depth could be detected for each such interpolated surface, by an appropriate $\nabla^2 G$ operator. This would result in a representation of the visible surfaces in which multiple levels of scale are explicitly maintained. This may prove to be useful for higher level visual modules which require depth descriptions at different resolutions.

9.9 Psychophysics and Neurophysiology

We began this book by suggesting that the computational paradigm would provide a useful context in which to state research questions for neurophysiology and psychophysics. Indeed, by determining what computation the visual system is attempting to perform, specific predictions concerning the behavior or structure of the computation can be stated. For example, Marr and Poggio [1979] list 15 psychophysical predictions and 6 physiological predictions based on their model of the human stereo system. Throughout this book, we have frequently relied on psychophysical evidence to determine characteristics of the algorithms being developed. We also based our interpolation algorithms on a set of algorithmic criteria which are based in part on the neurophysiological structure of the human visual system. In this final section, we list some of the other ways in which the computational theories discussed in this book can be related to the neurophysiology and psychophysics.

Since the psychophysical predictions of the stereo algorithm have been dealt with previously [Marr and Poggio, 1979], we concentrate here on psychophysical ramifications of the interpolation algorithm. These include:

1.   What is the form of the surface perceived in occluded regions? In particular, the minimization of quadratic variation suggests that if a portion of a curved object is occluded, then the surface in the occluded region should also be curved, and should minimize the quadratic variation across that region (similar to Figure 5.2).

2.   Figure 9.1 suggests that if discontinuities are not explicitly demarked in the interpolation process, a warping of the reconstructed surface (similar to Gibb's phenomena) will result. While, in principle, such ripples in the surface are undesirable, it is worth asking whether the human system specifically accounts for discontinuities before interpolation occurs. This may be rephrased by asking whether in stereoscopic situations similar to Figure 9.1, we perceive a Mach band-like warping of the surface in depth?

3.   We have suggested that there are several possible functionals which could be used to determine the most consistent surface. Based on algorithmic and mathematical arguments, we choose the quadratic variation. Can we test the shape of the reconstructed surface psychophysically? In particular, can we distinguish psychophysically between the minimum surface under quadratic variation and the minimum surface under some other functional, such as the square Laplacian? Is the reconstructed surface psychophysically consistent with the surface computed by quadratic variation?

4.   What is the spatial resolution of the reconstructed surface? That is, what is the spacing of the grid upon which the values of the reconstructed surface are computed?

Although we have used general characteristics of human neurophysiology to provide constraints on the architecture of the algorithms used to solve our computational theory (see Section 7.1, also Ullman, [1979b]), we would also like to be able to determine the specific neural mechanisms which perform the different stages of our computation. While no specific neural models for the Marr-Poggio stereo algorithm have yet been proposed (in part because to do so would require some knowledge about the neural mechanisms involved in the earlier stages)

Richter and Ullman [1980] have proposed a neural model for the early stages of the Primal Sketch computation. In particular, they propose that the convolution of the image with a series of $\nabla^2 G$ filters (or their approximation with a series of difference-of-Gaussian filters) takes place in the retinal ganglion cells. They show that the predicted responses of their model of the retina, to a series of visual stimuli, closely compare with electrophysiological recordings of the retinal cells. Based on these initial results, it is hoped that the neural mechanisms involved in the computation of zero-crossings, in the stereo matching process, and in the surface interpolation process may also be identified.

EPILOGUE

In this book, we have investigated the early visual processes of stereopsis and surface interpolation within the context of Marr's computational paradigm. Throughout this investigation, we have had two goals in mind. The first was to develop both computational theories and specific algorithms for converting pairs of images into three-dimensional representations of the shapes of the surfaces represented in the images. The second was to illustrate the computational approach to visual processing, by providing evidence of the fruitfulness of the approach. In some sense, it is the latter goal which is more important, since the basic concepts derived in the process of creating the algorithms will survive the specific details of the stereo algorithm, the interpolation algorithm, and so forth.

The strength of the computational approach lies in providing a framework within which one can combine the tools of Mathematics, Physics, Neurobiology, and Pyschophysics. Each of these areas provides valuable information about the problem at hand. Yet, taken alone, each is impoverished in providing an understanding of the processing of the system at all levels: computational theory, algorithm and implementation. By providing a coherent bridge between the different fields, the computational paradigm facilitates the statement of appropriate research questions, and separates the level of interaction of the different types of information. The initial success of the computational approach leads to the hope that future work will provide an even deeper understanding of the function and components of the human early visual system.

DISTRIBUTIONS OF ZERO-CROSSINGS

Assume that $f(x, y) = \nabla^2 G * E(x, y)$ is a white Gaussian process, where $E(x, y)$ is the image intensity. The problem is to find the distribution of intervals between alternate zero-crossings, taken along a horizontal slice of the image.

Assume that there is a zero-crossing at the origin, and let $P_1(\tau)$, $P_2(\tau)$ be the probability densities of the distances to the first and second zero-crossings. P_1 and P_2 are approximated by the following formulae [Rice 1945, section 3.4; Longuet-Higgins 1962, equations 1.2.1 and 1.2.3; Leadbetter 1969].

$$P_1(\tau) = \frac{1}{2\pi}\sqrt{\frac{\psi(0)}{-\psi''(0)}}\frac{M_{23}(\tau)}{H(\tau)}\left[\psi^2(0) - \psi^2(\tau)\right]\left\{1 + H(\tau)\cot^{-1}\left[-H(\tau)\right]\right\},$$

$$P_2(\tau) = \frac{1}{2\pi}\sqrt{\frac{\psi(0)}{-\psi''(0)}}\frac{M_{23}(\tau)}{H(\tau)}\left[\psi^2(0) - \psi^2(\tau)\right]\left\{1 - H(\tau)\cot^{-1}\left[H(\tau)\right]\right\},$$

where $\psi(\tau)$ is the autocorrelation of the filter $\nabla^2 G$, a prime denotes differentiation with respect to τ, and

$$H(\tau) = \frac{M_{23}(\tau)}{\sqrt{M_{22}(\tau) - M_{23}(\tau)}},$$

$$M_{22}(\tau) = -\psi''(0)\left[\psi^2(0) - \psi^2(\tau)\right] - \psi(0)\psi'^2(\tau),$$

$$M_{23}(\tau) = \psi''(\tau)\left[\psi^2(0) - \psi^2(\tau)\right] + \psi(\tau)\psi'^2(\tau).$$

It is now necessary to compute the autocorrelation $\psi(\tau)$. The filter is given by

$$\nabla^2 G(r) = \left(\frac{r^2 - 2\sigma^2}{\sigma^4}\right)\exp\left(-\frac{r^2}{2\sigma^2}\right).$$

The two-dimensional Fourier transform of this filter is given by

$$F(w) = -2\pi\sigma^2 w^2 \exp\left(-\frac{\sigma^2 w^2}{2}\right).$$

Since the interest is in the distribution of zero-crossing intervals along a horizontal slice of the image, it is necessary to obtain the portion of the spectrum corresponding to that slice. This is done by projecting the two-dimensional spectrum onto a line of similar orientation through the origin [Mersereau and Oppenheim, 1974]. This compression of the spectrum yields

$$F_1(u) = -(2\pi)^{\frac{3}{2}}\sigma\left(\frac{1 + \sigma^2 u^2}{\sigma}\right)\exp\left(-\frac{\sigma^2 u^2}{2}\right).$$

The power spectrum is then given by

$$F_1^2(u) = (2\pi)^3\left(\frac{1 + 2\sigma^2 u^2 + \sigma^4 u^4}{\sigma^2}\right)\exp\left(-\sigma^2 u^2\right).$$

Taking the inverse transform of the power spectrum yields the autocorrelation function

$$\psi(\tau) = \pi^{\frac{5}{2}}\sigma\left(\frac{11}{\sigma} - 5\frac{\tau^2}{\sigma^3} + \frac{1}{4}\frac{\tau^4}{\sigma^5}\right)\exp\left(-\frac{\tau^2}{4\sigma^2}\right).$$

The formulae of Rice may then be applied to this autocorrelation function, and the probability distributions obtained in this way are shown in Figures 4.15 and 4.16.

ZERO-CROSSING THEOREMS

Theorem 1 proved a relationship between any general two-dimensional surface and the probability of a zero-crossing occuring in the corresponding convolved intensities. Because the theorem dealt with any surface, the relationship was somewhat weak. In this appendix, a set of alternate theorems are given which apply in cases where the surface can be considered roughly cylindrical (or developable). The proofs of these theorems are included for completeness.

Theorem 7: Consider a portion of a second differentiable, developable surface oriented along the y axis such that $f_y(x, y) = q = c$, for some constant c. If the following conditions are true:

1.   *The surface portion contains exactly two inflection points in the x direction, at x_1 and x_2,*

2.   *At the points x_1 and x_2, normalized changes in albedo are dominated by normalized changes in reflectance,*

$$\left| \frac{\nabla^2 \rho}{\rho} \right| < \left| \frac{R_p p_{xx}}{R} \right|,$$

3.   *The reflectance map R does not pass through an extremum in this region of the surface,*

4.   *The reflectance map R is not constant over this region of the surface,*

5.   *The albedo ρ is non-zero,*

then there exists a point $x_1 < x' < x_2$ such that $\nabla^2 E(x') = 0$.

   Proof: The signum function is defined by:

$$sgn(x) = \begin{cases} 1 & \text{if } x > 0 \\ -1 & \text{if } x < 0 \\ 0 & \text{if } x = 0 \end{cases}$$

From the derivatives of the image equation,

$$\nabla^2 E = (\nabla^2 \rho)R + 2\rho_x R_p p_x + \rho(R_{pp}p_x^2 + R_p p_{xx}).$$

At the inflection points x_1 and x_2, $p_x(x_i) = 0$. Hence, evaluation of the equation yields

$$\nabla^2 E(x_i) = \nabla^2 \rho(x_i)R(p(x_i)) + \rho(x_i)R_p(p(x_i))p_{xx}(x_i) \quad \text{for } i = 1, 2$$

Condition (2) implies that the albedo changes are negligible in this region, so that the first term may be ignored,

$$sgn(\nabla^2 E(x_i)) = sgn(\rho(x_i) R_p(p(x_i)) p_{xx}(x_i)).$$

Condition (5) implies that $sgn(\rho) = 1$. Observing that

$$sgn(xy) = sgn(x)\, sgn(y),$$

the sign of the convolved intensity function at the surface inflection points is given by

$$sgn(\nabla^2 E(x_i)) = sgn(R_p(p(x_i)) p_{xx}(x_i)).$$

Condition (3) implies that R_p does not change sign in this region of the surface and hence

$$sgn(R_p(p(x_1))) = sgn(R_p(p(x_2))).$$

Note that $p_x = 0$ at x_1, x_2. The fact that there are exactly two inflections on the surface implies that $p_x \not\equiv 0$ over the neighbourhood (x_1, x_2). Thus,

$$sgn(p_{xx}(x_1)) \neq sgn(p_{xx}(x_2)),$$

and thus

$$sgn(\nabla^2 E(x_1)) \neq sgn(\nabla^2 E(x_2)).$$

The second differentiability of the surface implies that there exists a point $x' \in (x_1, x_2)$ such that $\nabla^2 E(x') = 0$. ∎

Corollary 7.1: Suppose one is given a set of known depth points at a set of zero-crossings, along a developable surface. If the albedo ρ is non-zero and the reflectance map R is not constant for this region of the surface, then the surface cannot contain two or more inflection points between any pair of adjacent zero-crossings. ∎

Theorem 8: Consider a portion of a second differentiable developable surface oriented along the y axis such that $f_y(x, y) = c$, for some constant c. If the following conditions are true:

1.   The surface contains exactly one inflection point in the x direction at x_1, and the reflectivity R achieves an extremum at the point x_2, $x_1 \neq x_2$.

2.   At the point x_1 the normalized changes in albedo are dominated by normalized changes in reflectance of the form,

$$\left| \frac{\nabla^2 \rho}{\rho} \right| < \left| \frac{R_p p_{xx}}{R} \right|,$$

and at the point x_2 the normalized changes in albedo are dominated by normalized changes in reflectance of the form,

$$\left| \frac{\nabla^2 \rho}{\rho} \right| < \left| \frac{R_{pp}p_x^2}{R} \right|,$$

3. The reflectance map R is not constant,
4. The albedo ρ is non-zero,

then there exists a point $x_1 < x' < x_2$ such that $\nabla^2 E(x') = 0$.

Proof: As in the proof of the previous theorem, at the point x_1,

$$sgn(\nabla^2 E(x_1)) = sgn(R_p(p(x_1))p_{xx}(x_1)).$$

At the point x_2, $R_p = 0$ so that

$$\nabla^2 E(x_2) = \nabla^2 \rho(x_2) R(p(x_2)) + \rho(x_2) R_{pp}(p(x_2)) p_x^2(x_2).$$

Condition (2) then implies that at this point, the normalized albedo changes are dominated by the normalized reflectance changes,

$$sgn(\nabla^2 E(x_2)) = sgn(\rho(x_2)) sgn(R_{pp}(p(x_2))) sgn(p_x^2(x_2)).$$

Condition (4) implies that $sgn(\rho) = 1$, so that

$$sgn(\nabla^2 E(x_2)) = sgn(R_{pp}(p(x_2))) sgn(p_x^2(x_2))$$
$$= sgn(R_{pp}(p(x_2))).$$

There are two subcases. In the first subcase, $p_{xx}(x_1) > 0$. Since there is only one inflection point in the surface, this implies that $p(x_1) < p(x_2)$. Then $R_{pp}(p(x_2)) < 0$ implies that

$$R_p(p(x_1)) > R_p(p(x_2)) = 0.$$

Conversely, $R_{pp}(p(x_2)) > 0$ implies that

$$R_p(p(x_1)) < R_p(p(x_2)) = 0.$$

In either case,

$$sgn(R_{pp}(p(x_2))) \neq sgn(R_p(p(x_1))p_{xx}(x_1)).$$

In the second subcase, suppose that $p_{xx}(x_1) < 0$. This implies that $p(x_1) > p(x_2)$. Then $R_{pp}(p(x_2)) < 0$ implies that

$$R_p(p(x_1)) < R_p(p(x_2)) = 0.$$

Conversely, $R_{pp}(p(x_2)) > 0$ implies that

$$R_p(p(x_1)) > R_p(p(x_2)) = 0.$$

In either case,

$$sgn\big(R_{pp}(p(x_2))\big) \neq sgn\big(R_p(p(x_1))p_{xx}(x_1)\big).$$

Thus, we see that

$$sgn\big(\nabla^2 E(x_1)\big) \neq sgn\big(\nabla^2 E(x_2)\big)$$

and as before the second differentiability of the surface implies that there exists a point $x' \in (x_1, x_2)$ such that $\nabla^2 E(x') = 0$. ∎

Corollary 8.1: Suppose one is given a set of known depth points at a set of zero-crossings, along a developable surface. If the albedo ρ is non-zero and the reflectance map R is not constant for this region of the surface, then if the reflectance map R passes through an extremum, the surface cannot contain any inflection points between any pair of zero-crossings. ∎

Theorem 9: Consider a second differentiable developable surface oriented along the y axis such that $f_y(x, y) = c$, for some constant c. If the following conditions are true:

1.   At the point x_1, the surface becomes self-shadowing, that is $R(x_1) = 0$,
2.   The reflectivity R achieves an extremum at the point x_2, $x_1 \neq x_2$,
3.   At the point x_2 normalized changes in albedo are dominated by normalized changes in reflectance,

$$\left|\frac{\nabla^2 \rho}{\rho}\right| < \left|\frac{R_{pp}p_x^2}{R}\right|,$$

4.   The reflectance map R is not constant over this region,
5.   The albedo ρ is non-zero,

then there exists a point $x_1 < x' < x_2$ such that $\nabla^2 E(x') = 0$.

Proof: The fact that the surface becomes self-shadowing implies that there is a region of the surface, beginning at x_1, such that R is constantly zero. The fact that there is an extremum in R for some other point implies that the intensity function must be concave down in the region of the extremum and concave up in the region of self-shadowing. There must be an inflection point in between and hence there must be a point x' such that $\nabla^2 E(x') = 0$. ∎

Theorem 10: Consider a second differentiable developable surface oriented along the y axis such that $f_y(x, y) = c$, for some constant c. If the following conditions are true:

1. At the point x_1, the reflectivity R achieves an inflection point,
2. There exist points $x_0 < x_1 < x_2$ such that reflectance changes dominate albedo changes,

$$\left| \frac{\nabla^2 \rho}{\rho} + \frac{R_p}{R}\left(2\frac{\rho_x}{\rho}p_x + p_{xx} \right) \right| < \left| \frac{R_{pp}}{R}p_x^2 \right|,$$

3. The first derivative of the surface, p, is monotonic in this region, (i.e. it does not achieve an extremum),
4. The reflectance map R is not constant over this region,
5. The albedo ρ is non-zero,

then there exists a point $x_1 < x' < x_2$ such that $\nabla^2 E(x') = 0$.

Proof: The proof is very similar to the previous ones, except that in this case, by condition (2),

$$sgn(\nabla^2 E) = sgn(\rho)sgn(R_{pp})sgn(p_x^2).$$

at the points x_0, x_2. Then condition (4) implies that

$$sgn(\nabla^2 E) = sgn(R_{pp}).$$

Condition (3) implies that

$$p(x_0) < p(x_1) < p(x_2)$$

or

$$p(x_2) < p(x_1) < p(x_0)$$

In either case, condition (1) then implies that

$$sgn(R_{pp}(p(x_0))) \neq sgn(R_{pp}(p(x_2))).$$

Hence,

$$sgn(\nabla^2 E(x_0)) \neq sgn(\nabla^2 E(x_2)),$$

and as before, the second differentiability of the surface implies that there exists a point $x' \in (x_0, x_2)$ such that $\nabla^2 E(x') = 0.$ ∎

VECTOR SPACES AND NORMS

This appendix contains a basic introduction to the notation of vector spaces and norms, taken for the most part from Rudin [1973].

A vector space V over a field Φ is a set, whose elements are called vectors, in which two operations, addition and scalar multiplication, are defined with the following algebraic properties.

1. To every pair of vectors v and w correponds a vector $v + w$ such that

$$v + w = w + v \qquad \text{and} \qquad v + (w + u) = (v + w) + u;$$

V contains a unique vector 0, called the origin, such that $v + 0 = v$ for every $v \in V$; and to each $v \in V$ corresponds a unique vector $-v$ such that $v + (-v) = 0$.

2. To every pair (a, v) with $a \in \Phi$ and $v \in V$ corresponds a vector av such that

$$1v = v, \qquad a(\beta v) = (a\beta)v,$$

and such that the distributive laws hold,

$$a(v + x) = av + aw, \qquad (a + \beta)v = av + \beta v.$$

If V is a vector space, $W \subset V, U \subset V, v \in V$, and $\lambda \in \Phi$, the following notations are often used:

$$W + U = \{w + u : w \in W, u \in U\}$$
$$\lambda W = \{\lambda w : w \in W\}.$$

A set $W \subset V$ is a *subspace* of V if

$$aW + \beta W \subset W, \qquad \text{for all scalars} \quad a, \beta.$$

A set $W \subset V$ is called *convex* if

$$tW + (1 - t)W \subset W, \qquad 0 \leq t \leq 1.$$

A vector space V is called a *normed space* if there exists a function, called the *norm*, from the vector space to the nonnegative reals, $\Theta : V \mapsto \Re^+$, such that

(a) $\quad \Theta(v + w) \le \Theta(v) + \Theta(w) \qquad \forall v, w \in V$

(b) $\quad \Theta(av) = |a|\Theta(v) \qquad v \in V, a$ scalar

(c) $\quad \Theta(v) > 0 \qquad$ if $\quad v \ne 0$.

Condition (a) is called the triangle inequality and is the generalization of the observation in Euclidean space that the length of one side of a triangle is never larger than the sum of the other two sides.

A *semi-norm* on V is a real-valued function p on V such that

(a) $\quad p(v + w) \le p(v) + p(w)$

(b) $\quad p(av) = |a|p(v)$.

Condition (a) is called the subadditivity property.

It is straightforward to show (see for example Rudin, 1973) that the set

$$\mathcal{N} = \{v : p(v) = 0\}$$

is a subspace of V.

Any space with a semi-norm defined on it can be associated with an equivalent normed space. To see this, let W be a subspace of a vector space V. For every $v \in V$, let $\pi(v)$ be the coset of W that contains v,

$$\pi(v) = v + W.$$

These cosets are elements of a vector space V/W called the *quotient space of V modulo W*. In this space, addition is defined by

$$\pi(v) + \pi(w) = \pi(v + w)$$

and scalar multiplication is defined by

$$a\pi(v) = \pi(av).$$

The origin of the space V/W is $\pi(0) = W$. Thus, π is a linear map of V onto V/W with W as its null space, called the *quotient map of V onto V/W*.

The important point about quotient spaces is the following. Suppose p is a semi-norm on a vector space V. Let

$$\mathcal{N} = \{v : p(v) = 0\}.$$

This is a subspace, by the above discussion. Let π be the quotient map from V onto $V/\mathcal{N}$, and define a mapping $p':V/\mathcal{N} \mapsto \Re$,

$$p'(\pi(v)) = p(v).$$

If $\pi(v) = \pi(w)$ then $p(v - w) = 0$. Since $|p(v) - p(w)| \le p(v - w)$, then $p'(\pi(v)) = p'(\pi(w))$ and p' is well-defined on $V/\mathcal{N}$. It is straightforward to show that p' is a norm on $V/\mathcal{N}$.

The point of the previous discussion is that now all facts about normed spaces apply to semi-normed spaces, to within a factor of the null space $\mathcal{N}$, since the quotient space defined by a semi-norm is always a normed space.

Given a sequence of vectors, $\{v_n\}$ in a vector space V and a norm Θ on that space, the sequence is said to be *Cauchy* if for all $\epsilon > 0$ there is an integer M such that

$$\Theta(v_m - v_n) < \epsilon \qquad \forall m, n > M.$$

For a sequence of vectors $\{v_n\}$ to converge, there must exist some vector v such that for every $\epsilon > 0$, there exists some integer M such that for all $m > M$, $\Theta(v - v_m) < \epsilon$. If every Cauchy sequence converges in a normed space, then the norm is said to be *complete*.

A norm is said to satisfy the *parallelogram law* if

$$[\Theta(v + w)]^2 + [\Theta(v - w)]^2 = 2[\Theta(v)]^2 + 2[\Theta(w)]^2.$$

Finally, note that given a set of functions, $\mathcal{F}$, defined on some vector space V, the set $\mathcal{F}$ also forms a vector space. To see this, let $f, g \in \mathcal{F}$ and define the vector $f + g$ by

$$(f + g)(v) = f(v) + g(v).$$

Similarly, if α is an element of the scalar field, define the vector αf by

$$(\alpha f)(v) = \alpha f(v).$$

Using these definitions of addition and scalar multiplication, it can easily be shown that $\mathcal{F}$ forms a vector space.

INNER PRODUCTS AND HILBERT SPACES

This appendix contains basic definitions of inner products and Hilbert spaces, taken for the most part from Rudin [1973].

An inner product is a function $\mu: V \times V \mapsto \Re$ written $\mu(v, w)$, satisfying

1. $\mu(y, x) = \mu(x, y)$
2. $\mu(x + y, z) = \mu(x, z) + \mu(y, z)$
3. $\mu(ax, y) = a\mu(x, y) \quad a \in \Re$
4. $\mu(x, x) \geq 0$
5. $\mu(x, x) = 0$ if and only if $x = 0$.

A real vector space V is called an *inner product space* if there is an inner product defined on it. Note that if condition (5) does not hold, then the function is called a semi-inner product, and the space is a semi-inner product space. If μ is an inner product, then $\Theta(v) = \mu(v, v)^{\frac{1}{2}}$ is a norm on the space. This can easily be shown; a more difficult criterion to check is the triangle inequality.

To see this, note the following. It is easy to determine that

$$0 \leq \Theta^2(\lambda v + w) = |\lambda|^2 \Theta^2(v) + 2\mu(v, w)\lambda + \Theta^2(w).$$

If $v \neq 0$, take

$$\lambda = \frac{-\mu(v, w)}{\Theta^2(v)}.$$

Then the above expression becomes

$$0 \leq \Theta^2(\lambda v + w) = \Theta^2(w) - \frac{|\mu(v, w)|^2}{\Theta^2(v)}.$$

Hence,

$$|\mu(v, w)| \leq \Theta(v)\Theta(w).$$

To show the triangle inequality, note that

$$\Theta^2(v + w) = \Theta^2(v) + \Theta^2(w) + 2\mu(v, w)$$
$$\leq \Theta^2(v) + \Theta^2(w) + 2\Theta(v)\Theta(w)$$
$$= (\Theta(v) + \Theta(w))^2.$$

Thus, every inner product space can be converted to a normed space. If the resulting normed space is complete, then it is called a *Hilbert space*.

CALCULUS OF VARIATIONS

The calculus of variations is frequently used to solve problems of mathematical physics, and is potentially applicable to our surface interpolation problem. In this appendix, we outline the basic methods of the calculus of variations, and show how they apply to the problem of visual surface interpolation. (For further details on the calculus of variations, the reader is referred to Courant and Hilbert [1953] or Forsyth [1960].)

The calculus of variations is, in essence, a generalization of the elementary theory of extrema, or stationary values, of a function. Its object, however, is to find extrema of functionals rather than extrema of functions of a finite number of independent variables. Thus, we seek the argument function in a given domain of admissible functions for which the functional assumes the stationary value or extremum in question. In differential calculus, we are usually concerned with extremum with respect to values of the function in the vicinity of the extremum point, rather than with absolute extrema. The same holds true for variational calculus. A neighbourhood of a function is defined in the following manner. If ϵ is a positive constant, a function $g(x, y, \ldots)$ is said to lie in the ϵ-neighbourhood of the function $f(x, y, \ldots)$ if $|f - g| < \epsilon$ in the region of definition.

The *fundamental problem of the calculus of variations* states: In a given domain of admissible argument functions, find an argument function (or functions) of a given functional for which the latter is an extremum with respect to all argument functions of the domain lying in a sufficiently small ϵ-neighbourhood of the extremal argument function. If the functional depends explicitly on variable parameters in addition to the argument functions, then we must determine these parameters as well as the argument functions, in order to obtain the extremum.

There are many methods of dealing with the fundamental problem. One of the most common is to transform the variational problem into a set of differential equations. The solution to the variational problem will then be characterized by the solution to the differential equations.

The Euler equations of a variational problem represent necessary but not sufficient conditions that a function must satisfy if it is to furnish the extremum of a given integral. The equations can be obtained by reducing the variational problem to a problem in the differential calculus. We shall illustrate the equations for a simple problem, and then indicate how the results may be generalized.

The simplest problem of the calculus of variations is to determine the minimum of the integral

$$J[y] = \int_{x_0}^{x_1} F(x, y, y') \, dx,$$

where the values x_0, x_1, $y(x_0)$, $y(x_1)$ are given, and where $y' = dy/dx$. The function F is twice continuously differentiable with respect to its three arguments and the second derivative y'' of the function y is assumed to be continuous. Suppose $y = f(x)$ is the desired extremal function. Now consider a function $\eta(s)$ that is defined in the interval $x_0 \leq x \leq x_1$, is continuously second differentiable, and vanishes at the end points, but is otherwise arbitrary. Let ϵ be an arbitrary small constant. The *variation* of the function $y = f(x)$ is defined as the quantity $\delta y = \epsilon \eta(x)$. We can construct the function $y_1 = y + \delta y = y + \epsilon \eta(x)$, where ϵ is a parameter. If ϵ is sufficiently small, all the varied functions y_1 lie in an arbitrarily small neighbourhood of the extremal function $y = f(x)$. Therefore, the integral $J[y_1] = J[y + \epsilon \eta(x)]$, which may be regarded as a function $\Phi(\epsilon)$ of ϵ, must have a minimum at $\epsilon = 0$ relative to all values of ϵ in a sufficiently small neighbourhood of 0. Therefore, $\Phi'(0) = 0$. Differentiating the integral $\Phi(\epsilon)$ with respect to ϵ under the integral sign yields the necessary condition:

$$\Phi'(0) = \int_{x_0}^{x_1} \left(\frac{dF}{dy} \eta + \frac{dF}{dy'} \eta' \right) dx = 0,$$

which must hold for all functions $\eta(x)$ that satisfy the above conditions. Integration by parts yields

$$\int_{x_0}^{x_1} \eta \left(\frac{dF}{dy} - \frac{d}{dx} \frac{dF}{dy'} \right) dx + \frac{dF}{dy'} \eta(x) \Big|_{x_0}^{x_1} = 0.$$

The second term vanishes, since $\eta(x_0) = \eta(x_1) = 0$. The above integral equations holds for all functions η.

The *fundamental lemma of the calculus of variations* states: If the relation $\int_{x_0}^{x_1} \eta(x)\phi(x) \, dx = 0$, with $\phi(x)$ a continuous function of x, holds for all functions $\eta(x)$ that vanish at the boundary and are continuous together with their first two derivatives, it follows that $\phi(x) = 0$ identically. This holds equally well for multiple integrals.

The lemma can readily be applied to the equation above, implying that

$$\frac{d}{dx} \frac{dF}{dy'} - \frac{dF}{dy} = 0.$$

This is the fundamental differential equation of Euler, which states a necessary condition for the existence of an extremum. Every solution of this differential equation is called an *extremal* of the minimum problem.

The essential idea in the above discussion is to imbed the extremal $y(x)$ in a family of functions $y(x) + \epsilon\eta(x)$ with the parameter ϵ. The linear occurence of the parameter is not important. Thus, we can imbed the function in a more general family of functions $y(x, \epsilon)$; the above discussion remains valid if we set

$$\eta(x) = \frac{\partial}{\partial\epsilon} y(x, \epsilon)|_{\epsilon=0}.$$

We now introduce a useful terminology. We called the function $\epsilon\eta = \delta y$ the variation of $y(x)$; similarly the expression

$$\delta J = \int_{x_0}^{x_1} \left(\frac{dF}{dy} - \frac{d}{dx}\frac{dF}{dy'}\right) dx + \frac{dF}{dy'}\eta(x)\Big|_{x_0}^{x_1},$$

is called the *first variation* of the integral J, even if η does not vanish at the boundary.

The Euler equations can be extended in a number of ways. Consider the case in which the value of the desired extremal function $y(x)$ is not known at the boundary points x_0, x_1. In this case, we can consider *natural boundary conditions* for the free boundaries. As before, a necessary condition for the existence of a stationary value is that the first varation of J must vanish. Hence, the Euler equations must still hold. In order to ensure that the second term in the expression for δJ also vanishes, we must impose as a necessary condition, the "natural boundary condition"

$$\frac{dF}{dy'} = 0 \qquad \text{for } x = x_0, x = x_1.$$

The entire discussion above, based on the simplest problem of the calculus of variations, can be extended to deal with functions of several derivatives, functions of several variables, and functions of several derivatives and several variables.

The Differential Equations of Mathematical Physics

The calculus of variations is a useful tool in formulating differential equations of mathematical physics, especially when combined with the variational principle of *minimum potential energy*. This principle applies to problems of stable equilibrium and states that the position of stable equilibrium of a system is governed by the conditions necessary to ensure mimimum potential energy.

We can consider our problem of visual surface interpolation as a problem of mathematical physics in the following manner. Suppose we are given a thin elastic plate, whose equilibrium position is a plane, and whose potential energy under deformation is given by an integral of the quadratic form in the principal curvatures of the plate. We can consider the interpolation problem as one of determining the surface formed by fitting a thin elastic plate over a region $\mathfrak{R}$ (with boundary Γ) and through the known points.

We want to determine the Euler equations and the boundary conditions for this situation. If the principal radii of curvature of the deformed plate are denoted by ρ_1, ρ_2 the potential energy density is given by an expression of the form [Courant and Hilbert, 1953, p.250]

$$A\left(\frac{1}{\rho_1^2} + \frac{1}{\rho_2^2}\right) + \frac{2B}{\rho_1\rho_2},$$

where A and B are constants determined by the material of the plate. The radii of principal curvature are the reciprocals of the principal curvatures κ_1, κ_2. Hence, the potential energy density is given equivalently by

$$A(\kappa_1^2+\kappa_2^2)+2B\kappa_1\kappa_2 = A\left[(\kappa_1+\kappa_2)^2 - 2\kappa_1\kappa_2\right]+2B\kappa_1\kappa_2 = AJ^2-2(A-B)K$$

where J is the first or mean curvature of the surface, and K is the second or Gaussian curvature of the surface.

Let the deformation normal to the equilibrium plane of the plate be denoted by $f(x, y)$, and suppose this deformation to be small in the sense that higher powers of f, f_x, f_y are negligible compared with lower ones. We have already seen that in this case, we may then write

$$J = f_{xx} + f_{yy} = \nabla^2 f$$
$$K = f_{xx}f_{yy} - f_{xy}^2.$$

Thus the desired potential energy of deformation is given by

$$U = \int\int_{\mathcal{R}}\left[(\nabla^2 f)^2 - 2(1-\mu)(f_{xx}f_{yy} - f_{xy}^2)\right]dxdy,$$

apart from a constant factor (which we set to one). The coefficient μ represents a constant of proportionality, and is equal to the tension in the plate. To find the Euler equations and the natural boundary conditions for our minimum problem, we must set the variation δU to zero. Applying the techniques discussed above, this variation can be derived as

$$\delta U = \int\int_{\mathcal{R}}(\nabla^4 f)\,dxdy - \int_{\Gamma} M\delta\frac{\partial f}{\partial n}\,ds - \int_{\Gamma} P\delta f\,ds.$$

Here, s is the arc length along the boundary contour Γ, $\partial/\partial n$ is a derivative normal to the boundary contour, $\partial/\partial s$ is a derivative with respect to arclength along the boundary contour, and

$$M(f) = -\nabla^2 f + (1-\mu)\left(f_{xx}x_s^2 + 2f_{xy}x_sy_s + f_{yy}y_s^2\right),$$
$$P(f) = \frac{\partial}{\partial n}\nabla^2 f + (1-\mu)\frac{\partial}{\partial s}\left(f_{xx}x_nx_s + f_{xy}(x_ny_s + x_sy_n) + f_{yy}y_ny_s\right).$$

Here, x_n, y_n and x_s, y_s are the direction cosines of the outward normal and the tangent vector, respectively. Thus, the Euler differential equation is

$$\nabla^4 f = \nabla^2\nabla^2 f = f_{xxxx} + 2f_{xxyy} + f_{yyyy} = 0$$

and the natural boundary conditions are that

$$M(f) = 0 \qquad P(f) = 0.$$

There are two subcases of particular interest. In the first case, suppose that the tension factor is given by $\mu = 1$. The energy equation reduces to

$$\int\int_{\mathcal{R}} \left(\nabla^2 f\right)^2 dx\, dy$$

which is simply the square Laplacian condition derived previously. The Euler equation is simply the biharmonic equation $\nabla^4 f = 0$ while the natural boundary conditions are

$$\nabla^2 f = 0$$
$$\frac{\partial}{\partial n}\nabla^2 f = 0,$$

along the boundary contour Γ. In the second case, suppose that the tension factor is given by $\mu = 0$. The energy equation reduces to

$$\int\int_{\mathcal{R}} \left(f_{xx}^2 + 2f_{xy}^2 + f_{yy}^2\right) dx\, dy$$

which is simply the quadratic variation condition also derived previously. The Euler equation is indentical to that of the square Laplacian, namely the biharmonic equation $\nabla^4 f = 0$. The natural boundary conditions are different, however. They are given by

$$-\nabla^2 f + \left(f_{xx}x_s^2 + 2f_{xy}x_s y_s + f_{yy}y_s^2\right) = 0,$$
$$\frac{\partial}{\partial n}\nabla^2 f + \frac{\partial}{\partial s}\left(f_{xx}x_n x_s + f_{xy}(x_n y_s + x_s y_n) + f_{yy}y_n y_s\right) = 0.$$

In the simple case of a square boundary, oriented with respect to the coordinate axes, the boundary conditions reduce to:

$$f_{yy} = 0$$
$$2f_{xxy} + f_{yyy} = 0$$

along the boundary segments parallel to the x axis, and

$$f_{xx} = 0$$
$$2f_{yyx} + f_{xxx} = 0$$

along the boundary segments parallel to the y axis.

These boundary conditions can be straightforwardly simplified to:

$$f_{yy} = 0$$

$$f_{xxy} = 0$$

along the boundary segments parallel to the x axis, and

$$f_{xx} = 0$$

$$f_{yyx} = 0$$

along the boundary segments parallel to the y axis.

INTERPOLATION TECHNIQUES

In this appendix, several possible methods of solving constrained optimization problems will be outlined. (The review article of Schumaker [1976] contains more information about possible methods of solving interpolation and approximation problems.) In discussing these methods, we will consider their relevance to the visual interpolation problem. Two factors will be important for this point of view. In Chapter 7, we saw that to be biologically feasible, an algorithm should satisfy the algorithmic criteria of locality, parallelism and uniformity. Further, many of the methods described below rely on a particular form of input data, which generally will not be satisfied by the output of the stereo algorithm.

Many of the methods studied in the literature are global methods, where the value of the surface at any point depends on all the known values. The algorithmic constraints imply that local methods, where the value of the surface at any point depends only on the nearby known points, are of particular interest. In general, global interpolation methods can be made local by partitioning the domain D into subdomains and patching together the interpolation functions for each subdomain. That is, to define the surface function f, one defines the surface in local patches, f_i over the subdomain D_i. There are, however, frequent problems in how to optimally define the subregions, and in the effect of the subdivision on the performance of the algorithm.

Note also that many of the methods for interpolation which are to be found in the literature require regular grids of known data points. Clearly, the Marr-Poggio algorithm, as well as other visual processes, such as Ullman's structure-from-motion algorithm, supplies data at scattered points or along isolated contour segments. Hence, the concentration will be on methods applicable to such data. It is possible to circumvent this problem by using a two stage process — a first stage to construct a surface g based on the scattered data, and then a second stage using the regular data of g for the construction of a smoother surface f.

0.1 Partitions

The most common subdomains for defining surface patches are rectangles (for gridded data) and triangles (for scattered data). When dealing with scattered data, one must consider methods for triangulating the domain into subdomains. The major problem with irregular or scattered data is that the triangularization of the field is a difficult problem. Moreover, the triangularization is not unique and in many cases (such as this) it is difficult to avoid long, thin triangles, which are poorly suited for interpolation. Some algorithms for triangularization are given in Cavendish [1974] and Lawson [1972].

0.2 Piecewise Linear Interpolation

The simplest method for defining a local interpolating surface is to construct each surface patch $f_i(x, y)$ to be of the form $a_1 + a_2x + a_3y$. The data at the corners of the triangle are sufficient to determine the coefficients for that piece of f. This results in a piecewise linear surface which is globally continuous. The major problem with this method is that no higher order smoothness will be attained. Thus, along each side of a triangle, the resulting surface will be discontinuous in first and all higher order derivatives. This is clearly unacceptable for this situation. Examples of the use of this method for data fitting can be found in Lawson [1972] and Whitten and Koelling [1974].

0.3 Polynomial Interpolation

The theory of finite dimensional interpolation is well known (for example, see Davis, [1963].) In general, it works as follows:

Let $\{\phi_i\}_1^N$ be a set of N functions on a domain D. Then

$$f(x, y) = \sum_{j=1}^{N} a_j\phi_j(x, y)$$

will satisfy the constraints $f(x_i, y_i) = F_i, i = 1, \ldots, N$ if and only if $\{a_j\}_1^N$ is a solution of the linear system

$$\sum_{j=1}^{N} a_j\phi_j(x_i, y_i) = F_i \qquad i = 1, \ldots, N,$$

which has a unique solution if and only if it is nonsingular.

Standard choices for the ϕ_j are polynomials in x, y. Problems with such a choice include guaranteeing that the system is nonsingular, or even when it is, guaranteeing that it is not ill-conditioned, and the fact that polynomials tend to exhibit a considerable oscillatory behaviour, yielding unacceptable undulating surfaces, likely to introduce inflections in the image intensities inconsistent with the zero-crossings.

In general, polynomial interpolation has not been applied to scattered data. Some treatment, however, can be found, for example in Ciarlet and Raviart [1971, 1972a, 1972b, 1972c], Guenther and Roetman [1970], Kunz [1957], Prenter [1975], Steffensen [1927], Thacher [1960], Thacher and Milne [1960], and Whaples [1958].

Polynomial interpolation is somewhat simplified, in the case of known data on a grid. By this, the following is meant. Let H be the rectangle $[a, b] \times [c, d]$ and let

$$a = x_0 < x_1 < \ldots < x_{k+1} = b$$

$$c = y_0 < y_1 < \ldots < y_{l+1} = d$$

Let F be defined on H and let the known values be

$$F_{ij} = F(x_i, y_j) \quad i = 0, \ldots, k+1 \quad j = 0, \ldots, l+1.$$

As noted, however, gridded data is only applicable in a two-stage process. Gridded polynomial fitting has been well studied in the literature, see for example, Prenter [1975] or Steffensen [1927].

If we do not require that the surface exactly interpolate the known data, but only approximate it, then the polynomial method may be extended to that of polynomial least squares fitting.

The general theory of discrete least-squares fitting is very well known. To review, suppose that $\{\phi_j\}_1^n$ are n given functions on D. Let

$$\Phi(a) = \sum_{i=1}^{N} \left(\sum_{j=1}^{n} a_j \phi_j(x_i, y_i) - F_i \right)^2$$

where $a = (a_1, \ldots, a_n)^T$ is an arbitrary vector in $\Re^n$. The problem is to find an a' such that

$$\Phi(a') = \min_a \Phi(a).$$

Then

$$f(x, y) = \sum_{j=1}^{n} a'_j \phi_j(x, y)$$

is the discrete least-squares approximation of $\{F_i\}_1^N$. Usually, $n \ll N$.

There are several methods for solving this problem. For example, if the $\{\phi_j\}_1^n$ are orthonormal relative to the inner product

$$(\phi, \psi) = \sum_{i=1}^{N} \phi(x_i, y_i)\psi(x_i, y_i)$$

then the solution is given by

$$f(x, y) = \sum_{j=1}^{N} F_j \phi_j(x, y).$$

One can also solve this problem by using normal equations or by using general matrix methods on $Aa = F$, where

$$F = (F_1, \ldots, F_N)^T$$

$$A = (\phi_j(x_i, y_i))$$

Polynomial discrete least-squares fitting has been widely studied for scattered data. For example, see Cadwell and Williams [1962], Crain and Bhattacharyya [1967], Whitten [1970, 1972].

Polynomial least squares methods can be considered as multi-dimensional regression (see Effroymson, [1960]). The method of weighted least squares can also be used. In this case, rather than using the function Φ, one uses

$$\Phi(a) = \sum_{i=1}^{N} w_i \left(\sum_{j=1}^{n} a_j \phi_j(x_i, y_i) - F_i \right)^2$$

where $a = (a_1, \ldots, a_n)^T$ is an arbitrary vector in $\Re^n$. The problem is again to find an a' such that

$$\Phi(a') = \min_a \Phi(a).$$

Then

$$f(x, y) = \sum_{j=1}^{n} a_j' \phi_j(x, y)$$

is the discrete least-squares approximation of $\{F_i\}_1^N$, [Pelto, Elkins and Boyd, 1968].

Since discrete least-squares fitting can be carried out with any finite set of functions, many authors have used tensor products of splines [Hayes and Halliday 1974, Whitten 1971].

Also, rather than using least-squares fitting, one can use ℓ_1 or ℓ_∞ approximation. In other words, given $\{\phi_j\}_1^n$ defined on D, the vector a' is sought such that

$$\Phi(a) = \sum_{i=1}^{N} \left| \sum_{j-1}^{n} a_j \phi_j(x_i, y_i) - F_i \right|$$

is minimized or such that

$$\Phi(a) = \max_{1 \leq i \leq N} \left| \sum_{j=i}^{n} a_j \phi_j(x_i, y_i) - F_i \right|$$

is minimized. Both of these approximations can be solved as linear programming problems [Rabinowitz 1968, 1970, Rosen 1971].

All of the above discussion applies to the general global case. In the local case, if functions $\{\phi_j(x, y)\}_1^N$ are constructed with the property that

$$\phi_j(x_i, y_i) = \delta_{ij} \qquad i, j = 1, \ldots, N,$$

then these functions can be constructed as pyramids in such a way that the function ϕ_j has support only on the triangles surrounding the data point (x_i, y_i). These functions are usually referred to as Lagrangian functions.

The Lagrangian approach to local interpolation is similar to the finite element method, which is concerned with the solution of an operator equation in the form of a linear combination of a set of functions (called elements) with the above property. The functions need not be restricted to polynomials, but may be rational functions or more complicated functions. In fact, it is possible to construct Lagrangian functions (or elements) with small support but higher global smoothness.

There are a great many papers in the finite-element literature concerned with defining convenient smooth elements. Included are the books of Aziz [1972], de Boor [1975], Strang and Fix [1973], Whiteman [1973], and the papers of Barnhill, Birkhoff and Gordon [1973], Barnhill and Gregory [1972, 1975], Barnhill and Mansfield [1974], Birkhoff and Mansfield [1974], Bramble and Zlamal [1970], Goel [1968], Hall [1969], Mitchell [1973], Mitchell and Phillips [1972], Nicolaidis [1972, 1973], Zenisek [1970], Zienkiewicz [1970], Zlamal [1968, 1970, 1974].

It should be noted that the construction of elements with higher-order smoothness becomes increasingly difficult. For example, Mansfield [1976] notes that to get an element with support on a triangle and achieve global continuity, it is necessary to use polynomials of degree at least 5. Akima [1978] gives an algorithm for accomplishing this.

0.4 Shepard's Method

Shepard [1968] has developed a method specifically intended for the case of scattered data. In brief, the method consists of the following.

Let ρ be a metric in the plane. Given a point (x, y), let

$$r_i = \rho((x, y), (x_i, y_i)) \qquad i = 1, \ldots, N.$$

Let $\mathcal{F}$ be a linear space of functions on D, and $\{\lambda_i\}_1^N$ be a set of linear functionals on $\mathcal{F}$. Let $\{\phi_i\}_1^N$ be a prescribed set of functions on D. Then we are interested in approximation schemes of the form:

$$QF(x, y) = \sum_{i=1}^N \lambda_i F \phi_i(x, y).$$

This is a surface fitting problem, where the data are given by $F_i = \lambda_i F$ for $i = 1, \ldots, N$. If the ϕ_i have support on small subsets of D, and if each λ_i has support on the same set, then the above computation is local. For example, if we let λ_i be point evaluation at (x_i, y_i) and $\phi_i(x, y)$ be a function with support in a neighbourhood of (x_i, y_i) then the approximation formula is given by

$$QF(x, y) = \sum_{i=1}^N F_i \phi_i(x, y).$$

This is similar to the Lagrange form of interpolation, but unless the ϕ_i satisfy $\phi_j(x_i, y_i) = \delta_{ij}$, QF will not be an interpolant. As a consequence, they are called quasi-interpolants. The main problem with this method involves a careful choice of $\{\phi_i\}_1^N$ in order to ensure appropriate accuracy and smoothness. Usually this excludes cases of scattered data. For an example of this method, see Lyche and Schumaker [1975].

Other examples of local approximation schemes include Babuska [1970], de Boor and Fix [1973], Fix and Strang [1969], Fredrickson [1971].

0.6 Spline Interpolation

Let X be a linear space of "smooth" functions defined on the domain D. Let

$$U = \{f \in X : f(x_i, y_i) = F_i, \quad i = 1, \ldots, N\}$$

so that U is the set of smooth functions which interpolate the data. Now let Θ be a functional on X which measures the smoothness of a function $f \in X$ — the smaller $\Theta(f)$ is, the smoother f is.

Consider the minimization problem of finding $s \in U$ such that $\Theta(s) = \inf_{u \in U} \Theta(u)$, assuming that such an s exists. Then s will be the "smoothest" interpolant, and in view of the similarity with classical spline approximation, s is called a spline function interpolating F. For a general theory of spline interpolation, see Laurent [1972]. The general method used in solving such minimization problems globally is to define a functional Θ, frequently as a pseudo-norm, and

Let $0 < \mu < \infty$. Then Shepard's interpolation formula is given by:

$$f(x,y) = \begin{cases} \sum_{i=1}^{N} \frac{F_i}{r_i\mu} \Big/ \sum_{i=1}^{N} \frac{1}{r_i\mu}, & \text{if all} \quad r_i \neq 0, \\ F_i, & \text{if some} \quad r_i = 0. \end{cases}$$

To determine the value of the surface at a point, this method essentially
all the data points according to their distance from that point.

The problem with Shepard's method is that it is very sensitive to the
μ. For $0 < \mu \leq 1$, the surface f has cusps at the data points. For $1 <$
flat spots at the data points. Thus, to avoid cusps, one needs $1 < \mu$. B
relatively large, then the surface is very flat near the data points, and very
between. In this situation this is undesirable. Note that the usual value f
(see Poeppelmeir, [1975] and Shepard, [1968]).

Other problems with Shepard's method are: first, if N is large, a grea
calculation is required to compute the surface; second, the weights are t
distance, but not on direction, although this can be corrected [Shepard, 19
third, the extremal points of the interpolated surface must lie at the know
(which implies that the cylinder of Figure 5.2 would be incorrectly interp
Of course, this method is a global one. Shepard modifies the method to
local in the following manner.

Fix $0 < R$, and define

$$\psi(r) = \begin{cases} \frac{1}{r}, & 0 < r \leq \frac{R}{3}, \\ \frac{27}{4R}\left(\frac{r}{R} - 1\right)^2, & \frac{R}{3} < r \leq R, \\ 0, & R < r. \end{cases}$$

This function is continuously differentiable, and vanishes identically for j
Now define

$$f(x,y) = \begin{cases} \sum_{i=1}^{N} F_i[\psi(r_i)]^\mu \Big/ \sum_{i=1}^{N} [\psi(r_i)]^\mu, & \text{if all} \quad r_i \neq 0, \\ F_i, & \text{if some} \quad r_i = (\end{cases}$$

This function interpolates the values F_i at the data points, and elsewh
values are weighted averages of the data values which lie at points within
tance R of the point.

0.5 Quasi-interpolants

One way of creating local methods of interpolation and approximatio
apply global methods of small partitions of the domain. There are also
local methods which construct an approximate surface without solving a s
of equations.

then to construct a reproducing kernel K on $D \times D$, so that the surface is explicitly given by the form

$$s(x, y) = \sum_{i=1}^{N} a_i K((x, y); (x_i, y_i)) + \sum_{i=1}^{d} b_i p_i(x, y)$$

where the p_i are a basis for the null space of the norm. The coefficients $\{a_i\}$ and $\{b_i\}$ can be determined by solving a system of linear equations. Examples of this method include Atteia [1966a, 1966b, 1970], Duchon [1975, 1976], Mansfield [1971, 1972a, 1972b, 1974], Schaback [1973, 1974], Thomann [1970a, 1970b].

Spline approximation over gridded data has been extensively studied, with a wide body of literature. Here, the general method is to use the product of B-splines over each rectangular surface patch, together with a set of boundary conditions. Most common is bicubic spline interpolation (the two-dimensional blending of two one-dimensional cubic splines). Examples include Ahlberg, Nilson and Walsh [1965, 1967], Birkhoff and de Boor [1965], Birkhoff and Garabedian [1960], de Boor [1962], Koelling and Whitten [1973], Spath [1969] and Theilheimer and Starkweather [1969].

Many generalizations of the spline problem have been investigated. Some of the methods include Arthur [1974, 1975], Birkhoff, Schultz and Varga [1968], de Boor [1973], Delvos [1975a, 1975b], Delvos and Schempp [1975], Delvos and Schlosser [1974], Fisher and Jerome [1974, 1975], Haussman [1974], Haussman and Munch [1973], Manteanu [1973a, 1973b], Nielson [1970, 1973], Ritter [1969, 1970], Sard [1973, 1974], Schultz [1969a, 1969b], Spath [1971] and Zavialov [1973, 1974a, 1974b].

If we do not require exact interpolation, but only surface approximation, spline methods are also applicable. Let X be a linear space of "smooth" functions, and Θ be a functional on X that measures the smoothness of an element in X. Let E be a functional on X which measures how well a function fits the data. Then the problem is to find $s \in X$ such that

$$\rho(s) = \inf_{u \in X} \rho(u)$$

where

$$\rho(f) = \Theta(f) + E(f),$$

if such an s exists. As in the case of spline interpolation, the general theory of spline approximation may be found in Laurent [1972]. The methods used to find solutions to this problem globally are similar to those used to solve the global spline interpolation problem — constructing a reproducing kernel and solving a system of linear equations to determine the coefficients of the resulting equation for the surface. Examples of this method include Duchon [1975, 1976] and Pivovarova and Puknacheva [1975].

Local spline interpolation has been widely used, Birkhoff and de Boor, [1965]; Birkhoff and Garabedian, [1960]; de Boor, [1962]; Ahlberg, Nilson and Walsh, [1967]; Whitten and Koelling, [1974]; Arthur, [1974, 1975]; Birkhoff, Schultz and Varga, [1968]; Delvos, [1975]; Delvos and Kosters, [1975]; Schultz, [1969a, 1969b]; and many more. In general, given a partition of the domain into regions (defined by a set of knots), a spline function is a collection of functions, each defined on a different portion of the partition, which are pieced together to form the surface and which have continuous derivatives up to some order r. A standard example of a one-dimensional spline is the cubic spline, in which the individual functions are cubic polynomials, and the functions have identical zeroth, first and second order derivatives at the knots. In two dimensions, one can use the product of cubic splines, known as bicubic splines. There are, of course, many other possible functions which can be used besides cubics.

There are a number of problems associated with using splines. The first case concerns the use of interpolating splines, in which the knots are chosen to be the known data points. In order to compute such splines, it is necessary to know the directions of the tangents of the surface at the extreme points. This may not always be possible. As well, if the data are noisy, the interpolating splines usually show strong oscillations, which are not acceptable.

One way around this problem is to chose a partition in which the knots are variable, rather than fixed at the known points. Ideally, one would like to leave them as free parameters to be chosen during an optimization problem. However, this turns out to be a very unpleasant mathematical and computational problem. Whereas the curve fitting problem is linear for fixed knots, the case of variable knots is nonlinear. There are local descent methods for finding the curve iteratively. However, the computational effort required for splines of higher order than linear is prohibitive. (For a further discussion of the use of spline approximations and its problems, see Pavlidis, [1977].)

One final comment about the use of splines concerns the idea of spline blending. These methods are used for constructing surfaces in the case of gridded data. They interpolate not only function values at isolated points, but also along the grid lines themselves. Of course, in our situation, the fact that we are given scattered data makes such methods of little use. Examples of this method include Coons [1967], Barnhill and Reisenfeld [1974] (including many references), Earnshaw and Yuille [1971], Forrest [1972a, 1972b], Ferguson [1964] and Hosaka [1969].

BIBLIOGRAPHY

Abramowitz, M. and Stegun, I.A. *Handbook of Mathematical Functions*, Dover Publications, Inc., New York, 1965.

Agin, G.J. Representation and description of curved objects, Stanford Artificial Intelligence Laboratory, AIM-173, 1972.

Ahlberg, J.H., Nilson, E.N. and Walsh, J.L. "Extremal, orthogonality, and convergence properties of multidimensional splines," *J. Math. Anal. Appl.* **11** (1965), 27-48.

Ahlberg, J.H., Nilson, E.N. and Walsh, J.L. *The Theory of Splines and Their Applications*, Academic Press, New York, 1967.

Akima, H. "A method of bivariate interpolation and smooth surface fitting for irregularly distributed data points," *ACM Trans. on Math. Software* **4**, 2 (1978), 148-159.

Arnold, R.D. "Local context in matching edges for stereo vision," *Proceedings: Image Understanding Workshop, Cambridge, Ma.*, 1978, 65-72.

Arnold, R.D. and Binford, T.O. "Geometric constraints in stereo vision," *Proc. SPIE, San Diego, Ca.*, 1980.

Arrow, K.J. and Hurwicz, L. "Reduction of constrained maxima to saddle-point problems," *Proceedings of the Third Berkeley Symposium on Mathematical Statistics and Probability ed. J. Neyman. Berkeley and Los Angeles: University of California Press*, 1956, 1-20.

Arrow, K.J., Hurwicz, L., and Uzawa, H. *Studies in Linear and Non-linear Programming*, Stanford University Press, Stanford, Ca., 1958.

Arthur, D.W. "Multivariate spline functions, I. Construction, properties, and computation," *J. Approximation Theory* **12** (1974), 396-411.

Arthur, D.W. "Multivariate spline functions, II. Best error bounds," *J. Approximation Theory* **15** (1975), 1-10.

Atteia, M. Etude de certains noyaux et theorie des fonctions (spline) en Analysis Numerique, Univ. of Grenoble, 1966a.

Atteia, M. "Existence et determination des fonctions splines a plusieurs variables," *C. R. Acad. Sci. Paris* **262** (1966b), 575-578.

Atteia, M. "Fonctions (spline) et noyaux reproduisants D'Aronszajn-Bergman," *Rev. Francaise Informat, Recherche Operationnelle 4E Annee* **R-3** (1970), 31-43.

Aziz, A.K. (ed) *The Mathematical Foundations of the Finite Element Method with Applications to Partial Differential Equations* , Academic Press, New York, 1972.

Babuska, I. "Approximation by hill functions," *Comment. Math. Univ. Carolinae* **11**, 4 (1970), 787-811.

Bajcsy, R. Computer identification of textured visual scenes, Stanford Artificial Intelligence Laboratory, AIM-180, 1972.

Bajcsy, R. and Lieberman, L. "Texture gradients as a depth cue," *Computer Graphics and Image Processing* **5** (1976), 52-67.

Baker, H. "Edge-based stereo correlation," *Proceedings: Image Understanding Workshop* , 1980, 168-175.

Baker, H.H. and Binford, T.O. "Depth from edge and intensity based stereo," *Seventh International Joint Conference on Artificial Intelligence* , 1981, 583.

Barlow, H.B., Blakemore, C. and Pettigrew, J.D. "The neural mechanism of binocular depth discrimination," *J. Physiol.* **193** (1967), 327-342.

Barnard, S.T. and Thompson, W.B. "Disparity analysis of images," *IEEE Trans. on Pattern Analysis and Machine Intelligence* **PAMI-2**, 4 (1980), 333-340.

Barnea, D.I. and Silverman, H.F. "A class of algorithms for fast image registration," *IEEE Trans. Comput.* **C-21** (1972), 179-186.

Barnhill, R.E. Birkhoff, G. and Gordon, W.J. "Smooth interpolation in triangles," *J. Approximation Theory* **8** (1973), 114-128.

Barnhill, R.E. and Gregory, J.A. Blending function interpolation to boundary data on triangles, Department of Math. Brunel Univ., TR 14, 1972.

Barnhill, R.E. and Gregory, J.A. "Compatible smooth interpolation in triangles," *J. Approximation Theory* **15** (1975), 214-225.

Barnhill, R.E. and Mansfield, L. "Error bounds for smooth interpolation in triangles," *J. Approximation Theory* **11** (1974), 306-318.

Barnhill, R.E. and Riesenfeld, R.F. *Computer Aided Geometric Design* , Academic Press, New York, 1974.

Barrow, H.G. and Tenenbaum, J.M. "Recovering intrinsic scene characteristics from images," *in Computer Vision Systems, A.R. Hanson and E.M. Riseman (eds), Academic Press, New York* (1978).

Barrow, H.G. and Tenenbaum, J.M. "Interpreting line drawings as three-dimensional surfaces," *Artificial Intelligence (Special Issue on Computer Vision)* **17** (1981).

Beck, J. and Schwartz, T. "Vernier acuity with test dot objects," *Vision Research* **19** (1978), 313-319.

Berry, R.N. "Quantitative relations among vernier, real depth, and stereoscopic depth acuities," *J. Exp. Psychol.* **38** (1948), 708-721.

Binford, T.O. "Spatial Understanding," *Proceedings: Image Understanding Workshop, Palo Alto, Cal.* , 1979, 4-11.

Birkhoff, G. and de Boor, C. "Piecewise polynomial interpolation and approximation," *Approximation of Functions, H.L. Garabedian, ed., Elsevier, Amsterdam* (1965), 164-190.

Birkhoff, G. and Garabedian, H. "Smooth surface interpolation," *J. Math. Phys.* **39** (1960), 258-268.

Birkhoff, G. and Mansfield, L. "Compatible triangular finite elements," *J. Math. Anal. Appl.* **47** (1974), 531-553.

Birkhoff, G., Schultz, M.H. and Varga, R.S. "Piecewise Hermite interpolation in one and two variables with applications to partial differential equations," *Numer. Math.* **11** (1968), 232-256.

Bishop, P.O., Henry, G.H. and Smith, C.J. "Binocular interaction fields of single units in the cat striate cortex," *J. Physiol.* **216** (1971), 39-68.

de Boor, C. "Bicubic spline interpolation," *J. Math. and Phys.* **41** (1962), 212-218.

de Boor, C. "On calculating with B-splines," *J. Approximation Theory* **6** (1972), 50-62.

de Boor, C. (ed) *Mathematical Aspects of Finite Elements in Partial Differential Equations* , Academic Press, New York, 1975.

de Boor, C. and Fix, G.J. "Spline approximation by quasi-interpolants," *J. Approximation Theory* **8** (1975), 19-45.

Braddick, O. Multiple matching in stereopsis, unpublished MIT report, 1978.

Brady, J.M., Grimson, W.E.L. and Langridge, D.J. "Shape encoding and subjective contours," *Proceedings of the First AIII Conference*, 1980.

Brady, J.M and Horn, B.K.P "Rotationally symmetric operators for surface interpolation," (1981), to appear.

Bramble, J. and Zlamal, M. "Triangular elements in the finite element method," *Math. Comp.* 24 (1970), 809-820.

Braunstein, M.L. *Depth Perception Through Motion*, Academic Press, London, 1976.

Brewster, D. *The Stereoscope*, John Murray, London, 1856.

Brigner, W.I. and Gallagher, M.B. "Subjective contour: Apparent depth or simultaneous brightness contrast?," *Perceptual and Motor Skills* 38 (1974), 1047-1053.

Brucke, E. "Uber die stereoskopischen Erscheinungen," *J. Muller's Archiv für Anat. und Physiol.* (1841), 259.

Burr, D.C. "Acuity for apparent vernier offset," *Vision Research* 19 (1979), 835-837.

Burr, D.J. and Chien, R.T. "A system for stereo computer vision with geometric models," *Fifth International Joint Conference on Artificial Intelligence*, 1977, 583.

Cadwell, J.H. and Williams, D.E. "Some orthogonal methods of curve and surface fitting," *Computer Journal* 4 (1961).

Campbell, F.W. and Robson, J.G. "Applications of Fourier analysis to the visibility of gratings," *J. Physiol. (Lond.)* 197 (1968), 551-556.

Cavendish, J. C. "Automatic triangulation of arbitrary planar domains for the finite element method," *Int. J. for Numer. Methods in Engineering* 8 (1974), 697-696.

Ciarlet, P.G. and Raviart, P.A. "Interpolation de Lagrange dans $\Re^n$," *C. R. Acad. Sci. Paris Ser.* A273 (1971), 578-581.

Ciarlet, P.G. and Raviart, P.A. "General Lagrange and Hermite interpolation in $\Re^N$ with applications to finite element methods.," *Arch. Rational Mech. Anal.* 46 (1972a), 177-199.

Ciarlet, P.G. and Raviart, P.A. "Interpolation de Lagrange sur des elements finis courbes dans $\Re^n$," *C. R. Acad. Sci. Paris Ser.* A274 (1972b), 640-643.

Ciarlet, P.G. and Raviart, P.A. "Interpolation theory over curved elements with applications to finite element methods," *Comp. Meth. Appl. Mech. Eng.* 1 (1972c), 217-249.

Clarke, P. G. H., Donaldson, I. M. L. and Whitteridge, D. "Binocular mechanisms in cortical areas I and II of the sheep," *J. Physiol. (Lond.)* 256 (1979), 509-526.

Collatz, L. "Uber die konvergenzkriterien bei iterationsverfahren fur lineare gleichungssysteme," *Math. Z.* 53 (1950), 149-161.

Coons, S.A. Surfaces for computer-aided design of space forms, MIT Project MAC, TR 41, 1967.

Coren, S. "Subjective contours and apparent depth," *Psychological Review* 79, 4 (1972), 359-367.

Coren, S. and Theodor, L.H. "Subjective contour: the inadequacy of brightness contrast as an explanation," *Bulletin of the Psychonomic Society* 6 (1975), 87-89.

Cornsweet, T.N. *Visual Perception*, Academic Press, New York, NY., 1970.

Courant, R. and Hilbert D. *Methods of Mathematical Physics, Volume I*, Interscience Publishers, Inc., New York, 1953.

Crain, I.K. and Bhattacharyya, B.K. "Treatment of non-equispaced two-dimensional data with a digital computer," *Geoexploration* 5 (1967), 173-194.

Crick, F.H.C., Marr, D. and Poggio, T. "An information processing approach to understanding the visual cortex," *in The Cerebral Cortex, Neurosciences Research Program* (1980).

Davis, J.C. *Interpolation and Approximation*, Blaisdell, New York, N.Y., 1963.

Davis, L. "A survey of edge detection techniques," *Computer Graphics and Image Processing* 4 (1975), 248-270.

Delvos, F.J. "On surface interpolation," *J. Approximation Theory* 15 (1975), 129-137.

Delvos, F.J. and Kosters, H.W. "On the variational characterization of bivariate interpolation methods," *Math. Z.* 145 (1975), 129-137.

Delvos, F.J. and Schempp, W. "Sard's method and the theory of spline systems," *J. Approximation Theory* 14 (1975), 230-243.

Delvos, F.J. and Schlosser, K.H. "Das tensorproduktschema von spline systemen," *in Splinefunktionen, K. Bohmer, G. Meinardus, and W. Schempp, (eds.), Bibliographisches Institut, Zurich* (1974), 59-74.

Dev, P. "Perception of depth surfaces in random-dot stereograms: a neural model," *Int. J. Man-Machine Studies* 7 (1975), 511-528.

Duchon, J. Fonctions-spline du type plaque mince en dimension 2, Univ. of Grenoble, Rpt. 231, 1975.

Duchon, J. Fonctions-spline a energie invariante par rotation, Univ. of Grenoble, Rpt. 27, 1976.

Earnshaw, J.L., and Yuille, I.M. "A method of fitting parametric equations for curves and surfaces to sets of points defining them approximately," *Computer Aided Design* 3 (1971), 19-22.

Effroymson, M.A. "Multiple regression analysis," *in Mathematical Methods for Digital Computers, A. Ralston and H. Wilff (eds.) Wiley, New York* (1960), 191-203.

Evans, C.R. and Clegg, J.M. "Binocular depth perception of Julesz patterns viewed as perfectly stabilized images," *Nature* 215 (1967), 893-895.

Felton, T.B., Richards, W. and Smith, R.A. Jr. "Disparity processing of spatial frequencies in man," *J. Physiol.* 225 (1972), 349-362.

Fender, D. and Julesz, B. "Extension of Panum's fusional area in binocularly stabilized vision," *J. Opt. Soc. Am.* 57 (1967), 819-830.

Ferguson, J. "Multivariable curve interpolation," *J. Assoc. Comput. Mach.* 11 (1964), 221-228.

Fisher, S.D. and Jerome, J.W. "Elliptic variational problems in L^2 and L^∞," *Indiana J. Math.* 23 (1974), 685-698.

Fisher, S.D. and Jerome, J.W. "Spline solutions to L^1 extremal problems in one and several variables," *J. Approximation Theory* 13 (1975), 73-83.

Fix, G. and Strang, G. "Fourier analysis of the finite element method in Ritz-Galerkin theory," *Studies in Appl. Math.* 48 (1969), 265-273.

Forrest, A.R. "On Coons and other methods for the representation of curved surfaces," *Computer Graphics and Image Processing* 1 (1972a), 341-359.

Forrest, A.R. "Interactive interpolation and approximation by Bezier polynomials," *Computer Journal* 15, 1 (1972b), 71-79.

Forsyth, A.R. *Calculus of Variations*, Dover Publications, Inc., New York, 1960.

Forsythe, G. and Wasow, W. *Finite-difference Methods for Partial Differential Equations*, John Wiley and Sons, New York, 1960.

Frederickson, P.O. "Quasi-interpolation, extrapolation, and approximation on the plane," *Conf. Numerical Math.*, Winnipeg, 1971, 159-167.

Frisby, J. P. and Clatworthy, J. L. "Learning to see complex random-dot stereograms," *Perception* 4 (1975), 173-178.

Gennery, D.B. "A stereo vision system for an autonomous vehicle," *Fifth International Joint Conference on Artificial Intelligence, Cambridge*, 1977, 576-582.

Gibson, J.J. *The Perception of the Visual World*, Houghton Mifflin, Boston, 1950a.

Gibson, J.J. "The perception of visual surfaces," *American Journal of Psychology* 63 (1950b), 367-384.

Gibson, J.J. *The Senses Considered as Perceptual Systems*, Houghton Mifflin, Boston, 1966.

Goel, J.J. "Construction of basic functions for numerical utilization of Ritz's method," *Numer. Math.* 12 (1968), 435-447.

Gregory, R.L. "Cognitive contours," *Nature* 238 (1972), 51-52.

Gregory, R.L. and Harris, J.P. "Illusory contours and stereo depth," *Perception and Psychopysics* 15, 3 (1974), 411-416.

Grimson, W.E.L. A computer implementation of a theory of human stereo vision, MIT Artificial Intelligence Laboratory, Memo 565, 1980a.

Grimson, W.E.L. Computing shape using a theory of human stereo vision, Ph.D. Thesis, Department of Mathematics, Massachusetts Institute of Technology, 1980b.

Grimson, W.E.L. "A computer implementation of a theory of human stereo vision," *Phil. Trans. Royal Society of London, B.* 292 (1981a), 217-253.

Grimson, W.E.L. A computational theory of visual surface interpolation, MIT Artificial Intelligence Laboratory, Memo 613, 1981b.

Grimson, W.E.L. and Marr, D. "A computer implementation of a theory of human stereo vision," *Proceedings: Image Understanding Workshop*, Palo Alto, Cal., 1979, 41-47.

Guenther, R.B. and Roetman, E.L. "Some observations on interpolation in higher dimensions," *Math. Comp.* **24** (1970), 517-522.

Gulick, W.L. and Lawson, R.B. *Human Stereopsis: A Psychophysical Analysis* , Oxford University Press, New York, 1976.

Haber, R.N. & Hershenson, M. *The psychology of visual perception* , Holt, Rinehart, and Winston, New York, 1973.

Hannah, M.J. Computer matching of areas in stereo images, Stanford Artificial Intelligence Laboratory, AIM-239, 1974.

Hall, C.A. "Bicubic interpolation over triangles," *J. Math. Mech.* **19** (1969), 1-11.

Haussman, W. "On multivariate spline systems," *J. Approximation Theory* **11** (1974), 285-305.

Haussman, W. and Munch, H.J. "On construction of multivariate spline systems," *in Approximation Theory, G.G. Lorentz, (ed.), Academic Press, New York* (1973), 373-378.

Hayes, J.G. and Halliday, J. "The least squares fitting of cubic spline surfaces to general data sets," *J. Inst. Math. Applic.* **14** (1974), 89-103.

Helmholtz, H. *Physiological Optics, Vol. 3* , Optical Society of America, New York, 1925.

Hildreth, E.C. Implementation of a theory of edge detection, S.M. Thesis, Department of Computer Science and Electrical Engineering, Massachusetts Institute of Technology, 1980.

Hirai, Y. and Fukushima, K. "An inference upon the neural network finding binocular correspondence," *Trans. IECE* **J59-d** (1976), 133-140.

Horn, B.K.P. Focusing, MIT Artificial Intelligence Laboratory, Memo 160, 1968.

Horn, B.K.P. Shape from shading: a method for obtaining the shape of a smooth opaque object from one view, MIT Project MAC Technical Report, MAC TR-79, 1970.

Horn, B.K.P. "Obtaining shape from shading information," *The Psychology of Computer Vision, P.H. Winston (ed), McGraw-Hill* (1975), 115-155.

Horn, B.K.P. "Understanding image intensities," *Artificial Intelligence* **8** (1977), 201-231.

Horn, B.K.P. and Bachman, B.L. Using synthetic images to register real images with surface models, MIT Artificial Intelligence Laboratory, Memo 437, 1977.

Horn, B.K.P. and Sjoberg, R.W. Calculating the reflectance map, 1979, 1770-1779.

Hosaka, M. "Theory of curve and surface synthesis and their smooth fitting," *Information Processing in Japan* **9** (1969), 60-68.

Howard, J.H. "A test for the judgement of distance," *Am. J. Ophthal.* **2** (1919), 656-675.

Hubel, D.H. and Weisel, T.N. "Receptive fields, binocular interaction and functional architecture in the cat's visual cortex," *J. Physiol. (Lond.)* **160** (1962), 385-398.

Hubel, D.H. and Weisel, T.N. "Receptive fields and functional architecture of monkey striate cortex," *J. Physiol. (Lond.)* **195** (1968), 215-243.

Hubel, D.H. and Weisel, T.N. "Cells sensitive to binocular depth in area 18 of the Macaque monkey cortex," *Nature* **225** (1970), 41-42.

Hubel, D.H. and Weisel, T.N. "A reexamination of stereoscopic mechanisms in area 17 of the cat," *J. Physiol.* **232** (1973), 29-30.

Huffman, D.A. "Impossible objects as nonsense sentences," *Machine Intelligence 6, B. Meltzer and D. Michie (eds), Edinburgh University Press* (1971), 295-393.

Hummel, R.A. and Zucker, S.W. On the foundations of relaxation labeling processes, Computer Vision and Graphics Lab., McGill University, TR-80-7, 1980.

Ikeuchi, K. Numerical shape from shading and occluding contours in a single view, MIT Artificial Intelligence Laboratory, Memo 566, 1979.

Ikeuchi, K. Shape from regular patterns (an example of constraint propagation in vision), MIT Artificial Intelligence Laboratory, Memo 567, 1980.

Jacobi, C.G.J. "Ueber eine neue auflosungsart der bei der methode der kleinsten quadrate vorkommenden linearen gleichungen," *Astr. Nachr.* **22** (1845), 297-306.

Johansson, G. "Perception of motion and changing form," *Scandinavian Journal of Psychology* **5** (1964), 181-208.

Johansson, G. "Visual motion perception," *Scientific American* **232**, 6 (1975), 76-88.

Julesz, B. "Binocular depth perception of computer-generated patterns," *Bell System Tech. J.* **39** (1960), 1125-1162.

Julesz, B. "Towards the automation of binocular depth perception (AUTOMAP-1)," *Bell System Tech. J.* (1963a).

Julesz, B. "Stereopsis and binocular rivalry of contours," *J. Opt. Soc. Am.* **53** (1963b), 994-999.

Julesz, B. *Foundations of Cyclopean Perception*, The University of Chicago Press, Chicago, 1971.

Julesz, B. and Chang, J.J. "Interaction between pools of binocular disparity detectors tuned to different disparities," *Biol. Cybernetics* **22** (1976), 107-120.

Julesz, B. and Miller, J.E. "Independent spatial-frequence-tuned channels in binocular fusion and rivalry," *Perception* **4** (1975), 125-143.

Kahan, W. Gauss-Seidel methods of solving large systems of linear equations, University of Toronto, 1958.

Kahl, D.J., Rosenfeld, A. and Danker, A. Some experiments in point pattern matching, University of Maryland Technical Report, TR-690, 1978.

Kamal al-Din Abul-Hasan al-Farisi *Kitab al-basair fiiilm al-manazir (Book of Reflexions on the Science of Optics)*, (from The Vertegrate Visual System, S. Polyak, Univ. of Chicago Press, 1957), 1433.

Kanizsa, G. "Subjective contours," *Scientific American* **234**, 4 (1976), 48-52.

Kaufman, L. "On the nature of binocular disparity," *Am. J. Psychol.* **77** (1964), 393-40.

Kender, J.R. "Shape from texture: a brief overview and a new aggregation transform," *Proceedings: Image Understanding Workshop*, 1978.

Kender, J.R. Shape from texture, Ph.D. Thesis, Department of Computer Science, Carnegie-Mellon Univ., Pittsburgh, 1979.

Kidd, A.L., Frisby, J.P., and Mayhew, J.E.W. "Texture contours can facilitate stereopsis by initiating appropriate vergence eye movements," *Nature* **280** (1979), 829-832.

Knight, T.F., Moon, D.A., Holloway, J. and Steele, G.L. CADR, MIT Artificial Intelligence Laboratory, Memo 528, 1979.

Koelling, M.E.V. and Whitten, E.H.T. "Fortran IV program for spline surface interpolation and contour map production," *Geocomprograms* **9** (1973), 1-12.

Koffka, K. *Principles of Gestalt Psychology*, Harcourt, Brace and Co., New York, 1935.

Kuhn, H.W. and Tucker, A.W. "Nonlinear Programming," *Proceedings of the Second Berkeley Symposium on Mathematical Statistics and Probability ed. J. Neyman. Berkeley and Los Angeles: University of California Press* , Berkeley, Cal., 1951, 481-492.

Kunz, K.S. *Numerical Analysis* , McGraw-Hill, New York, 1957.

Laurent, P.J. *Approximation et Optimisation* , Hermann, Paris, 1972.

Lawson, C. Generation of a triangular grid with applications to contour plotting, JPL, T.M. 299, 1972.

Lawson, R.B. and Gulick, W.L. "Stereopsis and anomalous contour," *Vision Res.* 7 (1967), 271-297.

Leadbetter, M.R. "On the distributions of times between events in a stationary stream of events.," *J. R. Statist. Soc. B* 31 (1969), 295-302.

Leipnik, R. "The extended entropy uncertainty principle," *Inform. and Control* 3 (1960), 18-25.

Levine, M.D., O'Handley, D.A. and Yagi, G.M. "Computer determination of depth maps," *Computer Graphics and Image Processing* 2 (1973), 131-150.

Lewis, R.A. and Johnston, A.R. "A scanning laser rangefinder for a robotic vehicle," *Proceedings of the Fifth International Joint Conference on Artificial Intelligence* , Cambridge, Mass., 1977, 762-768.

Lillestrand, R.L. "Techniques of change detection," *IEEE Trans. Comput.* C-21, 7 (1972), 654-659.

Longuet-Higgins, M.S. "The distribution of intervals between zeros of a stationary random function.," *Phil. Trans. R. Soc. Lond. A* 254 (1962), 557-599.

Longuet-Higgins, H.C. and Pradzny, K. "The interpretation of moving retinal images," *Proc. R. Soc. Lond., B* (1981), in press.

Luenberger, D.G. *Introduction to Linear and Nonlinear Programming* , Addison-Wesley Publishing Co., Reading, Mass., 1973.

Lyche, T., and Schumaker, L. "Local spline approximation methods," *J. Approximation Theory* 15 (1975), 294-325.

Mackworth, A.K. "Interpreting pictures of polyhedral scenes," *Artificial Intelligence* 4, 2 (1973), 121-137.

Mansfield, L.E. "On the optimal approximation of linear functionals in spaces of bivariate functions," *SIAM J. Numer. Anal.* 8 (1971), 115-126.

Mansfield, L.E. "On the variational characterization and convergence of bivariate splines," *Numer. Math.* **20** (1972a), 99-114.

Mansfield, L.E. "Optimal approximation and error bounds in spaces of bivariate functions," *J. Approximation Theory* **5** (1972b), 77-96.

Mansfield, L.E. "On the variational approach to defining splines on L-shaped regions," *J. Approximation Theory* **12** (1974), 99-112.

Mansfield, L.E. "Interpolation to boundary data in triangles with application to compatible finite elements," *Approximation Theory II, ed. G.G. Lorentz, C.K. Chui, L.L. Schumaker, Academic Press* (1976).

Marr, D. "A theory of cerebellar cortex," *J. Physiol.* **202** (1969), 437-470.

Marr, D. A note on the computation of binocular disparity in a symbolic, low-level visual processor, MIT Artificial Intelligence Laboratory, Memo 327, 1974.

Marr, D. "Artificial Intelligence – a personal view," *Artificial Intelligence* **9** (1976a), 37-48.

Marr, D. "Early processing of visual information," *Phil. Trans. R. Soc. Lond.* **275**, 942 (1976b), 483-534.

Marr, D. "Analysis of occluding contour," *Proc. R. Soc. Lond. B* **197** (1977), 441-475.

Marr, D. "Representing visual information," *AAS 143rd Annual Meeting, Symposium on Some Mathematical Questions in Biology, February 1977. Published in Lectures in the Life Sciences* **10** (1978), 101-180.

Marr, D. *VISION: A computational investigation in the human representation and processing of visual information*, W.H. Freeman, San Francisco, 1981.

Marr, D. and Hildreth, E.C. "Theory of edge detection," *Proc. R. Soc. Lond. B* **207** (1980), 187-217.

Marr, D. and Nishihara, H.K. "Representation and recognition of the spatial organization of three-dimensional shapes," *Proc. R. Soc. Lond. B.* **200** (1978), 269-294.

Marr, D. and Poggio, T. "From understanding computation to understanding neural circuitry," *Neuroscience Research Program Bulletin* **15**, 3 (1977a), 470-488.

Marr, D. and Poggio, T. "Cooperative computation of stereo disparity," *Science* **195** (1977b), 283-287.

Marr, D. and Poggio, T. "A theory of human stereo vision," *Proc. R. Soc. Lond. B* **204** (1979), 301-328.

Marr, D. and Poggio, T. Some comments on a recent theory of stereopsis, MIT AI Lab, Memo 558, 1980.

Marr, D., Poggio, T. and Hildreth, E. "The smallest channel in early human vision," *J. Opt. Soc. Am.* **70**, 7 (1979), 868-870.

Marr, D. and Ullman, S. "Directional selectivity and its use in early visual processing," *Proc. Roy. Soc. Lond., B* (1980), in press.

Mayhew, J. E. W. and Frisby, J. P. "Rivalrous texture stereograms," *Nature* **264** (1976), 53-56.

Mayhew, J. E. W. and Frisby, J. P. "Stereopsis masking in humans is not orientationally tuned," *Perception* 7 (1978a), 431-436.

Mayhew, J.E.W. and Frisby, J.P. "Relative depth discriminations in narrow-band-filtered random-dot stereograms," *Vision Res.* (1978b).

Mayhew, J. E. W. and Frisby, J. P. "Convergent disparity discriminations in narrow-band-filtered random-dot stereograms," *Vision Res.* **19** (1979), 63-71.

Mayhew, J.E.W. and Frisby, J.P. "Psychophysical and computational studies towards a theory of human stereopsis," *Artificial Intelligence (Special Issue on Computer Vision)* **17** (1981).

Mersereau, R.M. and Oppenheim, A.V. "Digital reconstruction of multi-dimensional signals from their projections," *Proc. IEEE* **62** (1974), 1319-1338.

Miles, W.R. "Movement interpretations of the silhouette of a revolving fan," *American Journal of Psychology* **43** (1931), 392-505.

Milne, W.E. *Numerical Solution of Differential Equations* , Dover Publications, Inc., New York, 1970.

Mitchell, A.R. "Introduction to the mathematics of finite elements," *in The Mathematics of Finite Elements, Academic Press, London* (1973), 37-58.

Mitchell, A.R. and Phillips, G.M. "Construction of basis functions in the finite element method," *Nord. Tidskr. Inform. BIT* **12** (1972), 81-89.

Moravec, H.P. "Towards automatic visual obstacle avoidance," *Fifth International Joint Conference on Artificial Intelligence, Cambridge* , 1977, 584.

Moravec, H.P. "Visual mapping by a robot rover," *Sixth International Joint Conference on Artificial Intelligence, Tokyo* , 1979, 598-600.

Mori, K., Kidode, M. and Asada, H. "An iterative prediction and correction method for automatic stereocomparison," *Computer Graphics and Image Processing* 2 (1973), 393-401.

Muller, J. *Zur vergleichenden Physiologie des gesichtssinnes des Menshen und der Thiere* , Cnoblock, Leipzig, 1826.

Munteanu, M.J. "Generalized smoothing spline functions for operators," *SIAM J. Numer. Anal.* 10 (1973), 28-34.

Munteanu, M.J. "On the construction of multidimensional splines," *in Spline Functions and Approximation Theory, A. Meir and A. Sharma, (eds.), ISNM 21, Birkhauser* (1973), 235-265.

Munteanu, M.J. and Schumaker, L.L. "Some multidimensional spline approximation methods," *J. Approximation Theory* 10 (1974), 23-40.

Nelson, J.I "Globality and stereoscopic fusion in binocular vision," *J. Theor. Biol.* 49 (1975), 1-88.

Nelson, J.I., Kato, H. and Bishop, P.O. "Discrimination of orientation and position disparities by binocularly activated neurons in cat striate cortex," *J. Neurophysiol.* 40 (1977), 260-283.

Nevatia, R. "Depth measurement by motion stereo," *Computer Graphics and Image Processing* 5 (1976), 203-214.

Nicodemus, F.E., Richmond, J.C., Hsia, J.J., Ginsberg, I.W. and Limperis, T. Geometrical considerations and nomenclature for reflectance, National Bureau of Standards. NBS Monograph 160, 1977.

Nicoliades, R.A. "On the class of finite elements generated by Lagrange interpolation," *SIAM J. Numer. Anal.* 9 (1972), 435-445.

Nicoliades, R.A. "On the class of finite elements generated by Lagrange interpolation, II," *SIAM J. Numer. Anal.* 10 (1973), 182-189.

Nielson, G.M. "Bivariate spline functions and the approximation of linear functionals," *Numer. Math.* 21 (1973), 138-160.

Nielson, G.M. Surface approximation and data smoothing using generalized spline functions, Univ. of Utah, 1970.

Nikara, T., Bishop, P.O. and Pettigrew, J.D. "Analysis of retinal correspondence by studying receptive fields of binocular single units in cat striate cortex," *Exp. Brain Res.* 6 (1968), 353-372.

O'Brien, B. "Vision and resolution in the central retina," *J. Opt. Soc. Am.* **41** (1951), 882-894.

Ogle, K.N. "Theory of stereoscopic vision" In *Psychology: A Study of a Science,* Vol. 1, S. Koch (ed), 362-394 , McGraw-Hill, New York, 1959.

Panum, P.L. *Physiological investigations concerning vision with two eyes* , Schwering's Bookstore, Kiel, 1858 (Translated by C. Hubscher, Darmouth Eye Institute, Hanover, N.H., 1940).

Pavlidis, T. *Structural Pattern Recognition* , Springer-Verlag, Berlin, 1977.

Pelto, C., Elkins, T. and Boyd, H. "Automatic contouring of irregularly spaced data," *Geophysics* 33 (1968), 424-430.

Pettigrew, J.D., Nikara, T. and Bishop, P.O. "Binocular interaction on single units in cat striate cortex: simultaneous stimulation by single moving slit with receptive fields in correspondence," *Exp. Brain Res.* 6 (1968), 391-410.

Pivovarova, N.B., and Puknacheva, T.B. "Smoothing experimental data with local splines," *Sem. Num. Methods of Applied Mathematics* , Novosibirsk, 1975.

Poeppelmeir, C. A Boolean sum interpolation scheme to random data for computer aided geometric design, Univ. Of Utah, 1975.

Poggio, G.F. and Fischer, B. "Binocular interaction and depth sensitivity of striate and prestriate cortical neurons of the behaving rhesus monkey," *J. Neurophysiol.* 40 (1978), 1392-1405.

Pratt, W. *Digitial Image Processing* , John Wiley and Sons, New York, 1978.

Prenter, P.M. *Splines and Variational Methods* , Wiley-Interscience, New York, 1975.

Price, K. and Reddy, D.R. "Change detection and analysis in multispectral images," *Fifth International Joint Conference on Artificial Intelligence, Cambridge, Ma.* , 1977, 619-625.

Purdy, W.C. "The hypothesis of psychophysical correspondence in space perception," *General Electric Technical Information Series, No. R60ELC56* (1960).

Quam, L.H. Computer comparison of pictures, Stanford Artificial Intelligence Laboratory, AIM-144, 1971.

Rabinowitz, P. "Applications of linear programming to numerical analysis," *SIAM Rev.* 10 (1968), 121-159.

Rabinowitz, P. "Mathematical programming and approximation," *Approximation Theory, A. Talbot (ed), Academic Press, London* (1970), 271-231.

Rashbass, C. and Westheimer, G. "Disjunctive eye movements," *J. Physiol. Lond.* **159** (1961), 339-360.

Reich, E. "On the convergence of the classical iterative method of solving linear simultaneous equations," *Ann. Math. Statis.* **20** (1949), 448-451.

Rice, S.O. "Mathematical analysis of random noise.," *Bell Syst. Tech. J.* **24** (1945), 46-156.

Richards, W. "Stereopsis and stereoblindness," *Exp. Brain Res.* **10** (1970), 380-388.

Richards, W. "Anomalous steroscopic depth perception," *J. Opt. Soc. Amer.* **61** (1971), 410-414.

Richards, W. "Visual space perception," *Chapter 10 of Handbook of Perception, Vol. 5, Seeing. Eds. E.C. Carterette and M.D. Freidman. New York: Academic Press* (1975), 351-386.

Richards, W. "Stereopsis with and without monocular cues," *Vision Res.* **17** (1977), 967-969.

Richards, W.A. and Polit, A. "Texture Matching," *Kybernetik* **16** (1974), 155-162.

Richards, W.A. and Regan, D. "A stereo field map with implications for disparity processing," *Investigative Ophthalmology* **12** (1973), 904-909.

Richter, J. and Ullman, S. A model for the spatio–temporal organization of X and Y–type ganglion cells in the primate retina, MIT Artificial Intelligence Laboratory, Memo 573, 1980.

Riggs, L. A. and Niehl, E. W. "Eye movements recorded during convergence and divergence," *J. Opt. Soc. Am.* **50** (1960), 913-920.

Ritter, K. "Two-dimensional splines and their extremal properties," *Z. Agnew. Math. Mech.* **49** (1969), 597-608.

Ritter, K. "Two-dimensional spline functions and best approximations of linear functionals," *J. Approximation Theory* **3** (1970), 352-368.

Rosen, J.B. "Minimum error bounds for multidimensional spline approximation," *J. Comput. System Sci.* **5** (1971), 430-452.

Rosenfeld, A. and Kak, A. *Digital Picture Processing*, Academic Press, New York, 1976.

Rosinski, R.R. "On the ambiguity of visual stimulation: A reply to Eriksson," *Perception and Psychophysics* 16 (1974), 259–263.

Rudin, W. *Functional Analysis*, McGraw-Hill Book Company, New York, 1973.

Sard, A. "Approximation based on nonscalar observations," *J. Approximation Theory* 8 (1973), 315-334.

Sard, A. "Instances of generalized splines," *in Splinefunctionen, K. Bohmer, G. Meinardus, W. Schempp, (eds.), Bibliographisches Institut, Mannheim* (1974), 215-241.

Saye, A. and Frisby, J. P. "The role of monocularly conspicuous features in facilitating stereopsis from random-dot stereograms," *Perception* 4 (1975), 159-171.

Schaback, R. "Konstruktion und algebraische eigenschaften von M-spline interpolierenden," *Numer. Math.* 21 (1973), 166-180.

Schaback, R. "Kollakation mit mehrdimensionalen spline-funktionen," *Numerische Behandlung nichtlinearer Integrodifferential und Differentialgleichungen, R. Ansorge and W. Tornig, eds., Lecture Notes 395., Springer-Verlag, Heidelberg* (1974), 291-300.

Schultz, M.H. "L-infinity-multivariate approximation theory," *SIAM J. Numer. Anal.* 6 (1969a), 161-183.

Schultz, M.H. "Multivariate L-spline interpolation," *J. Approximation Theory* 2 (1969b), 127-135.

Schumaker, L. L. "Fitting surfaces to scattered data," *Approximation Theory II, ed. G.G. Lorentz, C.K. Chui, L.L. Schumaker, Academic Press* (1976), 203-268.

Schumann, F. "Einige beobachtungen uber die zusammenfassung von gesichtseindrucken zu einheiten," *Psychologische Studien* 1 (1904), 1-32.

Schwartz, E.L. "Afferent geometry in the primate visual cortex and the generation of neuronal trigger features," *Biol. Cybernetics* 28 (1977), 1-14.

Seidel, L. "Ueber ein verfahren, die gleichungen, auf welche die methode der kleinsten quadrate fuhrt, sowie lineare gleichungen uberhaupt, durch successive annaherung aufzulosen," *Abh. Math.-Phys. Kl., Bayerische Akad. Wiss Munchen* 11 (III) (1874), 81-108.

Shepard, D. "A two-dimensional interpolation function for irregularly spaced data," *Proc. 1968 ACM Nat. Conf.*, 1968, 517-524.

Shirai, Y. and Suwa, M. "Recognition of polyhedrons with a range finder," *Second International Joint Conference on Artificial Intelligence, London* , 1971.

Silver, W. Determining shape and reflectance using multiple images, S.M. Thesis, Department of Electrical Engineering and Computer Science, Massachusetts Institute of Technology, 1980.

Spath, H. "Algorithmus 10-zweidimensionale glatte interpolation," *Computing* 4 (1969), 178-182.

Spath, H. "Two-dimensional exponential splines," *Computing* 7 (1971), 364-369.

Sperling, G. "Binocular vision: a physical and a neural theory," *Am. J. Psychol.* 83 (1970), 461-534.

Steffensen, J.F. *Interpolation* , Williams and Wilkins, Baltimore, Md., 1927.

Stevens, K.A. Surface perception from local analysis of texture and contour, MIT Artificial Intelligence Laboratory , TR 512, 1979.

Strang, G. and Fix, J. *An Analysis of the Finite Element Method* , Prentice-Hall, Englewood Cliffs, N.J., 1973.

Sugie, N. and Suwa, M. "A scheme for binocular depth perception suggested by neurophysiological evidence," *Biol. Cybernetics* 26 (1977), 1-15.

Sutro, L.L. and Lerman, J.B. Robot vision, Draper Laboratories, Cambridge, Ma., Report R-635, 1973.

Tanimoto, S.L. "A comparison of some image searching methods," *Proc. IEEE Comput. Soc. Conf. Pattern Recognition and Image Processing, Chicago* , 1978, 280-286.

Thacher, H.C.,Jr. "Derivation of interpolation formulas in several independent variables," *Annal. of the New York Acad. of Sciences* 86 (1960), 758-775.

Thacher, H.C.,Jr. and Milne, W.E. "Interpolation in several variables," *SIAM J. Appl. Math.* 8 (1960), 33-42.

Theilheimer, F. and Starkweather, W. "The fairing of ship lines on a high-speed computer," *Math. Comp.* 15 (1961), 338-355.

Thomann, J. Determination et construction de fonctions spline a deux variables defines sur un domaine rectangulaire ou circulaire, Univ. of Lille, 1970a.

Thomann, J. "Obtention de la fonction spline d'interpolation a deux variables sur un domaine rectangulaire ou circulaire," *Proc. Algol en analyse Numerique II* , Centre National de la Recherche Scientifique, Paris, 1970b, 83-94.

Tyler, C.W. "Spatial limitations of human stereoscopic vision," *SPIE* **120** (1977).

Ullman, S. "Filling in the gaps: The shape of subjective contours and a model for their generation," *Biol. Cybernetics* **25** (1976), 1-6.

Ullman, S. *The Interpretation of Visual Motion* , MIT Press, Cambridge, Ma., 1979a.

Ullman, S. "Relaxation and constrained optimization by local processes," *Computer Graphics and Image Processing* **10** (1979b), 115-125.

Wallach, H. "The perception of motion," *Scientific American* **210** (1959), 56-60.

Wallach, H. and O'Connell, D.N. "The kinetic depth effect," *J. Exp. Psych.* **52**, 5 (1953), 571-578.

Westheimer, G. "Diffraction theory and visual hyperacuity," *Am. J. Optometry and Physiol. Optics* **53** (1976), 362-364.

Westheimer, G. "Spatial frequency and light-spread descriptions of visual acuity and hyperacuity," *J. Opt. Soc. Am.* **67** (1977), 207-212.

Westheimer, G. and McKee, S. "Visual acuity in the presence of retinal image motion," *J. Opt. Soc. Am.* **65** (1975), 847-850.

Westheimer, G. and McKee, S. "Spatial configurations for visual hyperacuity," *Vision Research* **16** (1976), 941-947.

Westheimer, G. and McKee, S. "Integration regions for visual hyperacuity," *Vision Research* **17** (1977), 89-93.

Whaples, G.W. "A note on degree N independence," *SIAM J. Appl. Math.* **6** (1958), 300-301.

Wheatstone, C. "Contributions to the physiology of vision. Part I. On some remarkable, and hitherto unobserved, phenomena of binocular vision," *Phil. Trans. Royal Society of London* **128** (1838), 371-394.

Wheatstone, C. "Contributions to the physiology of vision. Part II. On some remarkable, and hitherto unobserved, phenomena of binocular vision (continued)," *The London, Edinburgh, and Dublin Phil. Mag. and J. of Sci.* **3**, 4 (1852), 504-523.

Whiteman, J.R. (ed) *The Mathematics of Finite Elements* , Academic Press, London, 1973.

Whitten, E.H.T. "Orthogonal polynomial trend surfaces for irregularly spaced data," *The Mathematics of Finite Elements* **2** (1970), 141-152.

Whitten, E.H.T. "The use of multi-dimensional cubic spline functions for regression and smoothing," *Austral. Comput. J.* 3 (1971), 81-88.

Whitten, E.H.T. "More on irregularly spaced data and orthogonal polynomial trend surfaces," *Int. Assoc. Math. Geol. J.* 4 (1972), 83.

Whitten, E.H.T. and Koelling, M.E.V. Computation of bicubic-spline surfaces for irregularly-spaced data, Northwestern Univ. Geology Dept., T.R. 3, 1974.

Wilson, H.R. and Bergen J.R. "A four mechanism model for threshold spatial vision," *Vision Research* 19 (1979), 19-32.

Wilson, H.R. and Giese, S.C. "Threshold visibility of frequency grating patterns," *Vision Research* 17 (1977), 1177-1190.

Witkin, A.P. Shape from contour, Ph.D. Thesis, Department of Psychology, Massachusetts Institute of Technology, 1980.

Woodburne, L.S. "The effect of a constant visual angle upon the binocular discrimination of depth differences," *Am. J. Psych.* 46 (1934), 273-286.

Woodham, R.J. Reflectance map techniques for analyzing surface defects in metal castings, MIT Artificial Intelligence Laboratory, TR 457, 1978.

Zavialov, Yu. S. "Interpolating L-splines in several variables," *Mat. Zametki* 14 (1973), 11-20.

Zavialov, Yu. S. "Smoothing L-splines in several variables," *Mat. Zametki* 15 (1974a), 371-379.

Zavialov, Yu. S. "L-spline functions of several variables," *Soviet Math. Dokl.* 15 (1974b), 338-341.

Zenisek, A. "Interpolation polynomials on the triangle," *Numer. Math.* 15 (1970), 283-296.

Zienkiewicz, O.C. "The finite element method: from intuition to generality," *Appl. Mech. Rev.* 23 (1970), 249-256.

Zlamal, M. "A finite element procedure of the second order of accuracy," *Numer. Math.* 14 (1970), 394-402.

Zlamal, M. "On the finite element method," *Numer. Math.* 12 (1968), 394-409.

Zlamal, M. "Curved elements in the finite element method, I," *SIAM J. Numer. Anal.* 10 (1973), 229-240.

Zlamal, M. "Curved elements in the finite element method, II," *SIAM J. Numer. Anal.* **11** (1974), 347-362.

NAME INDEX

SUBJECT INDEX

Acuity, 36, 39, 213-214
Albedo (ρ), 112-119, 121-123, 223-227
Algorithm, 7, 9-10
Algorithmic criteria, 10, 161, 163-164

Bi-directional reflectance-distribution function ($BRDF$), *see* reflectance function
Biharmonic equation, 155, 157
Biological feasibility, *see* algorithmic criteria
Brightness, apparent, 111-112

Calculus of variations, 140, 154-156, 232-237; natural boundary conditions for, 155-156, 236-237
Computational paradigm, 1, 5-10; constraints in, 7-8; levels of description of, 7-10;
Condition of linear variation, 23, 119
Conjugate directions; 170-172; theorem, 172
Conjugate gradient method, 169-172
Conjugate gradient algorithm, 172, 191, 196; examples, 197-202
Constrained optimization, 161-178
Constraint: continuity in stereo matching, 26; uniqueness in stereo matching, 26; surface consistency, 101, 106-109, 139-142, 159
Constraints: on false targets problem, 19; on correspondence problem, 26
Correspondence problem, 15-18, 26-31, 32; elements to be matched in, 17-18, 20-26
Curvature, of a curve, 148; principal directions of, of a surface, 149; principal, of a surface, (κ_a, κ_b) 149; first (or mean) (J), 149-150; second (or Gaussian) (K), 150

Depth, 15

Developable surface, 120-123, 127, 148-149, 223-227
Direction cosines, 126
Directional derivative ($\mathbf{v} \cdot \nabla$), 21-24, 37-39, 118-119, 126
Dirichlet problem, 158
Discontinuities in depth, 208-212
Disparity, 15, 16; crossed, 15, 16; measuring, 17; layers, 40-41; range versus resolution, 26, 28, 30-32; relation to surface shape, 94-99; uncrossed, 15, 16
Disparity map, examples, 57, 58, 64-75, 84, 85
Distance, 15, 94-96; relative, 96-97

Edge effects, 89-93
Euler equations, 155-156, 232-237
Eye movements, *see* vergence movements,

False targets problem, 18-20, 28, 32, 87-88; relationship range and resolution to, 28, 30, 31
Feasible: points, 166-167, 173; directions, 167, 169-172
Functional (Θ), 139-142; conditions for unique solution, 142-146; null space of, ($\mathcal{N}$), 141-145, 156-159; rotationally symmetric, 152-154
Functionals of surface consistency, 139; constraints on, 146-147, 151-152; difference between possible forms, 154-156; effect of null space on minimal solutions of, 156-159; possible forms, 146-151; vector space of possible forms, 152-154

Gaussian, 24, 32, 118
Gradient (p, q), *see also* surface orientation, 116
Gradient of hypersurface, 167

Minor
2